SOVIET PRESCHOOL
EDUCATION, Volume II:
Teacher's Commentary

SOVIET PRESCHOOL EDUCATION, Volume II:
Teacher's Commentary

EDUCATIONAL TESTING SERVICE
Henry Chauncey, Chief Editor

Holt, Rinehart and Winston, Inc.

NEW YORK   CHICAGO   SAN FRANCISCO   ATLANTA   DALLAS
MONTREAL   TORONTO   LONDON   SYDNEY

Preface

Not long ago, but long after I had completed my formal undergraduate and graduate training, I attended a seminar that proved to be one of the strangest and most stimulating in my career. Entitled: "What shall the values in American education be?", it was convened by William Kessen of Yale University for more than thirty people, all deeply committed to quality education through their disciplines, mainly psychology and education. Kessen made only one stipulation at the outset: that it would be a true seminar in that he would neither prime the meeting with his own ideas nor otherwise goad the participants to action, but would rather listen for the ideas that came from them.

A strange seminar indeed. Forty-five minutes passed, as I recall, in absolute silence, punctuated only by an occasional self-conscious giggle, enshrouded by anxious glances as one member looked to his peer for salvation from intellectual helplessness. The seminar terminated silently, profoundly. We went our ways.

What was it that sealed our mouths, fogged our wits? Lord knows we cared, for the issue of values goes right to the heart of educational programs, curricula and goals. We who were the planners, preachers, and implementers in American education, had nothing to say about the premises that underlay our work. Sad, indeed. Was it that we feared to speak openly lest we offend the sensibilities of an illustrious colleague?

Was it that the present turmoil in American education has shaken our values to the roots, to such a degree that the entire matter needs to be reconsidered and that the first approach to reconsideration is silence? Was it, perhaps, that no value consensus can be arrived at in a democracy such as our own that stresses individualism and the right of each man to have his own values? Was it, worst of all, that we had no values, that we traveled the American educational scene by the pragmatic seat of our pants, that we were carpenters rather than creators, implementors and not ideators?

This seminar (for it was truly that) was discussed heatedly for months to come. We never did answer these questions, nor did we finally come up with an educational Magna Carta upon which all could agree. We were, however, brought in that silence more poignantly than by words to examine the central issue of education: What shall our values be?

Our Soviet counterparts apparently have none of our problems in this regard. *Soviet Preschool Education: Teacher's Commentary* not only communicates clearly and in considerable detail the ways and means of proper education for children aged two months through seven years, but also the philosophies that should guide that education. I will not dilute your pleasure by describing at length those values here: they are amply and well interspersed among the educational instructions that are found in the volume. There are, however, tacit value metaphors hidden beneath the explicit philosophies and it will serve us some considerable gain to explicate some of these. Two that are most striking are what I would call the values of *precocity* and *intentional environmentalism.* They are, in many ways, overlapping categories and they emerge as forceful premises on the Soviet educational scene. Let us examine them in quite some detail.

It will surprise you, I am sure, as you peruse the first thirty pages of this volume, to find that the Soviets teach everything as early as they can. At four months, the rudiments of vocalization and sound discrimination are introduced; at eight months, the beginnings of toilet training. Play itself is ordered and designed to the child's capacity with a view to serving as the basis for what will come later. At one year of age, a full educational program is in swing: Esthetics—yes, esthetics!—through music appreciation; speech training; neatness and toilet training; obedience and self-control; active stimulation of interest in the environment—these and many others constitute the core curriculum for infants. It is a sensible program, tailored to the infant's capacities with considerable leeway given to individual differences. But its most striking hallmark is its emphasis on precocity: that which will be learned inevitably ought to be learned early.

It is not automatically evident why earlier is better, and extreme precocity best. Perhaps for the Soviets it is simply a matter of insurance. Soviet preschools, by our standards, seem understaffed and overworked (teachers and their assistants put in a twelve hour day with only a 30 minute break). A mandate for precocity may serve to assure society that Soviet children will be functioning as they should be functioning when the appropriate time arrives. A more interesting view, however, holds that the Soviet imagination, like our own, is captured by the notion that precocity augurs future achievement, that the earlier we start the further we go. On this matter, the evidence is ambiguous at best, and the measure of that ambiguity is amply reflected in our own society. On the one hand, we do have a vigorous nursery school movement and a Headstart program (albeit one whose merit and future are, at this writing, clouded). There is, moreover, a privately held norm of precocity, especially in the middle class, that permits us to take great pleasure in the child who walks, talks or tumbles before these are expected, and encourages us to teach him at home before he is taught in school.

Yet we are ambivalent about the virtues of precocity; this is seen mainly in the laissez-faire theories of development that are tacitly and overtly held in our public school systems. In these theories cognitive development is linked to age and physical development, these latter held to be immutable, and therefore cognitive development immutable also. Such thinking is buttressed from several sources. First are the normative studies, such as by Gesell and Ilg, which dominate the common mind such that it thinks only of that which is ordinarily achieved and turns away from that which is potentially achievable. Second are the oversimplified views of Piagetian psychology which see cognitive growth as a naturally unfolding process that cannot be hastened. Finally, there is fear, most evident in the writings of Dr. Spock, that appears to originate in the presumed fragility of the child and leads us to feel that in attempting anything we may attempt too much, and by attempting too much the child might be harmed. (Not to speak of parental aspiration: better not to aspire than to risk failure.) The sum of the matter is that while we take joy on the occasion of precocity, we are hesitant to facilitate it, and herein lies our first tacit value contrast with the Soviets.

The norm of precocity is linked in Soviet thinking to intentional environmentalism. This is to say that on the question of the relative contribution of nature and nurture to cognitive social and personality development, they opt strongly for nurture. But nurture is not a random thing: environments don't simply happen. They are created, willy-nilly, or intentionally, by those who live in them. The Soviets prefer to intentionally create their environments, to leave as little as possible to chance happening. One senses throughout this volume that they have not only a fair image of the kind of person they would have at each stage of development, but also of the manner in which he might be created. Correctly or incorrectly, they believe that for a child to be sociable, he needs to spend his infancy in a crib with other infants; for him to have an appreciation of music at eight years, he needs to be systematically exposed to melody at age eight months; for language to blossom, its elements need to be inculcated early. Toilet training, speech, moral behavior, muscular development, independence, curiosity, cognition and conformity are all analyzed into their elemental components, graded for their difficulty, and systematically fed to the child just as early as possible.

The American system, by contrast, is more casual. Of course, we have no nurseries for our infants: until they are three years old (and commonly until five), our children are raised at home. That fact alone guarantees a greater diversity of child-rearing approaches, if only because there are no systematic social controls and mothers are not usually professionally-trained infant teachers. These facts notwithstanding, there *are* manuals for mothers, one of the most widely used being Spock's *Baby and Child Care.* And even taking into consideration that Spock speaks to parents and this volume to teachers, the diversity of approach is remarkable. Confronted by a child whose development is irregular in some respects, the Soviet teacher is urged to concentrate on the weaknesses with a view to bringing them up to par. Compare this to Spock's advice to the American mother confronted with the same dilemma: "Enjoy him as he is. . .that's how he'll grow up best. . .enjoy your child for what he is. . .and forget about the qualities he doesn't have." (pp. 43–44) Indeed, the very notion of facilitating or encouraging development, particularly in a formal way during the early years, is anathema, the mark of an overly pushy parent. Hear Spock again: "A child becomes interested in dressing dolls properly, coloring carefully, playing trains realistically, each at a certain stage of his development. You can't hurry him. When you try, you only make him feel incompetent. This does more harm than good. . .let *him* show *you* how [to play]." (pp. 306–307) Compare this now to the Russian mandate, here in connection with language development: "Every moment in which the nurse and her assistant are in close contact with the child must be utilized: during care, feeding, independent games and outdoor play. . . .Name objects at the moment children seem to take a particular interest in them; name actions and movements while the child is performing them. . . .Develop in the child the ability to imitate sounds and words used by adults and create the necessary conditions to stimulate the children to pronounce various sounds as often as possible." (p. 48) Clearly the Soviet approach is one of active intervention, while ours is mainly one of appreciative watching.

Perhaps the critical difference between the Soviet approach and ours lies herein: that we are concerned to avoid pathology and they to promote development; that our manual for child-rearing is authored by a physician whose main concern is to interpret and prevent illness and harm (. . ."and when you try, you only make him feel incompetent. This does more harm than good.") while theirs is compiled by educators whose central mission is the promotion of talent (. . ."Create the necessary conditions to stimulate the child. . ."). My own judgment and that of many of my colleagues is increasingly on the side of educational intervention from the earliest years. Much as the absence of vice is no guarantor of virtue, the absence of illness in no way signifies the maximal development of educational potential. If we believe (and the scientific evidence is now too large to ignore) that early experience is critical for subsequent development, we may need to become intentional environmentalists ourselves, leaving development not to fortuitous chance (too many children are underprivileged in that regard), not even to avoidance of injury, but to the careful and orderly elaboration of ability.

There is a close and sensible relationship between the practices recommended in this book and psychological theory and practice. Not that *all* psychological research is translated into practice, nor that only matters that have been clearly researched are recommended. Far from it: scientific pyschology and scientific education are not so advanced that we can rely on them fully, but neither are they so retarded that they can teach us nothing. This volume, you will find, is a delightful blend of good sense and good science.

Take language development as a case in point. The common view, strongly buttressed by many normative studies, holds that language "develops": that at a certain age, the infant babbles "da-da," that somewhat later he acquires a more descriptive word or two, that by age two his vocabulary is larger, and by four, larger still. A moment's reflection, however, reminds us that language does not "develop," certainly not as second-year molars develop. It is acquired, learned, by exposure to speakers. And exposure to speakers is by no means equal for all children, as recent explorations into the language of underprivileged children have dramatically demonstrated. And if the child actively *learns* language (rather than passively developing it), language should be *teachable,* with better methods or with worse. The Soviets offer some concrete suggestions for language education.

For the infant, the words we speak have no meaning unless they are associated with things he somehow knows. Otherwise, words are quickly assimilated into the noisy and meaningless surroundings. Language teaching begins, reasonably enough, with precise pairing of familiar things with words. (Even before that, by training vocalization and sound discrimination). "Mommy has arrived," the nurse says to the five-month-old. "Let's go to Mommy." By nine months the nurse is pointing to familiar toys and naming them; hiding the toy and asking the infant to find it; giving commands ("bring me the rattle"). Subsequently, a program for naming actions and abstractions is implemented and finally, as the child approaches the time to learn reading and writing (about seven years old), consciousness of phonics and word structure is developed. The stress is not only on active teaching, but on *programmatic* teaching of language, such that the steps constitute a sensible progression from the simple to the complex.

Readers familiar with the works of Vygotsky or Piaget, or the more recent efforts of Roger Brown, George Miller and John Flavell, will easily understand the relations between language and thought, and abstract learning itself. Some of the relevant research in this area is, in fact, presented in Volume I of *Soviet Preschool Education.* Clearly, the simple message of all research in this area is that language is too important a matter for its acquisition to be left to chance or passive "development." The foundations of thought and facilitators of interpersonal relationship must be taught actively, sensibly, relentlessly.

Neither is moral development left to the accident of growing up, to chance learning. Concern for others, moral judgment and behavior, thoughtfulness, respect and courtesy are taught, again at early ages. There will be some disagreement about how far moral education can proceed at age three, but clearly the rudiments are inculcated then, to be developed later. The Soviet program is specific about how this is done. Not by preachments alone, but by *actions* performed by adults jointly with children. Adults influence children by their behavior, by their personal approach to other people around them, toward traditions, and toward the homeland. Such personal moral qualities as humility, modesty, truthfulness, diligence, sociability, goodwill, cooperativeness, thoughtfulness and cheerfulness form the foundation of a child's moral being. The evaluation and development of these qualities is aided by the example set by the teacher, by the consistent and fair attitude she maintains towards all the children of the group. Many of the techniques recommended here are supported by and consistent with research findings that have been available both in America and abroad. Many other techniques seem to be based more on good sense, or at least on good intentions, and will require further verification.

The matter of verification is critical for those who would propose educational procedures as for those who would borrow them. If education is too important a matter to be left to chance, it is also too important to be left to good intentions, however well those seem founded in common sense. What is critical is what works, and how and why it works. For determining these there are no easy substitutes for research. One cannot really assess from these volumes the degree to which a substantial research effort in education is ongoing in the Soviet Union. Clearly some progress is being made, as is evident in Volume I: how much and how successful are the questions. In any event, for those who would utilize these promising Soviet techniques for the solution of educational problems elsewhere, the message is clear and urgent: a program of evaluation, no less substantial in commitment and fiscal magnitude than that of the educational program itself, is required.

There is not, to my knowledge, a manual quite like this one presently available. For older children there is, of course, Marie Montessori's *The Montessori Method,* which describes her work in the *Casa dei Bambini* in the slums of Rome. Even earlier, there is the writing of Pestalozzi, who apparently greatly influenced Soviet thinking on education, and of Froebel. Readers familiar with those writings will immediately sense important commonalities and differences. All of these writers, along with authors of these volumes, hold that development is an unfolding process, and that education consists simply of not hindering that process, and of providing the child with precisely what it requires from the environment at each stage of development. There are differences in view about what the environment needs to supply and how it should do so. Montessori, you will recall, opts for structure, carefully designing all manner of educational apparatus to the presumed needs of the children. This volume suggests no special equipment, relying rather on what society naturally provides: a ball, a doll, a flower. Soviet conceptualization, on the other hand, stresses a matter that is considerably muted, if it is present at all, in these other writings: the critical importance of a warm teacher-child relationship. Throughout this volume where the Soviets criticize their teachers, it is entirely for neglect and abuse of this relationship: for their rudeness, their ordinary tendency to make invidious comparisons between children, their confusion of curiosity with disobedience, their failure to sustain a loving, caring relationship. It is no small mission that they assign their teachers, to retain and encourage that which is personal and facilitating midst that which is systematically required and anomic. It does us well to recall, as we revise our own curricula for young children, that care precedes technique, that positive regard is a necessary ingredient for intellectual maturation.

If there has been a central message in education during the past century, it is that the child is father to the man, that what is acquired early determines in good measure what will be learned later. How early is "early"? For us, education in kindergarten begins around age five. Is that early enough? Perhaps it is for privileged children, though I doubt it. But it is patently not early enough for underprivileged ones for whom enrichment programs such as Headstart now begin at age three, and even at this age show no real pattern of merit. Clearly we shall have to begin earlier, for the underprivileged as perhaps for the privileged, at home or in formal institutions. For such a program, *Soviet Preschool Education* is unique and will provide an excellent first approximation for a general program.

David Rosenhan

Swarthmore, Pennsylvania
May 1969

Contents

VI

VII

SOVIET PRESCHOOL EDUCATION, Volume II:
Teacher's Commentary

Introduction

This volume contains the operating instructions for the most extensive program of group upbringing in human history. Over 10 percent of all Soviet children under 2 years of age are currently enrolled in public nurseries. The corresponding percentage for children between 3 and 6 who attend preschool is about 20 percent. The enrollment is limited chiefly by the number of places available, with the demand far exceeding the supply. In Moscow, for example, which probably has more facilities than any other Soviet city, only 50 percent of all applicants can be accepted.

In the U.S.S.R. the use of communal facilities for the rearing of children is as old as the Soviet Union itself, but the program was considerably expanded in scope a decade ago with the creation of a new type of preschool institution, the *yasli-sad,* or *creche*-kindergarten, which provided for the upbringing of children from the age of two months to seven years (at which point the child is enrolled in regular school). The same Party resolution which established the *yasli-sad* commissioned the development of a new and detailed curriculum to be followed in all preschool institutions in the U.S.S.R. Responsibility for preparation of the new program was delegated jointly to the Academy of Pedagogical Sciences and the Academy of Medical Sciences. The present manual represents the outcome of that joint effort. It was first published in 1962. A second edition, with minor revisions and additions, appeared in 1965, and it is the latter version that is presented here in translation.

Although the manual was published by the Ministry of Education of the Russian Republic, it is in effect operative throughout all of the republics of the U.S.S.R. The Academy of Medical Sciences is an all-Union Academy; the Academy of Pedagogical Sciences recently became so. The writer has seen the procedures advocated in this volume employed, with only minor variations, in preschool centers ranging from

1

Tallin, Estonia to Alma Ata in Soviet Asia. The present manual is used as the basic text for the training of all preschool personnel. In addition, it serves as the prototype for dozens of other works on preschool education published in the Soviet Union and in the socialist countries generally. This means that millions of children throughout the Communist world are being brought up in accordance with the principles and procedures presented in the pages which follow.

But the significance of programs of this kind goes beyond the Communist world. Given the nature of the changes taking place in all large industrial societies, including our own, there is every reason to expect that programs of group upbringing will become increasingly common in the Western world as well. In the United States, we have already seen the beginnings of the new trend in the rapid development of Project Head Start, which in the first two years of its existence has had 2 million children in attendance. Even higher enrollment figures can be expected if the Administration carries out the provisions of the 1967 Social Security Act. This calls for the establishment of a nationwide network of daycare centers to provide for the children of mothers who, according to the new legislation, cannot qualify for welfare payments (regardless of how young their children may be) unless they take a job or receive job training. Nor is the development of preschool facilities likely to be limited to disadvantaged families. The growing number of working mothers, the increasing importance accorded to a mother having "a life of her own," the ever-greater difficulties encountered in taking the child along for shopping or social visits, the unavailability of qualified household help; all these considerations—coupled with the experts' stress on the need for enriched cognitive experience in the early years—increase the demand for preschool programs among middle class families as well. With such major developments in prospect, we do well to examine the Soviet program if only to become aware of the problems involved, and how our own solutions might differ.

Although, as will become apparent, the manual leaves little to the imagination in spelling out what is to be said and done from hour to hour in a Soviet nursery, the Western reader may feel mystified or even be misled as he seeks to understand how the program actually works, primarily because he lacks the frame of reference which the Soviet authors, and their readers, take for granted. It is the aim of this introduction to convey some of this context. To begin with, the very title of the manual—and its central theme—presents problems of communication. The manual describes a program of *vospitanie,* a household word in Russian, but with no equally familiar English equivalent. The dictionary translates it as "upbringing," but perhaps more of the flavor is conveyed by the expression *character education,* for *vospitanie* is the process of forming the character of the young. In the Soviet context, it has an even more specific meaning—the development of what is called *communist morality.*

It is this moral emphasis which gives Soviet education its distinctive cast, at least in comparison with public education in the West. Moreover, it is this same moral emphasis which distinguishes the present manual from its predecessors in the 1950s, which focused primarily on subject matter rather than conduct. This point is emphasized in the *Teacher's Commentary* on the *Program of Upbringing,* which has also been made available in translation as a companion piece to this volume.

> In the *Kindergarten Teacher's Manual* (published in 1953), practically all of the mental and esthetic instruction was based on formal study. Such an approach led to a situation in which extracurricular instruction was exceedingly poor and limited, with the children being for all intents and purposes left to their own devices in the periods between regularly scheduled activities. Experienced teachers knew how to direct and enrich the extracurricular activity of the children in accordance with the educational objectives, but for the majority of beginning teachers this proved to be an extremely difficult and vague area, inasmuch as the "manual" was very obscure on this matter. The intensive and at times exclusive attention of administrators, teachers, and curriculum and methods study groups to problems of instruction (in the narrow sense) was typical of this period, when preschool personnel were absorbing the principles of kindergarten instruction, and it did yield positive results. But one must still be careful never to underestimate the education of children through so-called everyday life and to place this process in an equal position with that of more formal instruction. [p. 2]

The frequent references in the manual to the virtues of respect for elders, obedience, self-discipline, proper conduct, modesty, manners, and the like represent the initial statement of themes that are to be presented again and again throughout the child's educational career in preschool, school, and youth organizations. This brings us to the second distinctive quality of Soviet preschool education: its carefully designed continuity with the experiences to follow in school and in the closely associated communist youth organizations; namely, the Octobrists (grades I through III; ages 7–9), the Pioneers (grades IV through VIII; ages 10–15), and the Komsomol, or Young Communist League, which enrolls youth up to the age of 28 and sometimes longer. This continuity is especially apparent in Chapter VII of the manual, which is virtually interchangeable with the first chapter of analogous handbooks on upbringing for the primary grades, prepared by the same Academy of Pedagogical Sciences.

A third distinctive feature is hardly apparent in the text, but captures the attention of the Western observer the moment he enters a Soviet nursery. The playpens which he will see there differ in two respects from their Western counterparts. First, instead of being at floor level, the pen is raised on legs so as to permit face-to-face interaction between infant and staff member. In fact, the pens are at different heights depending on the stage of the child's development—higher for the supine babies than for the crawlers who begin to pull themselves up by the bars. But even more striking to the Western eye is the fact that each playpen is the size of a small room, and contains not one but half a dozen infants. Soviet children must learn to live in a collective society, and they begin to do so in the first year of life.

Nor is the development of collective consciousness left to chance. As toys, dolls, and other objects are presented to the children, the upbringer makes a point of explaining their communal nature: "Children, here is our dolly. Vanya, you give our dolly to Katya, Katya, pass it to Marusya; now Marusya and Petya swing our dolly together." The banner hung over the archway proclaims: *"Moe eto nashe; nashe moe"* ("Mine is ours; ours is mine"). Group play is emphasized, and children are discouraged from playing alone. I recall an incident in a Kiev nursery. As I watched, two upbringers suddenly scurried toward a corner of the room. "Aha," I thought, "there's a scrap and two kids have to be separated." But I was wrong. The Soviet equivalent of an emergency was one child playing quietly by himself. Not just interaction but cooperation is emphasized. Children are taught to work together, to help each other, and to be responsible for disciplining each other. The effect of this training is reflected in two contrasting observations, one made by me in a Soviet nursery, the other by a Soviet colleague visiting an American preschool center. I was watching the 3-year-old group at lunch. Just imagine 20 preschoolers at mealtime—one child doesn't want to eat, another calls the teacher, still another takes something from a neighbor's plate while the victim shouts his protest, someone else sings a song—laughter, crying, noise! Nothing of the sort. What I heard was the hum of subdued, civilized conversation. But it was not sound so much as sight that distinguished the Soviet scene most sharply from its Western equivalent. In any American nursery school, there would have been an adult sitting at each table. Not so in Yasli No. 239. Here the upbringers had already made progress toward the goal of "forging a self-reliant collective." The children were themselves responsible for keeping order.

The members of the collective not only discipline each other, but work together. This point was brought home to me by the comments of a distinguished Soviet psychologist, an expert on development during the preschool years. He had been observing in an American day-care center for children of working mothers. The center was conducted under university auspices and reflected modern outlooks and methods in early childhood education. It was therefore with some concern that I noted how upset my colleague was on his return. "I wouldn't have believed it," he said, "if I hadn't seen it with my own eyes. There were four children sitting at a table, just as in our nurseries. But each one was doing something different. What's more, I watched them for a whole ten minutes, and not once did any child help another one. They didn't even talk to each other. Each one was busy in his own activity. You really are a nation of individualists!"

Complementing the emphasis on collectivism is a stress on self-reliance. From the very beginning children are taught to do things for themselves. The notion is that by learning how to be self-sufficient, the child not only furthers his own development but also shows his consideration for others. I saw 18-month-old children dressing themselves (except for buttoning). In the third year they are already helping and taking turns at chores, such as setting table, cleaning up, or gardening. The development of a proper attitude toward work is regarded as a major aim of Soviet upbringing. As soon as the child learns to talk, this objective is pursued actively through games involving the role playing of various tasks, trades, and occupations (for example, taking care of baby, playing farmer, miner, steel worker). Visits are made to local shops and factories so that children can see workers engaged at their jobs.

Another distinctive approach for acquainting the child with the world of people older than himself is the institution of *shevstvo*. Literally, the word means "being a chief over," or "having under one's supervision," but *shevstvo* is actually best described as a system of "group adoption" in which a collective in the neighborhood, such as a third-grade class, a shop in a factory, or a section of an office or institute, takes the nursery group as its ward. Members of the collective visit the center, become acquainted with the children, make toys for them, take them on outings, and invite them to their own place of work. By serving as aids and models for the young, these older children and adults fulfill their general social obligation to participate in "bringing up a generation that will live and work under communism."

But if the rest of the community is more in evidence in a Soviet nursery school than in its American counterpart, there is one group that is less influential: namely, parents. The fact that they are scarcely mentioned in the manual reflects the extent to which the Soviet nursery is viewed as the domain of the professional educator, who "knows what is best for the child." In the Soviet system of child rearing, the role of the family is clearly subordinate to that of communal institutions, who carry the primary responsibility for upbringing. This message comes through clearly in the only extended reference to the family which appears in the manual:

> Every kindergarten should serve as a model of the Communist education of children. The pedagogical staff of the kindergarten is faced with the task of disseminating pedagogical knowledge among parents, helping families to bring their children up properly, and sharing their invaluable experience in family upbringing. And, as is indicated in the Program of our Party, 'the educational influence of the family on children to a greater and greater extent becomes totally integrated with their public education.' [p. 6]

This, then, is the context—ideological and social—in which Soviet preschool education operates, and in which the instructions of the manual are to be carried out. As he examines the detailed specifications it contains, the reader may ask how closely reality lives up to the recommendations. Do Soviet upbringers actually do what the book says? In response one may ask the analogous question for the American scene: does the American mother actually do what Spock or Ginott recommends? The answer is the same for both societies: she tries. If anything, the Soviet upbringer tries harder. For one reason, it is her full-time career; for another, she is not bombarded with contradictory advice from a dozen experts who disagree. There are many Soviet guidebooks on upbringing; but they all emphasize the same objectives and the same methods for attaining the goals. It is comparatively simple. But there is a problem: the products may also be the same.

But before the Western reader dismisses the Soviet approach as too stereotyped for his taste, he would do well to ask about our own efforts in this sphere. Whatever else one may think about Soviet methods of education, it is clear that the Russians have worked hard to develop ways for teaching their children, early in life, the values and *behaviors* consistent with Communist ideals. Are we doing as well for American society? What values and behaviors do we teach in our preschool programs? Or, to put it more provocatively, what values and behaviors do our children learn when they participate in these programs?

The answers to these questions may not be altogether disappointing, but even so, they prompt us to ask what one might find in an American equivalent to the Soviet manual, if such a book existed. There may be those who would argue that such a book should not exist—not a single manual for all programs. Agreed, but let us then have more than one. And, in the meantime, until they are written, we can read this manual and, on every page, ask with profit: how would we do it differently?

Urie Bronfenbrenner
Cornell University

Ithaca, New York
March 1969

I

Concerning the Program of Instruction in the Kindergarten

The 22nd Congress of the Communist Party of the Soviet Union has taken concrete steps for the establishment of a communist society in our country. These grandiose perspectives induce every worker, wherever he may be, to persistent inspired effort. Kindergarten teachers are proud of the fact that to them has fallen the honor of educating the generation which will live and work in a communist society.

With the aim of achieving further improvement in public preschool instruction and of assuring the all-around and harmonious development of every child, the party and the government have passed a resolution concerning a new type of preschool institution in which children aged 2 months to 7 years will be educated. In accordance with this resolution, a new program of instruction in the kindergarten has been prepared which will help in solving the problem of achieving a fundamental improvement of the educational process.

The perfecting of instruction will be effected through the deeper and more subtle care of every child by a teacher fully equipped with pedagogical knowledge, so that the best qualities of man in a communist society will be instilled and developed in the child.

It is imperative that we overcome the inconsistencies which have been created by the separation of the developmental stages of the preschool child, as a result of which children up to 3 years of age are instructed in institutions using one approach whereas children from 3 to 7 years of age are instructed in institutions using a different educational system.

The new program has been created on the basis both of experience in using the most advanced techniques and of research in the pedagogical field (on general and particular problems of instruction, play, esthetic training and work, as well as in psychological areas). For the first time in the history of Soviet public preschool instruction, the program treats the instruction of children beginning with their first year of life and going up to the beginning of school, that is, the duration of the entire preschool childhood.

The continuity which is necessary for the child's natural process of development will be achieved in the favorable conditions of a single institution in a sequential and comprehensive program of instruction.

The program of instruction of children at every age is based on those concepts which the child has already assimilated and contains the new material which he is to acquire. In each group the children not only acquire new knowledge, skills and habits, but also perfect and strengthen those which have already been acquired.

The new program differs from the old not only in the fact that the lower age boundaries have been extended, but also in that it envisages a substantial revision of the inner structure of the educational process. This means a reconstruction of the interrelation between the education of children through formal study and activities (i.e., education in the narrow sense of the word) and the education of children in the broader sense, in less formalized activities.

In the *Kindergarten Teacher's Manual* (published in 1953) practically all of the mental and esthetic instruction was based on formal study. Such an approach led to a situation in which extracurricular instruction was exceedingly poor and limited, with the children being for all intents and purposes left to their own devices in the periods between regularly scheduled activities. Experienced teachers knew how to direct and enrich the extracurricular activity of the children in accordance with the educational objectives, but for the majority of beginning teachers this proved to be an extremely difficult and vague area, insomuch as the *Manual* was very obscure on this matter. The intensive and at times exclusive attention of administrators, teachers, and curriculum and method study groups to problems of instruction (in the narrow sense) was typical in this period when preschool personnel were absorbing the principles of kindergarten instruction, and it did yield positive results. But one must still be careful never to underestimate the education of children through so-called everyday life or to place this process in an unequal position with that of more formal instruction.

The new program will lead the teacher to a proper formulation of the entire pedagogical process and will facilitate its planning.

The whole way of life in the kindergarten (which is arranged differently in winter and in summer) must be permeated by the active happiness of each child, and must produce the most favorable conditions for the all-around development of children through the many different activities directed and supervised by the teacher. For some periods of the day the teacher directly organizes the activity of the children (teaches them formally, participates in sports and games with set rules, and so forth); at another time of day the children act independently, without the direct participation of the teacher but under his supervision (they play, build homemade toys, and the like). This independent activity of the children will be livelier and richer in proportion to the preparedness of the teacher; that is, the greater his store of pedagogical and general knowledge, the greater number of diverse skills he possesses.

II

The Care and Upbringing of Infants

OBJECTIVES

In the course of the early childhood years a child goes through an accelerated process of physical and neuropsychological development. He grows rapidly and gains in weight; in the structure and functioning of his organism significant changes occur.

This age is characterized by great vulnerability and little adaptability to the surrounding environment. The children's resistance to various diseases is weakly developed.

The fundamental objectives of work with children at an early age are the following: to strengthen health, to assure sound physical development of the body and to prevent diseases.

With proper care in this period of life intensive development of the sense organs (sight, hearing, touch, feel and taste) takes place in the child, and this is of great significance for his perception of his surroundings. Negative emotions first manifest themselves, and at a later stage of development positive ones occur.

Negative emotional manifestations appear from the first days in the life of the child and are expressed in his crying and in his restless gesticulations. The reasons for these are usually the following: cold, hunger, pain, lack of a schedule or of the necessary hygienic conditions, or the absence of an individual approach to the child.

Positive emotions, above all joy or a state of well being, have great significance in the life of small children. Such feelings stimulate the child to movement and babbling (and later to speech reactions), strengthen his breathing, improve his circulation and digestion, and promote the neuropsychological development of the child.

In the period of early childhood the child begins to master complex physical movement and speech. The power to think, to remember and to concentrate develops in the children, enabling them to establish ties with their surroundings. Ideal psychological development of every child is the most important objective in his care and instruction.

At an early age it is necessary to develop the child's ability to handle toys, to eat by himself, and to participate actively in dressing and undressing. It is important to train him to have good health habits, to obey the rules of proper behavior, and so forth. Developing friendly relations between children and the adults they meet in everyday life and developing positive character traits are among the objectives in the care of infants.

In order to fulfill the objectives which have been set, given conditions answering educative as well as sanitary demands must be met: a light, spacious building with furniture and equipment corresponding to the children's age; a correct schedule; a sensible diet corresponding to the needs of a growing organism; development of the children's resistance; and systematically planned educative work with them.

The observance of good health and sanitary habits; the orderly care of toys and equipment; a subtle, attentive, affectionate relationship of nurse and her assistant toward each child; a full knowledge of the contents of the program, educative methods and the peculiarities of each age group; and contact with the pedagogical and medical staff—all help to create in children the cheerful, happy disposition indispensable for their correct development and successful education.

III

The Care and Upbringing of Children During the First Year of Life

DAILY SCHEDULE

Strict adherence to a schedule is a necessary condition for insuring the proper growth and development of infants. If the life of children is regulated by a fixed schedule, if every day they eat, sleep and are kept awake at definite hours of the day, this will help to raise the children to be healthy and psychologically well balanced. The schedule must provide for sufficiently long periods of sleeping and of being awake at various times of the day, and for the proper alternation of these periods to fit in with feeding times.

In the course of the first years of life, a baby goes through a state of rapid and extensive development, and, therefore, the organization of his life during this period changes a number of times. In the course of the first three to five weeks of his life, a baby sleeps for a longer period of time than he is awake. As the baby grows, the length of time he sleeps within a 24-hour span is distributed according to the age of the children in the following manner:

The life of children up to 12 months is organized in such a way as to insure that the baby sleeps before feeding and is kept awake after the meal. A baby who has slept well eats well and, having satisfied his hunger, is active during his waking period, after which, having been settled in his crib, he quickly falls asleep and sleeps until the next feeding.

If together in one group there are children varying significantly in age, for example 2 months old and 6 months old, then a separate schedule is

13

	UP TO 2½–3 MONTHS	FROM 2½–3 TO 5–6 MONTHS	FROM 5–6 TO 9–10 MONTHS	FROM 9–10 MONTHS TO 1 YR.
Number of feedings	7	6	5	5–4
Length of intervals between feedings	3 hrs.	3½ hrs.	4 hrs.	3½–4½ hrs.
Length of each waking period	1–1½ hrs.	1½–2 hrs.	2–2½ hrs.	2½–3½ hrs.
Number of times child sleeps during daytime	4	4–3	3	2
Length of each period of daytime sleep	2–1½ hrs.	2–1½ hrs.	2–1½ hrs.	2–2½ hrs.
Amount of sleep during 24-hour period	18–16½ hrs.	16½–16 hrs.	16–15 hrs.	15–14½ hrs.

set up for the children of each age. In a case where the children being cared for in one group vary even more in age, let us say from 2 months to 1 year, it is absolutely necessary to provide three different schedules (one for each subgroup).

Sometimes it is even necessary to arrange two schedules for children within the very same age group. This will be necessary if the working conditions of some mothers are such that their children, having been awakened before the others and fed at home, must then be put to sleep earlier than the others.

Where there are two or three different schedules within one group, not all children are awake at the same time; one subgroup may sleep while the others are awake. This enables the nurse and the assistant to feed children without hurrying and give to each one of them more attention during playtime.

To determine a suitable schedule for each child, one must take into account not only his age but also the condition of his health and his physical development. Children who enjoy good health, are physically well developed, and have a stable nervous system can be moved ahead sooner than others to the schedule of the next older subgroup. Children in poor health are better suited to the schedule of children younger than themselves.

If the nurse notices that some of the children take a long time to fall asleep, do not wake up at the proper time, eat at the scheduled times without appetite, and do not finish the food served to them, she reports this fact to the doctor, who then introduces some sort of change into the child's schedule.

The nurse tries to insure that the necessary favorable conditions are created for the fulfillment of the schedule: regarding food, everything should be prepared beforehand; while the children are awake, they should be kept active and everything should be arranged so that the children can move about easily and use their toys. The guidance of the nurse, who keeps the children in a cheerful, happy frame of mind through all of this, is of the utmost importance.

It is important that the schedule and diet established at the kindergarten be also observed at home. To that aim, the nurse confers with the parents, makes clear to them the importance of a unified schedule for both home and school.

FEEDING

The correct breast feeding of infants has an exceptional importance for their normal growth and development.

Babies up to 3 months of age should be fed every three hours, or seven times in all in the course of a 24-hour period; from 3 to 5 months, babies should be fed every three and a half hours, or six times a day; from 5 to 12 months, every four hours, or five times in the course of a 24-hour period.

It is particularly important for a baby to be breast fed during his first year of life. Because of the ingredients it contains, this milk satisfies the needs of the child's organism and is easily assimilated. Sucking the milk directly from the mother's breast, the baby absorbs sterile food at the proper temperature. If the mother has sufficient milk, the baby grows and develops, is less likely to catch diseases, and, if he does fall sick, quickly recovers since the mother's milk contains substances which protect from diseases. This must be made clear to each mother, and she must be required to follow the schedule strictly and to obey the rules of breast feeding.

Moreover, when a baby is breast fed, a strong link is formed between the mother and the child. The first manifestations of mutual love and attachment between them are frequently linked with breast feeding.

Each time, only one breast must be used for feeding, thereby alternating breasts for each feeding. Care must be taken to see that the baby completely sucks out the milk from the breast. It is important for the mother to wash her hands carefully and clean her breast with boiled water before each breast feeding. For that purpose, the reception room must be equipped with a wash basin and towel for washing the hands, a pitcher of water which has been boiled, clean absorbent cotton in a closed container and a disposal container for the cotton that has been used.

If the baby is healthy, has spent enough time in the open air, has exerted himself physically, played and slept well, then he should feel hungry at the time scheduled for his feeding.

Even a 2-month baby reacts actively just before breast feeding time, turning his head toward the mother's breast and grabbing the nipple. This activity should be developed so that babies take hold of the nipple themselves, hold on to the mother's breast with their hands, and suck energetically. If the baby shows signs of fatigue and begins to suck indifferently, a break of two or three minutes should be taken, and then the feeding continued.

To avoid having the baby's attention distracted while sucking, the mother should not talk with either the baby or anyone else present during the breast feeding.

It is good if the mother can spare the time, once feeding is completed, to play or talk with the child for a while.

It is very important that the mother herself come to feed the infant. Only in cases of extreme emergency should she skip a scheduled feeding, and then either the head nurse or the assistant nurse should give the baby some of the mother's milk which has been preserved.

Before and following breast feeding, the baby must be weighed so as to know the precise quantity of milk he has consumed.

If the mother has sufficient milk, the baby puts on weight satisfactorily and develops normally. Up to 5 months of age, the baby should only be breast fed. If the mother has insufficient milk, the doctor prescribes supplementary feeding which the baby takes from a bottle, immediately following breast feeding. When mixed and artificial feeding is used, the baby must be held in the same position as when he is breast fed.

The nipple which is put on the bottle must have a small opening so that the milk flows gently; otherwise, if the baby swallows too rapidly, he does not have a feeling of satisfaction, a feeling of being "full." Besides, having become used to the rapid flow of milk, the baby will refuse to suck the mother's breast, which requires greater effort.

Before each feeding, the baby must be shown the bottle of milk, the sight of which sharpens his appetite. A 3-month-old baby by himself grabs the bottle nipple with his mouth. His hands should be put on the bottle so that by the time the baby is 5- to 5 ½-months-old, he is trained to hold it with his own hands, take the bottle out of his mouth and put the nipple back to his mouth.

In order to increase the number of vitamins in the baby's diet, one should start giving him by the third or fourth month raw (uncooked) berry or vegetable juice (strawberry, black currant, raspberry, carrot, cabbage).

After 4 to 5 months, breast feeding alone is no longer sufficient to insure the proper development of the child. He needs more albumen and mineral salts than are contained in the mother's milk. Therefore, semi-liquid food must be introduced in addition. This additional food must be introduced gradually, beginning with four or five teaspoonfuls once a day before breast feeding, and afterwards increasing the dose over a period of seven to eight days to bring the amount up to three-fourths of a glass. At that time, one breast feeding is replaced by 5 percent cooked semolina or mashed vegetable puree.

From the age of 4 ½ to 5 months, the baby must be fed from a spoon; as of the age of 7 to 8 months, he must be taught to drink from a cup held by an adult.

One must not attempt to teach the child to eat from a spoon at the same time as he is getting used to a new kind of food. Eating from a spoon requires complicated movements unknown to the baby up to that time. Therefore, at the beginning, a new kind of food is given to the baby in the manner to which he is accustomed. When the baby is accustomed to the taste of new foods, he is quite willing to eat it from a spoon.

At the time of feeding, a baby should be encouraged to participate actively in the process. He should open his mouth without any prompting from adults; he should swallow the food immediately without holding it in his mouth; at the age of 7 to 8 months, he should hold in his hand a piece of bread or a cookie and bite off pieces of his own accord.

Forcing a child to eat if he refuses to do so is useless and may even bring about aversion to food.

The position of a child at the time of feeding changes in relation to his growth. From the time the baby is 4 ½ to 5 months old, he no longer lies down during feeding time but gets fed while half seated in the arms of an adult; from 7 months on he may sit in the lap of the nurse or assistant; and 8- to 10-month-old babies, having learned how to sit up, can be fed sitting at the table (no more than two children at a time) and being given by turns one or two spoonfuls.

From the time the babies reach the age of 6 months, one should talk to them during mealtime, naming objects and actions linked with food and feeding: "open your mouth," "take the cookie," and so forth. The nurse or assistant should watch to make sure that when the baby's hands, lips or cheeks get dirty from eating, they are immediately wiped. This teaches the child personal cleanliness.

The children should not be kept waiting to be fed in turns. For both artificial and supplementary feeding everything should be prepared beforehand. Before children wake up, the bottles of food and vitamins (with name tags attached) and a pan containing warm water should be set on the serving table. While the assistant nurse brings a baby who has just awakened into the room and changes it, the head nurse puts its bottle in the pan in order to warm it up.

The bottle nipples should be of two kinds: one with a small opening for milk and milk mixtures, and the other with a somewhat larger opening for semiliquid cooked cereals and jellies. Each type of nipple is kept in a separate container covered with a lid. There should be a larger number of nipples than of children. For the older children in the younger group, small bowls or small soup plates should be provided. Again, the number of these should be greater than the number of children.

The table at which the children are fed should be placed in such a way that the nurses, busy feeding children, are at the same time able to supervise the children who are active in the playpen. For the younger group, three tables should be provided, one a serving table at which the nurse feeds those children who cannot sit up, and two double high chairs at which nurses feed the 7- and 8-month-old babies.

SLEEPING

To insure proper physical development, good health and general wellbeing of the baby, it is indispensable that he sleep soundly and peacefully every day for the length of time determined for his particular age and that the periods of sleep be properly scheduled.

Children up to 5 months should sleep three or four times a day for periods of one and a half to two hours; at 5 months, three times a day, one and a half to two hours each time; from 9 to 10 months, twice a day for periods of two to two and a half hours. At night they should sleep for ten to eleven hours.

The third period of sleep for babies of 5 to 6 months often overlaps the time of arrival of their parents. For this reason it is important to convince the parents to take their children home after they have had their sleep, and it must be explained to them why it is important not to disturb the child's sleep.

Care must be taken so that children fall asleep quickly, sleep soundly and wake up quietly. Those children who seem to feel the need of sleeping must be put to bed first. After play, babies become limp and sleepy and get difficult to handle. Children should not be permitted to fall asleep in unsuitable conditions (for example, in the play pen), as undressing the child and putting him in bed will disturb his sleep.

Out in the open, children fall asleep more quickly and sleep more soundly. For this reason, during the day the children should sleep out of doors, in the yard, on a patio or under an awning. Only in cases when means of organizing the children's daytime sleep outside are completely lacking should they be put to bed in a room with the windows wide open; the room should be separated so that the noise of children playing nearby does not disturb the children who are asleep.

Getting a young or newly admitted baby accustomed to sleeping in the open during the colder periods of the year must be brought about gradually. For the two-hour sleeping period, such children are taken out for periods of twenty to forty minutes at a time, with this time increased daily until after a period of some two weeks the one-and-a-half to two-hour sleep can be spent entirely in the open.

Babies of 3 to 6 months may sleep in the open when the temperature is $-12°$, and by the end of the first year when the temperature is $-15°$.[1]

Children born during the warm months of the year must be taken out from the very first day of life providing the outside temperature is not lower than $+12°$ to $+15°$.

During the summer when the weather is good, children may sleep in a fairly shady area, and when it rains, on the veranda. In very hot weather when there is no shady area available, children should of course be made to sleep in a room.

For sleeping, children should wear clothing appropriate to the season and the weather. In cold weather a small baby would wear a kerchief on his head and be wrapped up in a warm blanket, but in such a way that his freedom of movement is not restricted. Then the baby, having been put into a sleeping bag, is carried out to the veranda or yard where cots have already been prepared. The bedding, kept in a warm room, is taken out just before the babies are put to sleep.

Getting the child ready for bed, the person in charge talks to the baby in a quiet and gentle manner saying that he is going to be bundled up warmly and will go to sleep: "Bye bye, Olia." At the same time, the nurse does not forget to keep an eye on the children still playing in the playpen.

If the children are put to bed for their nap in rooms, then according to the air temperature they are either wrapped in blankets up to their underarms or wear overalls and are covered up above with a blanket or a sheet.

When put to bed in the open, children usually fall asleep rapidly and sleep soundly. The child who cannot fall asleep for a long time requires the attention of an adult and must be quieted down. Someone should stay near him for a while and talk gently to him.

---

[1]*Editor's Note:* all temperatures appearing in the text will be centigrade. To convert to the Fahrenheit scale, multiply the centigrade figure by 1.8 and add 32°. For example, $-15°C \times 1.8 + 32° = +5°F$.

In the hot summer weather some children get very excited before going to sleep; the older ones sit or stand up in their cots and refuse to lie down. Patiently but firmly, the nurse puts the baby down again, persuades him to go to sleep, calms him down by talking to him in a soothing tone of voice, saying for example: "Close yours eyes, Misha, all the children are already asleep." Usually the excited baby will react favorably.

Regarding those children recently admitted to the kindergarten and particularly those who have been used to artificial means of sleep inducements (a "pacifier," rocking, or being carried in the parent's arms), it is not advisable to change such habits suddenly and abruptly. For the first days, one may hold the baby in one's arms, carry him about the room for a while, or sit near him for a little longer than is normally advisable.

Children who have not become used to the schedule, do not fall asleep at the proper time, and cry should be put to bed after the others and apart from the sleeping children, as they can then be given more attention. Proper attention must be insured for the sleeping children.

Proper scheduling and a practice of working with the parents very soon show results, and children will fall asleep quickly at the appropriate time.

Usually children do not all wake up at the same time. The child who has awakened must be taken into a room, changed, fed, and put down in the playpen or on the floor behind a railing and given toys. If the baby does not wake up at the proper time, he should be awakened.

The bedding accessories of each baby (sleeping bags, blankets, etc.) must be marked and stored in closets with separate compartments. Mattresses and pillows must be brought into a warm area of the building at cold times during the year.

THE BABY'S HYGIENE, DRESS, AND TOILET

Small children require very thorough hygienic care. Accordingly, it is important to do the baby's toilet fully every day. This obligation rests with the mother, who must bring the baby to the kindergarten thoroughly washed.

The mother must be told and shown how to proceed correctly in taking care of the cleanliness of the baby. Having previously washed her own hands, the mother uses a clean piece of wet absorbent cotton to wash the face, eyes, ears, and hands of the child. This is done with warm running water from a faucet or pitcher. Drying must be done carefully with a soft towel or dry absorbent cotton so as not to leave any dampness in the folds of skin, behind the ears, and on the neck. The eyes must be washed with absorbent cotton, changing the piece of cotton for each eye, and going from the outer toward the inner corner of the eye. The outer parts of the ears and nose must be cleaned with twisted cotton, slightly moistened with vaseline. For this purpose, hard objects, such as matches covered with cotton, are never used. These may harm the delicate mucous membrane of the nose or the eardrums. If nails have grown on hands and feet, they must be carefully snipped off with scissors.

No attempt should be made to wipe the inner part of the baby's mouth, even in such cases when a white coating (or fur) is observed on the mucous membrane. This must be reported to the doctor who will indicate the proper medication.

The morning toilet concludes with the washing of the rest of the baby's body which must be done, like the washing of the face, under a stream of warm running water. When washing little girls, the movements of the hand of the adult must proceed from front to back so as not to introduce an infection in the sexual organs.

The toilet must proceed in a thorough and careful fashion without inflicting on the baby unpleasant sensations and without producing in him a negative attitude toward these procedures.

.   .   .

One should arrange with the parents to have babies up to 6 months of age bathed at home daily, and older babies every other day. If the necessary conditions cannot be met by the family, then the baby is bathed in the kindergarten. At home the bathing is done at night, while in the kindergarten it is performed before the afternoon nap.

Parents must be taught how to bathe babies correctly. A thoroughly clean tub must be used and the temperature should be 36–36.5°, as measured by a water thermometer. The temperature of the surrounding air should be not lower than 20°.

Two or three times a week the babies should be washed with soap. For rinsing after the baby is washed with soap, one should have water ready which is at a temperature of one degree lower than in the tub itself.

If 4- to 5-month-old babies are given a chance to splash around in the water, and older babies (8 or 9 months) to play with floating toys, they will enjoy the bath and thenceforth will wash with a feeling of joy.

Having been taken out of the bath, the baby is wrapped up in a bath towel from head to toe, put down on a little table, and carefully dried; he is patted through the towel with the hands, which are pressed into all the recesses and wrinkles of the skin. After this the baby is rubbed with boiled vegetable oil or vaseline behind the ears, under the armpits, between the legs, and in all the folds of the skin. He is then quickly dressed and put to sleep.

Clothing and diapers must be put on in such a way that children remain comfortable and their movements are not cramped. Babies wear a nightie of thin material which is fastened at the back, and on top of this a jacket of some warm cotton material which fastens in the front. These pieces of clothing are folded upward so that they will not get wet.

The lower part of the child's body is wrapped up in a diaper (which may be made out of muslin) folded into a triangle. The long part of the diaper is placed under the baby's buttocks, the lower end is placed between the legs, and the two other ends go around the baby's pelvis and join on the stomach. After this, the baby is wrapped up to the armpits in a light blanket, and over this is placed a heavier one, folded in such a way that the legs are well covered. If the baby must be wrapped up in a blanket, a small oilcloth (30 centimeters by 30 centimeters) is put under him. After two or three months, there is no need to put a diaper on the baby; instead he can wear a simple style of "combination" overalls-diapers.

Children must be taught cleanliness from a very early age. This depends above all on the extent to which adults concern themselves about changing the baby's clothing immediately when it is wet or dirty. This must be done carefully, without inflicting unpleasant sensations on the baby. In response to cheerful and gentle talk of adults, babies, while they are being changed, will move about in a lively manner and make sounds which they have learned to pronounce. Talking to older children (over 6 months), the nurse and her assistant name the clothing and the actions which they are performing; when the baby reaches 9 or 10 months, you can suggest to him that he sit down, lie down, stretch out an arm or leg and perform a large number of other movements required in dressing, and he will perform them with pleasure.

Babies who are used to having soiled clothing changed regularly express their discomfort and cry if they are again wet. This serves as a signal to adults that help is needed.

In kindergarten it is not possible to hold each baby on the toilet seat. Therefore they are put on the toilet only from the time when they are able to sit up well, typically by the time they are 8 months old.

Babies must be put on the toilet seat systematically from day to day, but only at the moment when they feel the need to pass water or have a bowel movement: before going to sleep, after sleeping, when the baby wakes up dry, and about fifteen or twenty minutes after feeding.

Babies must be put on the toilet at other times too, if they indicate a need through restless movements or by crying or acting upset. The practice of putting babies on the toilet must not be abused by frequent sittings. Until such time as the babies are used to this procedure, they should not be put on the toilet more than three or four times within a 24-hour period.

The nurse or her assistant should stay near babies for the whole time while they are sitting on the toilet and stimulate them to the physiological acts with appropriate sounds, calming them down when they indicate they are upset. No more than three or four babies should be sat down on toilets simultaneously.

As soon as the baby has excreted, he must be immediately taken off the toilet and wiped, and his clothing put in order. Should a sitting of three to four minutes on the toilet produce no results, the baby must be lifted off and sat down again after a little while. It is important to teach the babies to ask to use the toilet whenever they feel the need to do so.

The babies are put on the toilet in a bathroom or in some other area specially set aside for this purpose. The toilets must be small so that they are comfortable for babies to sit on, and have smooth edges without cracks or marks. Each toilet has its own brush, and the nurse and assistant must see to it that they are properly used.

INSTRUCTIONAL WORK IN THE WAKING HOURS

In working with the youngest babies (3 to 5 weeks to 3 to 5 months), the nurse must remember that they need not only hygienic care and breast feeding but also the development of their neuropsychological activity.

At this age, the main attention must be directed toward the formation of audiovisual reflexes, and the development of the positive happy emotions which determine the general animation of the baby and improve all of his physiological processes.

When the children are awake, it is important that they be put in a playpen. There should never be more than six to eight children in a playpen at one given time. Moreover, those who cannot move about must be placed in different areas of the playpen.

One should put children up to 2 months in the playpen immediately after feeding, having previously wrapped them in a blanket up to the underarms and having put a flat pillow or a folded diaper under their head. Toward the end of the waking period, overalls should be put on the babies to enable them to move about freely.

It is very important to take care that the child does not catch cold. Therefore the baby must not be put down right away on a spread covered with oilcloth, but rather on a blanket a corner of which is folded over to cover the baby. 2- to 3-month-old babies wear playsuits during their waking hours.

It is healthful for the child to be in different positions, that is, lying not only on his back, but also on his stomach. This contributes to the strengthening of the body muscles. Children must be put down on their stomachs before meals or toward the end of the waking period. After meals, this position might cause vomiting. If a baby who, lying on his stomach, gets tired of the same position and begins to fret, he must be turned over on his back.

As a result of lying down on his stomach every day, after two or three months the baby learns how to raise and hold up his head.

From time to time, the nurse does exercises with the babies who know how to hold their head erect (at 2 to 2 ½ months) to prepare them for more complicated movements, such as standing and walking. Holding the baby under the armpits, she gives the baby a chance to stretch out his legs from the hips and touch a table or the adult's knees, to do a sort of dance. In doing this, however, the nurse does not allow a baby under 4- or 5-months-old to stand on his legs. A playful exercise like this is not only healthful but gives the babies a great deal of pleasure.

While the babies are awake, the nurse keeps in close contact with them. She plays with them, talks affectionately to each of them, sings nursery rhymes, and endeavors to induce in the babies a happy mood. The nurse sees to it that the children who are lying down in the playpen are kept active and busy. Constant affection of the staff toward the babies creates in them a happy state. Seeing the nurse, the baby begins to smile and move about energetically, stretching out and bending his arms and legs and making sounds which are of great significance for the later development of speech. The person in charge must remember at all times that a prevailing state of happiness in small children is vital for their proper physical and psychological development.

From the very first months of life, the baby begins to be aware of surrounding sounds, and he reacts to them in different ways. Loud, shrill sounds usually evoke crying, while melodious sounds he will listen to attentively. For this reason, the nurse and her assistant must speak to the children in an even voice with a calm, soothing intonation. By calling the child's name and then coming up to him, the nurse and her assistant develop in the baby the ability to determine from which direction a sound is coming.

In the second month of life the baby begins to focus his sight on surrounding objects, especially on those which attract his attention by their bright color, as well as on the faces of adults when they are talking to him. Gradually babies begin to follow moving objects with their gaze. In order to help develop the ability to concentrate visual attention on objects and their movement, it is recommended that some bright large toy (balloon) be suspended above the baby's chest, at a distance of about 70 centimeters, or, if the toy is smaller, at a distance of 50 to 60 centimeters.

Pictures on the walls of the babies' rooms, large bright toys on the shelves, and low flowering plants at the windows all attract the babies' attention; the babies look at them while in a variety of different positions (lying on their backs, on their stomachs, or in a vertical position in the arms of an adult).

With babies from 3- to 3 ½-months-old the nurse continues to develop the ability to see and distinguish objects, and to listen and distinguish (and even imitate) sounds; she encourages attempts by the baby to use vocal chords. It is essential to encourage the development of the grasping movements of the hands as well as those movements which prepare the baby for crawling, sitting, and standing.

Babies at this age continue to be put in playpens while they are awake, but they need more space. As they are able to change their position, and later to move a little, they must be given this opportunity. For babies of this age (up to 7 months), experiments have demonstrated the convenience of a playpen on legs with sides made of vertical and horizontal boards.

Dressed in a baby's vest, a warm jacket and a playsuit, children can move their legs and arms around freely.

Celluloid rings with balls and other toys should be hung up above 3-month-old babies not only so that they can look at them, but also so that they can occasionally grasp them when their hands accidentally knock against them. Later on when, toward the age of 4 months, the baby can extend his arms all the way, the toys should be hung higher. At that point, the baby's movements can be made more complicated by providing such toys as parrots and rattles, which require greater coordination of movement.

Beginning when he is 3-months-old, each baby must be given, besides the suspended toys, something to hold in his hands such as pleasant sounding rattles of various shapes. From 5 to 6 months on, when the babies are able to grasp and hold an object in their hands, they no longer need the suspended toys.

While they are awake, the nurse keeps the babies happy by talking to them in a gentle voice, encouraging response, and giving them toys corresponding to their stage of development. She makes sure that babies are all spread out in the playpen so that they will not get in each other's way. The nurse helps those babies who still do not know how to change their position: some are put on their stomachs, others are turned over on their backs; the 5- to 6-month-old babies are encouraged to crawl by having brightly colored toys placed within easy reach.

With the help of the nurse in charge the baby gradually masters the movements preparatory to crawling: by the age of 4 months he begins to turn from his back onto his side; by 5 months, from his back onto his stomach; and by 6 months, from his stomach on to his back. A 5-month baby can stay a long time on his stomach with his arms extended, propping himself up with the palms of his hands, raising the upper part of his body, and arching his back. By the age of 6 months he stands on all fours, leaning on the palms of his hands and his knees. At that stage some children begin to crawl.

As of 4 to 5 months of age, a baby recognizes and distinguishes adults close to him (his mother, the nurse and her assistants). The nurse, taking advantage of the mother's arrival at the kindergarten (when the baby is brought to the kindergarten, is being breast fed or is about to leave), turns to the baby affectionately and says, "Mommy has arrived, let's go to Mommy," or "Mommy will come again for her little girl Olya," or "Misha will go home with Mommy now."

The nurse must do her best to see that all the time which the mother spends at the kindergarten is used for close personal contact between her and the baby. Suitable conditions must be established to permit the mother to spend a little time talking and playing with the baby after feeding.

Infants from 6 to 9 months develop the ability to perform a series of movements: crawling and changing position at will; sitting without the help of adults; lying down and then standing up; walking while leaning on something. For children over 7 months, the playpen must be replaced by a sufficiently large area of the floor which is covered with an oilcloth-covered spread. A specially made fence or various pieces of furniture (such as tables, sofas and climbing horses) may serve to enclose the area.

The nurse, leading various activities, encourages the children to be physically active. Pointing to a toy placed at some distance from the infant, the nurse gently urges him on: "Ivan, here is a ball, come on, crawl to it, come on!" She thereby stimulates in the baby the desire to get close to it."

A toy, placed on top of the railing, encourages the baby to stand up. If the toy is moved, the baby will try to move step by step to follow the toy. He will experience a great sense of satisfaction if, reaching the toy, he is able to take it in his hands.

Babies of 6 to 9 months of age show noticeably increased interest in their surroundings; they can, by moving around, get familiar with a large number of objects. By the age of 9 months, babies begin to walk holding on to surrounding objects.

The nurse then makes the babies' handling of toys more precise and intricate. If at the beginning the baby limits himself to inspecting the toy, shaking it, banging it, and shifting it from one hand to the other, then by eight or nine months of age, as a result of training, he masters various actions suggested by the object itself: he shakes a rattle, he rolls a ball, he squeezes a squeaking toy. The baby's interest in toys will increase significantly; he is able to play with them for a longer period, and when he drops them he is distressed.

The nurse develops the babies' speech and familiarizes them with the names of surrounding objects, pointing to them and naming them as she goes along: "clock," "cat," "dog." Changing the usual position of an object, she challenges the baby to find it. The baby will remember the names of things better if he is given an opportunity not only to look at them, but also to use them (to roll a ball, to shake a rattle).

If, wishing to attract a child's attention, the nurse calls him by his name, the baby begins to respond first by turning his head, and then later with sounds. Children recognize the names of the nurse and her assistant if they call themselves by name when playing hide and seek with the babies ("Where's Auntie Ann?") or challenge the baby to "give Auntie Mary the toy."

Babies of this age are not only interested in adults, people who are around them constantly, but also in babies their own age. The interest of a baby in the one next to him in the playpen is already obvious. A baby can, although not for very long at the beginning, observe what his neighbor does with this or that toy, the way he laughs or moves about. In answer to his laugh, the baby smiles and tries to get closer to him. These attempts at mutual communication are to be encouraged provided that they are inspired by good will and friendliness and give the babies pleasure.

These efforts will only be successful in cases where the mutual relationships are developed under the constant influence and guidance of the nurse. At this age, negative relationships between babies may also appear; a baby seeing a toy in the hands of another baby begins to take it away from him. One should then divert his attention to some other toy, take the baby into one's arms or talk to him gently.

To arouse the babies' interest in each other and to acquaint them with each other's names, the nurse may use various games such as hide and seek. She puts a muslin napkin over a baby's head and, turning to the other babies, says: "Where is Alyosha? Alyosha's gone, gone!"; then, taking off the napkin, she exclaims, "Here is our Alyosha." In this kind of game, the attention of a small group of babies is attracted toward a specific baby, and they hear and remember his name.

If the nurse accompanies with words the baby's actions, as well as her own when handling objects, the babies then quickly assimilate the name of these actions. Holding the baby in her arms, the nurse brings him up close to various objects and attracts his attention to their functions: "The clock goes tic-toc." Such instruction gives the babies new impressions and evokes a happy mood. On being told by the nurses "Give me your hand," "Bring me the ball," "Bring me the rattle," the baby begins actually to carry out the simple actions involved.

To give the babies practice in pronouncing sounds and syllables, the nurse encourages them to imitate. Some games will be found very useful for this purpose, especially those based on nursery rhymes.

To further improve the ability of the babies to look and listen, the teacher shows them winding toys and fish swimming in an aquarium, and hums or sings songs. The nurse's singing lends a special emotional feeling to her relationship with each baby, as well as to the games which she plays with the babies in small groups. At the beginning, the babies listen attentively, then begin to indicate their pleasure with a smile, a "coo," and animated movements.

The babies who already know how to follow moving objects with their eye particularly enjoy it when the teacher shows them some bright shining toy and sings a song at the same time. For example, one may sing a song and at the same time wave a flag or shake a rattle.

Babies at this age usually have three musical activities a week. Half an hour after feeding time, the babies are brought closer together in the playpen and everything that may distract their attention is removed, for example, suspended toys and the toys lying around in the playpen.

At the beginning of this period, the teacher sings or plays on some instrument (mirliton, mouth organ, metallophone), then for no more than five to six minutes performs rhythmical movements using any sort of toy, little flag, or rattle. This demonstration should proceed without hurry, so that all the babies can follow the moving object with their eyes.

In order for the teacher's singing to be enjoyed by the babies, it must be soft and melodious. Loud singing deafens babies and prevents them from listening attentively. Singing should be heard in the kindergarten not only during special activities, but also when relating to the babies individually, whenever they are being undressed, and on walks during the summer.

From 9 to 10 months up to 12 months of age, children must be taught to walk by themselves and to pronounce consciously about ten very simple words, such as mommy, pussy, and so on. ... As of 10 or 11 months, the babies move from one support to another, crawl, and climb up and down a three-step climber, while at about 12 months, they begin to walk without using any support.

At this age babies master movements in independent activity and therefore must have at hand suitable toys and sufficient room to be able to move about. For this reason, a space must be set aside which is partitioned off from the rest of the room by a railing. The furniture placed in this area, for instance a climber, a play table, or a little couch, will be used by the teacher for the babies' physical development and play.

It is also important that the babies be provided with brightly colored, pretty, washable toys: large and small colored balls for rolling, rings to lower onto a pole, rattles, rubber toys, and, later on, celluloid and rubber dolls as well as bits of colored materials.

Besides, it is important that toys should be so selected that the baby can use several of them at the same time. Examples are a box with two or three balls (so that babies can put the balls into the box, then take them out), a little stand with rings attached, and so forth.

Not all available toys should be given to the babies for play: some of them should be stored in a closet. From time to time it is good to change the set of toys with which the babies play. Otherwise they will no longer hold their attention. A baby should not be allowed to play with a broken toy. So that each baby can choose a toy easily, they should be spread out on tables, on the climber, on the couch, on top of or inside the toy box. The babies crawl or walk up to the toys and take them in their hands. While playing, the babies move about, take toys from one place to another, climb up on the little couch, or sit down on the floor.

If, by the age of 11 months, a baby does not make any attempts to walk, special exercises should be done with him. The nurse or assistant, sitting down in front of the baby, holds out her hands toward him and calls him to her: "Masha, come to me!" This encourages the child to walk by himself.

It is also possible, holding a toy in one's hands, to stimulate the baby's desire to come toward it and take it. It is very important to encourage the child at such a time, as this helps him to overcome the fear of falling. It is good to attract the attention of children and adults present to the success of the baby: "Look, children, how nicely Ivan is walking." One can also sing or beat out rhythmically "See how our Masha walks, top-da-top," etc. Giving him attention and encouraging his first steps makes the baby happy and stimulates his desire to move by himself.

From time to time, the nurse draws several babies into a motion game, for example "Hide and Seek." She "hides" right in front of the children and asks: "Who will go and look for Auntie Anya?" Some of the babies will set out to look for her.

The nature of the independent activity depends mainly on the way it is organized by the adults. Although the babies at this age are given enough time for such activity and have acquired some ability to move about and handle toys by themselves, they still cannot play for any length of time without the participation of adults. Therefore, the nurse must have her mind on the babies who are playing, mix with them, introduce variety into their activities and prevent negative relationships from springing up between them.

      ·   ·   ·

After some time the baby will attempt to carry over the actions he has learned to other similar objects; for instance, he will put together the two halves of a *matreshki*,[2] he will put the lid on a saucepan after looking for the lid by himself, etc. The nurse encourages the babies to play independently, but comes to the rescue herself when this seems necessary.

One cannot expect babies at this age to put the toys away. This the nurse and her assistant must do, and toys with which the babies are not playing should not be allowed to remain scattered on the floor. While the babies are asleep, the nurse or her assistant washes the toys and puts them back in their proper place.

A baby who has learned to move about independently has an opportunity to get better acquainted with surrounding objects, and to associate more with other babies his age as well as with adults. Babies enjoy this immensely. One should help babies at this age to develop their ability to see and distinguish objects, and to observe. This is an indispensable condition for the development of the children's speech.

Working with each baby individually and with small groups of babies (no more than five), the nurse strives to improve the babies' understanding of adult speech, and at the same time develops their own speech and their ability to communicate with adults for various reasons and on different occasions. To make the babies familiar with the names of objects, the nurse shows various objects to the baby and names them. Then she asks him to give her a toy, the name of which the baby knows by that time, and gives the name of a toy that is still unfamiliar to the baby.

A series of games can also be organized to this effect. For example, the nurse suggests that the babies bring this or that toy which is placed within easy view. When the baby brings the toy to the teacher, she names it, saying: "Here, Sergei has just brought the cat, purr-purr. Good boy, Sergei." In another variation, the nurse, together with the babies, "hides" toys, naming the toys and the place where they are hidden: "Let's put the chicken on the table, let's put the ball on the couch," and so on; then the group of babies, together with the nurse, "looks for" the toys, each time naming them.

After some time, the nurse begins to work on developing the babies' ability to generalize, having them find objects similar in name but different in appearance and in the material of which they are made. For

---

[2]A *matreshki* is a container in the shape of a peasant woman, containing smaller containers of the same shape, sometimes as many as twelve and as few as two.

instance, she asks them to bring dolls (made of rubber, celluloid, rag) or dogs (of papier-mâché, rubber, wood).

The teacher names the actions with which the babies are very familiar: the ball rolls, the rattle rattles, and so forth. Just as she did in the previous subgroup, the nurse continues to acquaint the babies with the names of the surrounding children and adults, and to develop in them friendly attitudes toward each other.

Further improving their babbling is very significant for the development of the active speech of the babies. The particular sounds uttered by the babies must be clearly and slowly repeated (*ma-ma, ba-ba*). New sounds are then introduced as well as such words as are within the ability of the baby to repeat, frequently those linked by similarity in sound: doggy (*av-av*), etc.

In order to arouse the babies' interest in the imitation of sounds and the pleasurable experiences related to this type of exercise, a simple dramatization can be organized using various toys. For example, holding a doll wrapped up in a blanket, the nurse sings a lullaby. Showing the babies a toy rooster, she says: "Here is our rooster! How beautiful he is! He sings loudly: 'koo-ka-re-koo.' The rooster wants to peck grain. Peck, Peter (the rooster), peck, peck. And now he sings his song again, 'koo-ka-re-koo'. Children, how does the rooster sing?"

Similar dramatizations may be shown with other toys. Doing this, one must keep in mind that the babies will want to play with the toy which has been shown, so it is important to prepare ahead of time a sufficient number of such toys to satisfy the desire of all the babies who want to play with them.

Much laughter and joy is brought about by showing winding toys. The nurse lets a winding car go on a slide or on the table. "Here goes the car, too-too-too," she says. The babies go on repeating the simple sounds, such as too-too, which the nurse pronounces with particular emphasis.

If the teacher-nurse sings or dances with little flags or a bright kerchief, tambourine or rattle, the babies will look on with great interest, laugh, babble and hop around, and, sitting either in the playpen or standing by a railing, draw close to the nurse, expressing their desire to dance. Imitating the nurse, the babies also try to hit the tambourine which is brought to them. When mixing with the children, the nurse sings songs, clapping the babies' hands or, having taken a baby in her arms, raises and lowers him gently in time with the dance music. Later, the baby will begin to make dancing movements as soon as he hears gay music.

In connection with such activities for babies of this age, the songs in the collection of Babadjan can be used. The best for listening are the following: "Ladooshki (Palms)," arranged by Rimsky-Korsakov, "The Rooster," arranged by Krasev, "The Little Bird" by Raukhverger, words by Barto, etc.

With babies of this age group, the teacher spends five to seven minutes doing musical exercises. If such training was performed regularly when the babies were in the previous age group, then the babies listen eagerly and look for the teacher who is playing or singing. At the age of nine to ten months the babies turn their head toward the side of the room from which the sound of song or music is coming.

The listening attention of babies at this age continues to develop. They can be attentive to music for 20 or 30 seconds without a break, and listen in a general way to music (with breaks) for two or three minutes. Singing, when accompanied by the showing of bright objects and toys or movements by the teacher, stimulates in the babies the desire to be active.

Much interest and happiness is experienced by the babies when observing animals: chickens, pigeons, sparrows, hens, a cat, a puppy, a rabbit, or a baby goat. The process of getting acquainted with these animals is usually accompanied by certain movements and the pronouncing of various sounds.

Gradually the babies must be acquainted with pictures of the objects and animals with which they are familiar. Pictures for babies must be drawn beautifully, clearly, and in bright colors (*Pictures for the Little Ones*, cardboard cubes with pictures on them may be used).

In addition to the regular activity periods, the nurse takes advantage of each time she is in close contact with the babies to develop their active speech and their understanding of adult speech.

STRENGTHENING THE BABY'S ORGANISM

The program for strengthening the baby's organism is directed at increasing its resistance to harmful influences in the environment and developing its capacity to adapt to sharp changes in the temperature of the surrounding air. In addition, special measures involving natural elements, such as air, water and sunshine, are applied to build up resistance.

In daily life maintenance of a normal temperature inside the building, the systematic exposure of the babies to the open air in clothing suited to the season, and washing of their hands and face in lukewarm water contribute to strengthening their organisms. In this strengthening process one must observe the following rules: proceed gradually and systematically and take into consideration the special individual characteristics of the babies.

The principle of proceeding gradually is applied in lowering the water temperature and the air temperature on the premises, in increasing the length of time spent in the open, and in partially shaded areas, and in lightening the babies' clothing.

The systematic repetition of the measures which have been initiated for strengthening their organisms develops corresponding habits in the babies and quickens the organism's adaptation to changing conditions. It is also essential to take into consideration the state of health and physical development of each baby as well as the specific characteristics of his nervous system and his degree of sensitivity to changes in the outside environment.

Of all means available in the kindergarten for strengthening the baby's organism, the most readily applicable is that involving the control of the air temperature. It is important to see to it that the buildings are constantly well aired. With this in mind, whenever the babies are out on a walk or during their sleep on the veranda, the room should be thoroughly ventilated. Besides, even when the babies are occupying the room, vents must be periodically opened, and when the air outside warms up, windows should be opened.

During warm days when the temperature in the shade is no lower than $+18°$ to $+20°$, the whole life of the babies is moved outside. For this purpose, awnings or roofs are built to provide shade in the play areas, flooring is laid down, and playpens are set up. Whenever the weather gets warmer, the babies wear lighter clothing corresponding to the air temperature.

In order to strengthen the body, babies are exposed to air for various lengths of time. At first this is done inside, limiting the experience to a predetermined air temperature. For very small babies, exposure to air is combined with change of clothing or diapers; moreover, in cold weather this operation takes place near a source of warm air. While this is going on, the air temperature in the babies' room must be $+20°$ to $+22°$. A rise in the temperature above normal increases babies' perspiring, and when it decreases, they show signs of catching cold.

As the baby grows, air exposure is gradually increased from three or four to ten minutes. Strengthening the baby's organism by exposing him to the open air when the weather is cold is done during the day sleep.

Babies must be warmly dressed for sleeping outside. Babies in their first month of life, on top of the usual underwear, are wrapped up in a warm blanket, then put into a sleeping bag. A kerchief is put on their head as well as a warm hood. Mattresses for day sleep are taken out just before the babies are put to sleep.

2- to 3-month-old babies sleep in the open two or three times a day whenever the weather is calm and the temperature not lower than $-5°$. At first, the babies are not exposed to air for more than 15 or 20 minutes;

gradually this time is increased up to one or one and a half hours. By the time they are 1 year old, children may sleep outside when the temperature is lower (up to − 10°). In cold weather the baby's face should be left exposed but rubbed with some oily cream. The nurse and her assistant keep watch over the condition of the baby while he is sleeping, and if his face becomes pale it is covered with a blanket.

As the weather warms up, the clothing is gradually lightened; the baby, put in a sleeping bag, is not wrapped up in a blanket any more, but in a cotton sheet, and finally he is put to bed not in a sleeping bag but simply in a woolen blanket.

Of the various types of water procedures for this age group, rubbing is the most recommended. To prepare an infant's organism for the water procedure, a daily dry rub is desirable, as is recommended by Professor Speranskii. The body of the baby is rubbed with a piece of clean flannel or some other material until it becomes slightly red. After two or three weeks of dry rubbing, one may progress to wet rubbing. This process should take place either in the morning after the child wakes up or after the second daytime nap; the baby's body should be warm before rubbing.

Wet rubbing is performed with a washcloth, dampened in water of suitable temperature and then squeezed out slightly. At first, the water temperature should be + 34° or + 35°. By lowering the water temperature every two or three days it is brought down to + 26° or + 27°.

Getting a small baby used to wet rubbing should be done with extreme care. When this is done for the first time, the baby's body is covered loosely with a blanket and only that part of the body which is to be rubbed down with water remains bare.

The rubbing process takes place in a definite order: first, the arms are rubbed (from hands to shoulder), then the chest and stomach. Then the child having been put over on his stomach, the back is rubbed as well as the buttocks and legs. After wet rubbing each part of the body, it is immediately dried completely. Then the whole body is rubbed with a dry soft towel until it becomes slightly red, and the baby is dressed in his usual clothing.

Whenever this operation is applied to babies of 8 months and older, they may sit down, and it is only at the time when their legs are rubbed that they have to lie down. The order in which the wet rubbing is performed for babies of this age and older remains the same as for the younger ones.

Showers for babies less than one year old are not recommended. They lead to a violent disturbance of the nervous system.

Sunbathing is not applied as a means of strengthening the organism of an infant. Babies under 1 year of age are not taken out under the direct rays of the sun, but after some time spent in the shade where the air temperature should not be lower than $+20°$, they should be placed in partly shaded areas to play quietly in playpens.

Massages and exercises are prescribed for babies in accordance with their age. For this purpose babies in their first year of life are divided into four groups: from 1½ to 3 months, from 3 to 6, from 6 to 9, and from 9 to 12 months. For each group the doctor prescribes a set of exercises and massages, taking into consideration the specific individual characteristics of the children, and then sees to it that they are carried out.[3]

Suggested Distribution of Duties between the Nurse and Her Assistant for the Group of Infants in Their First Year of Life

TIME OF DAY	NURSE	ASSISTANT
7:00–8:00 A.M.	Receives the incoming babies and keeps an eye on babies who are playing. Puts 3- to 6-month-old babies to bed.	Sets out equipment for playpen games. At 7:10 fetches the breakfast and feeds older babies—9 months to 1 year.
8:00–9:00 A.M.	Puts 6- to 9-month-old babies to bed. Helps assistant to feed older babies (from 9 months to 1 year) and organizes play and exercises for that group. Keeps an eye on babies who are sleeping.	Finishes feeding of older babies. Hands in and receives washing. Cleans up the place.
9:00–10:00 A.M.	Puts older babies (9 months to 1 year) on the toilet and then to bed. Prepares the equipment for playpen games. Wakes up 3- to 6-month-old babies. Passes them on to mothers for breast feeding. Gives additional food to those whose prescription calls for it. Organizes play for babies who have been fed.	Helps to put older babies to bed. Cleans up the place. Brings food for 6- to 9-month-old babies.
10:00–11:00 A.M.	Wakes up and feeds the 6- to 9-month-old babies. Passes them on to mothers for feeding. Organizes the waking period of the babies who have been fed. Does exercises with 3- to 6-month-old babies.	Helps the nurse to wake up and feed the older babies.

[3]K. D. Hubert and M. G. Reiss, *Exercises and Massages for Infants,* Leningrad, 1963.

*Suggested Distribution of Duties between the Nurse and Her
Assistant for the Group of Infants in Their First Year of Life*

TIME OF DAY	NURSE	ASSISTANT
11:00–12:00 P.M.	Leads activities with 6- to 9-month-old babies. Organizes their waking period. Wakes up and feeds babies 9 to 12 months old.	Puts to bed babies 3 to 6 months old. Does the dishes. Brings food and helps to feed the 9- to 12-month-old babies.
12:00–1:00 P.M.	Continues feeding babies from 9 to 12 months old. Organizes their waking period and leads activities. 30-minute break.	Puts 6- to 9-month-old babies to bed. Helps feeding of older babies. Puts them on the toilet. (At the time of nurse's break) washes dishes. Tidies up room. Keeps an eye on the babies who are playing and those who are sleeping.
1:00–2:00 P.M.	As mothers arrive, wakes 3- to 6-month-old babies and gives them to mothers for feeding. Watches after the babies who are sleeping. Organizes play and activities with older babies. Starts putting older babies to sleep.	Takes from mothers the babies who are finished feeding. Gets ready all things necessary for their play.
2:00–3:00 P.M.	Feeds the 6- to 9-month-old babies. Gives babies to mothers for breast feeding. Leads activities with the 3- to 6-month-old babies and puts them to bed.	Fetches food for 6- to 9-month-old babies. Puts older babies to bed. Helps feed 6- to 9-month-old babies. Washes dishes, watches after babies who are sleeping.
3:00–4:00 P.M.	Leads activities and organizes waking time for 6- to 9-month-old babies. Sets out equipment, etc., for play of the older babies.	30-minute break. Gets the afternoon snack for older babies. Puts 6- to 9-month-olds to bed.
4:00–5:00 P.M.	Picks up the older babies who are awake and feeds them. As mothers arrive, babies are passed on to them for feeding.	Helps to get older babies out of bed and feed them.
5:00–6:00 P.M.	Gives babies 3 to 6 and 9 to 12 months old to mothers who take them home. Supervises play of older babies and sleep of 6- to 9-month-old babies.	Does the dishes. Prepares dirty wash for dispatch to laundry. Tidies up the place. Gets food for 6- to 9-month-old babies.

Suggested Distribution of Duties between the Nurse and Her Assistant for the Group of Infants in Their First Year of Life

TIME OF DAY	NURSE	ASSISTANT
6:00–7:00 P.M.	Gets 6- to 9-month-old babies out of bed and feeds them. Supervises babies who are playing. Passes babies to mothers (who feed, change and take babies home). Gets everything ready for receiving the babies the next morning and for their playing.	Helps to get babies out of bed and to feed the 6- to 9-month-olds. Finishes up cleaning.

IV

The Care and Upbringing of Children in the Second Year of Life

THE CHILD'S DAY IN THE KINDERGARTEN

Strict observance of a daily schedule, providing for feeding at regulated times and the proper alternation of sleep and active periods, has a great influence on the health, physical development, feelings and behavior of a child in his second year of life.

The schedule is of great educational significance. Children get used to a definite order which is repeated from day to day. They fall asleep without fuss because, at the scheduled times, they feel the need for sleeping; at the accustomed time for feeding they feel the urge to eat and they eat willingly the appropriate amount of food. After being fed sufficiently, they play cheerfully, gaily and actively.

In connection with the development of the nervous system, the schedule for the second year of life provides for an increase in the waking period and a decrease in the amount of time devoted to daytime naps.

Children from 1- to 1 ½-years-old sleep twice a day for periods of one and a half to two and a half hours and are kept awake without interruption for periods of three and a half to four hours. Children over 1½ years old sleep only once a day for a period of three to three-and-a-half hours and are kept awake four-and-a-half to five hours.

The schedule of feeding times, sleeping and waking periods is altered for the children in the older subgroup—they sleep after their dinner.

For children in their second year of life who are being raised in a single group, two schedules are prescribed—one for the younger ones, that is up to 1 year and 6 months, and one for the others, from 1 year 6 months on. The sleeping and waking periods for the two groups do not coincide, which gives the nurse and her assistant the chance to devote more time to the small groups of children who are awake at a given time.

In order to determine the schedule for each child, not only his age but the condition of his health and general development must be taken into account. It is advisable to hold the weaker children with poorly balanced nervous systems back on the schedule of a younger subgroup of children. A child is moved to a different schedule when the nurse, after observing the child for some time, notices that he does not fall asleep on time or wakes up too soon, and that he has no appetite at meal time. She reports this to the doctor who, when he finds it necessary, gives instructions to transfer the child onto the next schedule.

When a child is moved on to the older subgroup, the nurse must carefully observe whether he adapts to the new schedule. If the child begins to fret, eats and sleeps poorly, or becomes disinterested and sluggish, he must be put back on the previous schedule for a little while (three or four days).

It is not recommended that a child who has just been changed to a new schedule be given food to which he is not accustomed. He may either be gradually accustomed to the food of the older group and then transferred to the new schedule, or the other way around, but to do both at the same time is not advisable.

The whole attitude of children during the course of the day may be influenced by a happy frame of mind when they arrive at the kindergarten. This often depends on the way the nurse or her assistant greets the child and the manner in which they ease his parting with the mother. Not only do they pay special attention to the child, but also to the parents, trying to establish contact with them and to stimulate reciprocal trust in questions of child upbringing and care.

Meeting the children in the reception room, the nurse welcomes and greets child and mother alike. In a brief business talk she finds out how the child slept, how he feels; checks the child's throat and skin, and takes his temperature. "All's well. Let's go inside, Sasha. Tanya is already waiting to play with you there. Good-bye, Mommy!" says the nurse in a gentle, cheerful voice and takes the child away. "Hi, Tanya, look, here is Sasha," says the nurse, giving the child over to her assistant. The latter changes the child and keeps an eye on the children's play while the nurse receives other children. The assistant greets every child enthusiastically and talks to him as she undresses him. Those children who have been brought early should be given breakfast and not have to wait for the others to assemble.

Should the nurse notice that a child is looking limp or pale, she questions the mother in greater detail regarding the condition of his health and his behavior at home. She finds out how he slept during the night, whether he had a temperature, what he was given to eat, if he went to the toilet, and so on; then she shows the child to the doctor and observes him particularly closely over the course of the day.

Toys which attract the children's attention are spread out at various places in the room; when the children arrive, they begin to play with pleasure.

Some find it difficult to get used to new conditions, and when parents leave they scream and cry. Such children require the special attention of the nurse and assistant. At their arrival, a bright toy (colored ball, doll) must be gotten ready to attract their attention, keep them away from tears, and calm them down. In such cases, it is also good to show a winding toy in action. Holding the child in one's arms and talking to him gently usually calms down the child. It is better to do this in a room where there are no children, lest others, seeing the crying child, may also burst out crying.

The nurse and her assistant continue to teach the children good health habits in their second year. It can be expected that a child of about 18 months will ask to use the toilet if he has previously been trained in this regard.

In order to establish in children the habit of using the toilet in time, definite times of day when the child is to be sat down on the toilet must be strictly observed: before and after a walk, before going to sleep and after waking up, when the child wakes up dry. At this age the habit of asking to be put on the toilet is only in the process of being formed. It can easily be broken if adults are not careful to remind the children about this. On the other hand, if the nurse or assistant lacks sufficient tact and tears the child away from an interesting game to put him on the toilet (when he has not yet learned to turn to the adults in time about this) not only will he not develop proper sanitary habits, but he will strongly resist being put on the toilet.

The children are put on the toilet in a separate room. Each toilet pot must be marked for a specific child, and they should be stored on shelves.

When the nurse brings food from the kitchen, the children begin to wash their hands. The nurse calls two or three children, saying: "Let's go, Misha, and wash our hands, Auntie Mary has already brought our dinner. Sasha's coming with us too, and so is Tanya." The nurse reminds the children that they must put away their toys. If the child does not pay any attention to the nurse's remark, she repeats gently or puts them away herself and leads the children toward the washbasin. The children must gradually be trained to go and wash voluntarily.

For children of this age group, low washbasins should be provided, and, should this be impossible, a stand should be built in front of an ordinary washbasin so that the children can stand on it and wash their hands easily.

An adult turns up the children's sleeves and urges them to wash their hands, to hold them under a stream of water and get them wet. Either the nurse or her assistant puts soap on both sides of the children's hands and then rinses it away. It is usually necessary not only to wash the hands, but also the face, especially in hot weather or when the baby's nose is running.

While washing the children, the adults talk to them and encourage their actions. Seeing a child put his hand under the running water, the nurse says: "look what a good boy Misha is, he washes his hands himself. Does Tanya know how to do this?" Many small children do not like to have someone wash their face; therefore this must be done gently and carefully with appropriate remarks made to encourage the child. The nurse then dries off the child's face and hands with a towel. The children's towels may be hung at a height suitable for adults as the children are not yet able to use them themselves. If the older children's napkins are kept at the same place, then immediately after washing they are put on the children.

While showing and helping one child to wash his hands, the nurse gives two or three other children, standing by the washbasin with their sleeves rolled up, the chance to proceed independently: to wet their hands, put some soap in the palms of the hands, spread the soap all over their hands and rinse it all off. The adults accompany their own actions and those of the baby with brief sentences explaining to him what to do: "Wet your hands, take the soap," and so on.

Children of this age cannot as yet manage the whole operation of washing up on their own. The goal of the adult is to associate a pleasant sensation with the process of washing, and to develop the children's desire to participate actively in it.

In order to determine which of the younger children should be fed first, the nurse must know which one of them woke up first and when he was fed breakfast at home. The basic rule which must be remembered is that a child must be fed no more than one hour after he has awoken.

Children of the younger and older subgroups are fed differently, since the younger ones cannot yet eat by themselves and therefore must be fed by adults. The nurse and her assistant cannot feed more than two or three of the younger children at one time.

The feeding of children in their second year of life significantly changes. Breast feeding ceases and the child begins to get varied, thicker and more solid foods requiring chewing. The adults' problem is to get the children accustomed to eating unfamiliar foods, eating the amount of food which they are given, and getting into the habit of eating on their own.

Feeding must take place in favorable conditions. The children of the younger subgroup must be sat down at a fairly high table in highchairs with footstands. The nurse puts spoons in their hands, brings the plates with the food closer to the children, and coaxes them to eat. Observing the children's actions, she stimulates their attempts to eat by themselves and helps to get the food onto the spoon and up to the mouth. All of this she accompanies with words. At first, when children are being shown how to eat by themselves, they are given fairly thick food.

Adult guidance in the feeding process of younger children consists in providing immediate help: correcting the position of the spoon in the child's hand, helping him to get some food on the spoon, taking it to his mouth, getting him to take the cup properly in both his hands, and, when absolutely necessary, helping him to hold it. In the course of the feeding process, adults accompany all their own actions and those of the children with speech.

Realizing that the children are just beginning to learn how to eat independently, adults help the feeding process along by using an extra spoon (one for each child), giving each child in turn one or two spoonfuls of food.

After eating, adults carefully wipe the small child's mouth, and, if need be, wash his hands and face and take him to where the toys are.

The older children are fed at tables with four seats, the tables corresponding in size to the size of the children. The tables should be covered with a bright colored oilcloth, fastened under the table.

For both the first and the second dishes, soup plates are used. The spoons used should be fairly small (dessert spoons). For small children, the cups provided should be durable, with broad bottoms and a handle which can be held conveniently.

The serving table, corresponding to the children's age, gives them a chance to manage their food independently, without spilling or throwing the food about. The adults should encourage any independent actions by the children. Adults must bring the children close enough so that they are sitting comfortably and do not bother each other. So that the children do not soil their clothing, long bibs must be provided, covering their chest and knees.

There should be no waiting for food. As soon as the child sits down at the table, the nurse serves him food and suggests that he begin to eat. At this age, children can respond to the teacher's instructions: "Pick up the spoon in your other hand"; "Hold your cup with both hands"; "Bite off a piece of bread." It is sometimes necessary for the adult to correct the way a spoon or a cup is being held and to show the children how to eat properly by holding the child's hand in his own. The staff tries to anticipate incorrect movements by the child so that he doesn't spill or crumble the food.

One should remember that the children have not yet achieved full coordination of their movements and cannot be expected to be perfectly orderly during the meal. Having satisfied their hunger, children tire quickly, become distracted, and stop eating. Adults help them to finish the meal, see that dirty faces and hands are soon wiped off, and clean up the table if there are crumbs or something has been spilled. After finishing eating, each child leaves the table without delay and is given a chance to play.

While the assistant finishes the feeding of older children, the nurse leads activities with the little ones, and then with the older ones, after which they both assist in preparing the younger children for sleep.

As a rule, first the younger children must be settled down, as well as those children who are weak or tire easily and therefore need prolonged periods of sleep. Bedclothes must be prepared beforehand, and only after this has been done is the child picked up and put to bed.

Before going to sleep, each child must be put on the toilet. It is not advisable for more than three or four children to be taken to the toilet at the same time. After using the toilet, the children come back to the common room where they are dressed for sleep.

In order to insure normal conditions for restful sleep, a separate room must be provided so that the noise of children who are awake will not be heard.

It is advisable for the day sleep to be in the fresh air, on the veranda or in covered area of the playground. It is important to keep in mind that in cold weather children up to 1 year and 6 months are not taken for walks, and the older group takes walks only for very short periods of time. Therefore, sleeping out of doors is indispensable for this age group.

If conditions necessitate having the children sleep indoors, good cross ventilation should be assured: vents and windows must be kept open for the period of sleep (opened to a degree determined by the time of year, the temperature and the circulation of the air outside), taking care that the children do not lie near a cold draft of air and do not catch cold.

For sleeping out of doors, the children must be dressed in such a way that they do not get cold or overly hot. For this purpose, padded sleeping bags are convenient for cold weather.

To get the child ready for sleeping out of doors, all his clothing must be taken off except his undershirt. Pajamas or loose trousers are then put on him, he is wrapped up in a blanket, a kerchief is put on his head, he is put in a sleeping bag and then taken out and put in a cot at the place appointed for the children's sleep. Mattresses and pillows are taken out just before putting the children to bed.

Changing the child, the nurse speaks to him in a gentle and soft voice: "Look how we are going to wrap up Tanya. Tanya will be nice and warm when he sleeps; we'll cover his head with a kerchief," etc.

It happens with some children, especially those who have recently arrived at the nursery, that difficulties are experienced at bedtime, especially if at home they are used to being given a pacifier or being rocked or carried about in parent's arms. It is not advisable to change such habits abruptly. In such cases, the child should be picked up or be given attention in other ways, such as by sitting near him or talking to him for a little longer than with other children. With correct scheduling, the child will soon get used to new conditions and will fall asleep at the same time as the other children.

The whole process of getting the children ready for bed must be performed calmly, without haste or fuss, in order to induce in the children a corresponding mood and not upset the feeling of drowsiness which occurs at the scheduled times.

There must be full agreement between the nurse and her assistant with regard to their duties; each one must know the extent of her obligations. While the nurse is getting the children ready to sleep (bundling them up in sleeping bags, if the children are to sleep out of doors, or else settling them in their beds) and keeping an eye on those who are playing, the assistant puts children on the toilet or takes those who are ready out to the veranda.

When children are sleeping on the veranda, all windows should be wide open. The coldest temperature at which children may sleep out of doors in the winter is $-15°$.

As the weather warms up, children's clothing for sleeping out of doors becomes lighter. The blanket is taken away, the heavy sleeping bag is replaced by a lighter one, and then just by a blanket laid over the child. A knitted sleeping cap is put on his head.

While the children are sleeping during the day, one must keep watch over them to make sure they feel all right and are lying down comfortably, and that nothing is disturbing them. Some children must be covered up, others put on the toilet, some changed, and so forth.

All of these basic processes—washing, feeding and putting the children to bed—should always be carried out in the same tempo and in a fixed order. The adults taking care of children must always make the same demands. The head nurse must make clear to her assistant what is to be done and how, convince her of the necessity of developing in the children a desire to participate in taking care of themselves, and patiently work on the development of habits and skills. The nurse is responsible for observing and supervising her assistant's work.

The older children who have finished their activities are made ready for their walk by the assistant. She organizes toilet procedures and dresses the children.

While dressing the children, adults speak with them, naming the various parts of the clothing as well as associated actions. This helps the children to recognize and remember words which are new to them and keeps up the children's desire to participate in dressing. "I'll do it myself," says the child, although in reality he cannot yet do anything by himself. However, the fact that the child shows signs of wishing to act by himself will have a great significance in the future development of independence. Adults are to encourage children to perform such actions as they are able to do by themselves. For example, putting on overalls, the nurse says: "Stretch your leg, Tanya; now the other. So, that's good!" Some children who are used to being dressed silently at home and not called upon to participate in the process wait motionless for the adults to dress them and do not make any attempts to perform these actions by themselves. It is essential for the nurse to call the assistant's attention to such children and, together with her, to use various means to stimulate activity on their part. For instance, having put some pants on the child, the nurse asks: "And now, Voloda, what are we going to put on?" Although the child cannot speak yet, he will point to his boots.

Parents must also be induced to participate in developing their children's self-reliance. This will quicken the children's acquisition of habits.

It is very important when dressing children to follow the same sequence each time. During the cold weather, when the outfit of clothing to be worn is somewhat more complicated, trousers are put on first, then shoes, then a sweater. The head is covered with a kerchief. Mittens and a coat are put on and finally a cap or fur hat. It is important to check and make sure there is a handkerchief in the coat pocket which can be gotten out easily if needed.

The temperature of the air outside must be watched closely so that the children can be dressed appropriately for the weather. Occasionally in the morning it is very cold and the mother dresses the child warmly, but by the time the children are to take their walk, the weather has warmed up; then the children's clothing must be lightened to prevent them from perspiring excessively and from easily catching a cold. In cases like these, children should not wear a sweater under their coat, nor a scarf; and if there is no wind there is no need to raise their collar. There should be regular talks with the parents so that they do not wrap up their children too much and in order to insure that they are dressing them according to the weather. When the children are dressed, they must not remain indoors or else they may get overheated and catch cold upon going out of doors. Therefore the nurse goes outside with five or six children, not waiting for the remaining ones who are being dressed by the assistant and who will eventually be led out to the nurse.

It is extremely important to take toys along outside. The nurse should attract the children's attention to the toys and show the children how to use them: how to put sand in a bucket, dig sand with a shovel, put a doll in a stroller and walk her about, and so forth.

Children of this age group do not always know how to occupy themselves. The nurse alternates fast-moving games for three or four children with ones involving less motion: "You Can't Catch Me," "Hide and Seek," etc. While out of doors, the nurse tries to keep all the children busy doing something, and, particularly in cold weather, moving about a great deal. She herself must be sure to take part in these games. She also organizes for the children the observation of the surroundings.

She watches carefully the emotions of the children and the state of their clothing—whether they are hot, whether noses are clean, whether coats are well fastened, whether some shoe lace is untied, and so on. If she notices that a child needs to use the toilet, she immediately takes him indoors and passes the child along to some adult (in warm weather, chamber pots with lids must be made available out of doors).

The nurse teaches the children to take care of the toys, and during the whole time they are outside observes how the children are handling them. At the end of the period of outside play, the nurse, together with the children, puts away the toys in the toy box, counts balls, spades, and so forth, and hunts for the missing items. Toward the end of the play period the assistant comes out to help the nurse; she takes in some of the children and carries in some of the toys.

Before entering the building, the children must be taught to wipe their feet on the mat. In winter, adults must shake the snow off children's clothing, using small clothes brushes.

While undressing the children, adults try to encourage them to participate, and suggest to the older children that they perform certain tasks. Winter clothing (coat, hat) is removed but children themselves get their footwear from the closet, and, putting it down by their chair, then try to take off their outdoor pants. Adults take these garments off the child's legs, change his shoes and accompany him to the bathroom; from there he goes on to the common room.

This is the hardest period in the staff's work. The older children are located in three areas: the place where they are undressing, the bathroom and the common room. Everywhere they must be watched and helped. By this time, the small children are all beginning to wake up and require attention.

With this in mind, the administration arranges the shift schedule in such a way that at about this time, the nurse and assistant for the following shift are arriving for work. Together they attend to the meal, put the older children to bed, and take the younger ones out of bed. While one of the adults undresses the children, it is possible to have the other watch over the proceedings in the bathroom, help in washing hands, and then take them into the main room. The nurses sit the children at the tables, serve the first course, supervise the meal, and help spoonfeed the children. The nurse who is now free helps out wherever needed.

Children are gradually taught to eat the whole meal by themselves. Usually, they willingly eat the first course, then tire and eat the second course sluggishly, get distracted and stop eating altogether. In such cases, the adult sits on a low stool beside the child, slowly feeds him, giving the child a chance to chew the food, and then goes on to another.

Should some child, despite prompting and persuading, obstinately refuse to eat, it is better not to insist, as forced feeding may only produce a feeling of repugnance toward food. While feeding children, the adults talk to them: "Eat, children, the soup is tasty." To younger children the nurse suggests biting off a piece of bread and holding it in their hands. "Look, Aunt Nastya, Kathy has eaten her soup; give her a cutlet with potatoes. The cutlet is very good. Eat up, little girl." Thus in the process of being fed children learn the names of courses: soup, jelly, compote, tea, etc.

When the meal is over, the children leave the table. The nurse reminds each of them that he must wipe off his mouth with the napkin and say "thank you." She herself wipes off the children who don't know how, and helps pull back their chairs; then they go off and play.

Gradually, the older children are put to bed, following the same pattern as for the younger ones. The assistant takes the children to the bathroom and puts them on the toilets, all the while supervising the children who are playing. The nurse wraps each child up in a sleeping bag if they are to sleep outside, or undresses the children if they are to sleep indoors.

While undressing, the older children are taught to do things for themselves insofar as they are able: to bring up a low chair, take off shoes which are already unlaced and place them under the chair, take off an unfastened dress or shirt, panties, undershirts, or stockings, and lay them down on the chair.

Undressing the children, the nurse carefully folds up their clothing on a chair, making each child take notice of what he is doing.

At about this time, the younger children begin to wake up. They must be picked up gradually as they do this. A child who has awoken is dressed, fed and taken to that part of the room which has been set aside for play. Those children who are not accustomed to waking up on time must be awakened so as not to upset the feeding schedule.

The assistant brings the child who has awoken into the room where the nurse unwraps him and talks to him gently while changing him: "Tanya, how did you sleep? Well, let's get dressed quickly. Where is your hand?" "Where did you hide your legs?" the nurse jokes while holding the child's overalls.

If the children wake up without being wet, they must be put on the toilet, then have their hands washed, be fed and set to playing. While the assistant finishes lifting the children out of their beds and feeding them, the nurse begins to lead activities with small groups of children.

In warm weather, after activities, the younger children are taken outside for a play period; in summer they spend the whole day out of doors. In the winter, the little ones are not taken out for walks, as children who are heavily dressed because of the cold weather find it difficult to move about. If children move little, they tend to catch cold.

In the course of conversations with parents, the nurse endeavors to make them realize the importance of a little walk in the evening, in the morning as well if possible, and, on days when parents do not work, both in the morning and in the evening.

The younger children are undressed after playing outside, then they are taken to the toilet, their hands are washed, they are fed and put to sleep. It is important to make sure that these operations proceed in the proper order.

According to the schedule, when the younger children are put to sleep for their second sleep of the day, the older ones are beginning to wake up gradually. If the children sleep indoors, clothing is given to them as they wake up. They look it over and try to put it on, while the adults are dressing other children. This time should be utilized for close individual contact with the children. Children love it when adults take notice of their clothing: "What a beautiful dress, and there is a pocket too, and a handkerchief in it. What a nice Mommy Olya must have." Such conversations bring children closer to adults, arouse good feelings toward the mother and a love for the beautiful. Once dressed, the child is directed toward the bathroom, after which he plays in the main room until he is called and told to wash his hands before the afternoon snack.

One should never permit a situation in which children who are sitting at the table have to wait for the food to be brought in: being forced to sit still in the same position and to be inactive in general tire children and take away their appetite.

When the assistant brings the food, the children, after having washed their hands, sit at the tables. After the afternoon snack, the older group has activities. At that time, the younger children are taken out of their beds, and after going to the bathroom, they are fed and are given a chance to play. Both subgroups are awake at the same time.

The nurse plays and entertains the children, seeing off those for whom the parents have come. If the children are quiet and the assistant is able to look after them, the nurse goes to the parents to tell them briefly how the child feels, communicate to them whatever is new in the child's behavior, or give a piece of advice to the mother.

THE ORGANIZATION AND CONTENT OF THE CHILDREN'S ACTIVITIES

In the second year of a child's life, the period of time he is awake increases significantly. Children 1 year and 2 or 3 months can be kept awake for three to four hours without a break, and by 1 year and 10 months this period extends to four or five hours. This makes it possible to render the child's activities more meaningful and varied.

At this period of their life, having learned to walk, the children show exceptional mobility. Walking for them becomes a real need. In order to satisfy the child's yearning to move about independently, a sufficient area must be provided for that purpose. In a large room, it is good to make use of a climber with a large surrounding area and a slide (a device which is useful and important for exercising children in various forms of movement).

Walking is often linked with the child's desire to move objects from one place to another. For this purpose, the children may be given large cubes of various sizes, each with a hole in the middle for them to get their hand through, big soft dolls, baskets with handles, bags capable of holding a number of toys, balls, and boxes on wheels big enough for a child to fit in. In order to give the children a chance to roll, throw and chase, medium and larger-sized balls should be provided.

Observing the children's activities, the nurse teaches them to perform some actions upon command, such as to bring a ball or roll it, or climb up on a bench in order to reach a toy. The children must have a great deal of space in which to play when they are out of doors.

The playground should be planted with trees and the ground should be even and clean. There should be no possibility of children finding a piece of glass or stumbling over a stone.

.   .   .

On part of the playground, a low hill should be built up out of earth, and also banks and hollows. All of these should be planted with grass. The children will walk around on these. Balls, hoops, and all kinds of moving toys will stimulate the children's physical activity.

In the winter, most of the playground must be kept clear of snow. The little hill and hollows that are left covered with snow may be used for developing the children's sense of balance. Sleds with tall backs are used for rides and as a means of transporting them from one area of the playground to another.

During the time the children spend out of doors, they learn to overcome a number of natural obstacles. It is much more difficult for them to walk on grass in the summer, to walk in winter in heavy clothing on snow, or to climb to the top of a grassy mound or a snow bank, than to walk on a smooth floor, or even to climb on and off the various climbing devices in the room. At this period of their life, children need help in improving certain of their movements, and they must be encouraged in their attempts to overcome the obstacles.

During the time the children spend on the playground, the nurse must make sure that all children are active, moving about and playing. She involves the children in fast-moving games, suggesting that they try to catch her or look for children who have hidden behind the hill.

The time children spend out of doors in the playground must be used to enrich their store of impressions and to broaden their orientation with their surroundings. The teacher-nurse turns the children's attention toward natural phenomena (snow falling, sun shining); together with her the children look at trees, admire and smell flowers, observe birds flying onto the playground, and look at animals.

During the play period, the children should be made to observe the various surrounding adult activities: the milkman delivering milk, the bread man delivering bread; the assistant hanging clothes on the line, the janitor shovelling off snow and sweeping the paths. Such observations should be planned and made systematically. By this means the teacher-nurse attracts the children's attention to the actions performed by various people and the objects which they use.

Familiarizing the children with their surroundings can be done in small groups (three to five children) while the other children are busy playing independently. However, excessive fatigue must never be allowed to occur; it is important to know how to alternate skillfully periods of observation, relaxed play and activity. Toward this end, the playground should be provided with low benches with backs and tables on which children can play quiet games with various toys.

The ability of the children to move about independently makes it possible for them to become better oriented to their surroundings. The nurse now faces, therefore, the problem of improving their developing power of observation. With this purpose in mind, it is good occasionally to change the arrangement of the furniture, of the toys in the playroom and the pictures on the walls; and to create meaningful but simple tableaus with a few of the toys, introducing new characters from time to time. The children's attention should be drawn to these projects. For example, a tableau representing children sledding down the hill may be replaced by another of interest to the children, such as rabbits dancing around a Christmas tree.

Children must be given a chance to observe what is going on in the street from the common room by standing, for example, on the climber. They watch birds flying, streetcars passing by, rain falling, and so forth. The child develops the ability to imitate the sounds he hears and the actions he sees. This is very important for his general development, for speech formation, and for his play activity.

At this age children cannot as yet play as a group, since their speech is not sufficiently advanced to communicate with other children to agree upon the purposes and conditions of a game. The nurse trains the children to play sitting side by side with other children, without bothering them, and teaches them to share toys. During the period of independent play, children play with dolls and building materials, and look at pictures.

In the course of independent play, children in their second year of life show considerable interest in pictures, but as yet they cannot stay with them for long at a time. Therefore, pictures should not be used for long periods or else the children will begin to wrinkle, tear and throw them. It is essential to create conditions in which the children will use this kind of material and activity to advantage. The teacher-nurse must teach the children how to leaf carefully through picture books and how to use pictures pasted on plywood or cardboard, putting them away after use in the box on the shelf.

For play time, soft toys representing animals (cat, dog, bears), as well as dolls with cloth bodies and celluloid heads and rubber figures of people and animals must be provided. One addition should be sets of aluminum dishes, doll furniture (tables, beds), bits of material for wrapping dolls in, and odd garments for the children themselves to dress up in (colored kerchiefs, white smocks, aprons, crowns, caps and hats).

To help develop the children's ability to handle objects, they must be provided also with wooden boxes with lids, bowls with and without lids, wooded devices with holes for inserting plugs, and so forth. For playing with sand and water, they need spades, buckets, trowels, various sand toys as well as floating toys.

The activities of children in this age group are shaped by such objects that fall into their field of vision. Therefore, toys must be placed in various areas of the room in such a way that they are likely to be noticed by the children and so that the children, without bothering each other, can play with them. When toys are placed in sets (furniture and dishes, building material, balls and slides), it induces the children to perform more than one operation: take the dishes and set them down on the table, roll balls down the slide.

It is important to vary the children's play by introducing thematic elements into it. For example, the nurse might suggest to the child who is pulling an empty truck that he give his doll or teddy bear a ride. Children must be taught to use toys correctly: to pull cars, to carry dolls with care, to roll balls or throw them, and so on.

In their play, children reproduce things and activities from impressions they have received from their surroundings. They need to be helped in trying to illustrate in play what they observe in everyday life: mother nurses a baby, a driver drives a car, a doctor examines, and so forth. Afterwards, their play becomes more intricate through the addition of actions that have been shown during activity periods or in periods of individual attention to the children (how to pull a truck, how to carry a doll, etc.). Whenever possible, adults must actively participate in children's games by taking one of the roles.

The nurse and her assistant try to maintain some order within the group; they put away discarded toys, gradually teaching the children to do so too.

In the course of the day, the children's games take on a variety of aspects. In the morning and evening hours, when both subgroups are awake and the nurse must devote considerable time in attending to hygiene, it is advisable to give the children toys and equipment which they know how to handle with ease. Some of the toys, such as large cars and carts, must be taken away at that time since if some of the children play with them they will get in the other children's way.

When both subgroups are playing at the same time, special attention must be devoted to the establishing of friendly relations between them. Children of the older group will learn to be kind to the younger group and help them search for the toys they need. The little ones must learn not to bother the older ones.

Separate waking periods for the older and younger subgroups give the staff the opportunity to organize their independent activities in a suitable way. Through individual attention, the nurse improves the child's skill in handling a new toy and then shows him new ways to use it.

Waking periods must be used to develop the children's ability to speak. This is helped along by providing the following conditions: greater opportunity for individual attention toward the child and relative quiet which allows the child to hear distinctly the teacher's and his own voice.

A great role is played in the child's development by independent activity. However, special exercises are needed. Benefiting from the teacher's influence, the child is able to acquire skills, habits and knowledge more rapidly. The organization and content of children's activities at an early age are substantially different than for older children of preschool age. Exercises are conducted with small subgroups of children or individually. To achieve success, it is very important to stimulate in the children an interest in what they are learning. This can be produced by the unexpected appearance and disappearance of objects, a sudden change in an action, and astute questions put by the adults.

In the course of training, the children must be taught to observe the elementary rules of behavior. From the very first (from 1 year and 2 to 4 months), children must be expected to remain still during the activity period and listen carefully to the nurse while she is speaking, look at the objects which are shown to them, and give proper answers. Observance of the rules of behavior soon becomes a habit; success in performing a given movement or action or in pronouncing a word begins to produce a sense of satisfaction and joy in the child.

The ability to imitate adults and obey spoken suggestions is first really observed in the course of the second year of a child's life. This still is only vaguely formulated, and thus children usually answer questions or suggestions from adults only after repeated practice. In order to maintain interest in a given activity and the desire to do something suggested by an adult, it is necessary to repeat previously learned material along with introducing new material.

During group activities it is important to use an individual approach to the children, especially those who need it most, such as the newcomers, the shy, and the underdeveloped. These children are asked to participate actively when they begin to show signs of interest and the desire to take part. During activities, these children must be constantly in the field of vision of the adults, as they need help more than others.

The difficulty of an exercise can be increased when the children develop skill in performing the previous material, answering questions correctly or performing particular actions as requested by the teacher-nurse.

For activities and play with the children of the younger subgroup, the most favorable time is considered to be the period following the second feeding, just before that group is put to sleep for the second time, i.e., when the older children are asleep.

Besides activities indoors, the nurse plans and carries on activities in the playground; in the winter these will consist of fast-moving games as well as the systematic observations of surrounding life which are within the capacity of the child. In the summer, activities are moved out of doors, but in doing this conditions must be set up so that the children will not be distracted and so that they can sit comfortably, hear the nurse, and act independently.

For the older subgroup, the nurse leads activities in winter inside the building. These occur after the third feeding. The younger children are also awake at that time, and therefore the nurse gets the assistant to supervise their play. On those days when the outdoor playtime must be cancelled, activities can be held with the older children during the time when the younger group is asleep.

Play in the older subgroup is organized in groups of no more than six to eight children: they take apart and put together various toys, work with building materials, catch balls and walk along boards.

If there are only a few (four to six) children in the younger subgroup, they can all have activities at the same time: the teacher points to pictures and names the things illustrated, familiarizes the children with new toys, tells them stories about the toys, and shows them how they work and how one can play with them. For activities with children of 1 year 6 months and over, as many as eight may be assembled in a group. Musical activities, showing animals, and so forth are carried on at the same time for both groups. The teacher-nurse must plan ahead how to organize the children and how to place them during activities. In the course of activities, during which given actions are performed, children must be arranged so that each child has enough room at the table so that neighbors will not shove each other and so that all have sufficient playing material.

For little dramatizations, children should be seated on one side of a table so that all of them can see. For observing animals in natural settings, if is more convenient for the children to sit in a ring at some distance from the animals so that they will not be afraid and will not prevent each other from seeing. Some activities do not require any special arrangement of the children: for example, the nurse throws a ball and children run to pick it up.

The nurse must be prepared for each activity: she must prepare all the necessary equipment, know how many children can participate, know in her mind how to proceed.

Exercises for speech development are performed with a small group of children (four or five). Some types of activities and exercises—for example, imitating sounds—definitely have to be done individually. This facilitates the understanding of speech and helps to establish that feeling of intimacy between the child and the adult which is so necessary to small children.

Skills which the child has acquired in the course of organized activities are developed and improved in the periods of independent activity.

With children in their second year, exercises and activities are conducted in the following areas: speech development, orientation to surroundings, physical development, the manipulation of objects, music and entertaining demonstrations.

EXERCISES FOR SPEECH DEVELOPMENT
AND ORIENTATION TO THE SURROUNDINGS

For children in their second year, a whole series of exercises is conducted which helps along the development of the ability to imitate in the pronunciation of sounds and words, contribute to the development of active speech and the understanding of adult speech.

Children are acquainted with objects which are within their range of understanding. For this purpose, toys may be used as well as pictures (in addition to talks and observations made during walks). Every day there are four or five activities periods. Let's mention some of the exercises simply as an example: the game "The Magic Bag" can be played with children over 18 months old. The purpose of the game is to sharpen the children's imagination and recollection of familiar objects and to stimulate speech activity. For this game the teacher prepares a bright beautiful bag in which she puts toys with which the child is quite familiar, such as a doll, rooster, top, etc. It is better if the toys are made of various materials (wood, celluloid, rag dolls). The teacher shows the bag to the children and gives them time to examine it. Then she takes out one toy after the other, attracting the children's attention to each and saying: "Look, this is a rooster. What kind of a noise does it make?" The children answer. Then the teacher says: "Anna, feed the rooster!" The baby puts out her hand pretending the rooster is pecking grain.

The sudden appearance of the toys will interest the children. The teacher gives each child a chance to touch the toy, and if he wants to, to pat it and feed it. Then the rooster "hides." "Oh, the rooster has run away," says the nurse. "Oh well, what else do we have here?" And she takes out another toy. If children experience difficulties in recognizing the toy, the teacher helps by giving hints. Proceeding in this way, the teacher shows all the toys one by one, talks about each one, stimulates the children to imitate some sounds, and then gives the toys to the children to play with.

From the time they are about 1 year 5 to 6 months, the children play with dolls. The nurse seats four to six children on chairs. Next to her is a table with doll furniture; first a bed with bedding accessories, and next to this a set of dolls's dishes—a saucepan, a spoon, a plate, a pitcher. The teacher takes the doll and, turning to the children says: "Children, let's give our doll Tanya some porridge. Let's take the porridge out of the saucepan." (She puts imaginary porridge on the plate.) "Eat, Tanya, the porridge tastes good." (She feeds the doll and wipes its mouth with a napkin lying nearby.) "How nicely Tanya is eating the porridge!" The teacher-nurse suggests that some children should feed the doll. The children do so. The teacher watches the operation, taking care that the children hold the spoon properly, place the "porridge" in the doll's mouth, make it drink from a mug, and wipe its mouth with a napkin. As soon as the children are finished, the teacher says: "Now that Tanya has eaten so well, let's put her to bed." Taking off the doll's clothing, the nurse says: "Let's undress Tanya; we'll hang the dress on a chair and we'll put the slippers under the bed. Lie down, Tanya, go to sleep; we are going to cover you up with a blanket. Your head goes on the pillow, just so. Good! Children, Tanya is asleep. Let's sing her a lullaby nice and gently."

Through all of this the teacher must encourage the spoken activity on the part of the children. For example, when the children feed the doll, she asks: "What are you giving to Tanya?" The children answer, "porridge." At a later date, the children must be helped to apply the actions learned in the course of these activities (feeding dolls, putting them to bed) to their independent play.

Exercises with pictures (already begun in the previous age group) are at first organized on an individual basis every other day for periods of one to two minutes, then in small groups. Pictures must be of average size, be brightly colored and present illustrations of familiar objects.

To begin the exercises, the child's attention must be attracted by the unexpected appearance of a picture; enough time must be allowed for him to examine it, and only then should the object it represents be named. The picture must be shown to the child several times until he can answer the appropriate questions by imitating sounds and words.

When the exercise includes two pictures, the familiar picture is shown first, then the new one, on which the child must focus his attention for some time. Afterwards, the teacher names the object. During the next exercise the nurse shows both pictures simultaneously and says: "Point to the dog," or "Take the picture with the watch and give it to me. What sound does a watch make?" In succeeding exercises, the number of pictures progresses to between five and eight. When a large number of pictures are used (four to five and more), exercises should begin with the new picture to create a stronger impression, then return to the repetitive showing of familiar pictures.

Starting at the age of 1 year 3 months, a child should be taught to generalize. For this purpose, a number of pictures are selected which represent the same object in various positions. The teacher emphasizes: "This is a dog, and this one is a dog, and also this one."

There is no need to spend too long on pictures representing objects. As the child assimilates the material, it is better to pass on to pictures representing actions. At first they must be very simple actions: cat lapping milk, a boy washing his hands, and so on.

From the age of 18 months on, it is possible not only to show pictures but to tell the children about related events in which they themselves have participated. For example, remind them or talk about the fact that they saw birds while they were out on a walk. The birds were pecking grain (how did they peck?) and then flew away (how?).

Children like to listen to short verses or nursery rhymes. The nurse may use popular nursery rhymes or jingles within the children's range of understanding, such as the collection of Fedaevskaya entitled "For the Little One's Joy."

A good device for getting children to pronounce many sounds and words is the so-called "children's movie", a hand-manipulated wooden device through which a paper tape moves with painted animals, children, etc. (designed by N. R. Eigess). The teacher herself names the objects and actions to the younger children: "There goes a dog, here is a little girl playing with a ball;" the older children are asked: "What is this?" or "Who is this?"

To develop the children's powers of attention, observation and concentration, and to familiarize them with their surroundings, dramatizations with dolls and toys are effective. In a dramatization, the nurse shows a series of actions to the children, accompanying them with words. Such performances attract the children's attention, provide a considerably long period of observation, acquaint the children with the names of objects and the corresponding actions, stimulate the children to answer with appropriate words, and finally, contribute to development of more complicated variations in the children's own play. These shows may be of various types. For example, the nurse brings to the group a beautiful doll and a big car. The doll rides in the car, then comes out of it, talks to the children, dances, sings songs, and so on.

In order for the development of active speech in the children to proceed, the following principles are indispensable:

(1) Every moment in which the nurse and her assistant are in close contact with a child must be utilized: during care, feeding, independent games, and outdoor play.

(2) A secure intimacy between the staff and the child must be established.

(3) One must talk with the children, preferably individually (except for special group activities).

(4) Objects must be named at the moment children seem to take a particular interest in them, actions and movements named while the child is performing them.

(5) One must develop in the child the ability to imitate sounds and words used by adults, and create the necessary conditions to stimulate the children to pronounce various sounds as often as possible.

(6) It is very important to use objects which particularly attract the child's attention (moving, sounding objects, and living animals).

As the child's understanding of adult speech develops, he must be given various spoken commands, demanding the performance of simple actions and encouraging the child to express things himself: "Give Auntie the ball," "Ask Auntie to give you the ball," "Say, 'Give me the ball, Auntie!' ", etc.

(7) To encourage children to turn to adults on various occasions, one must understand children's indistinct speech and answer the child attentively each time he tries to say something, thereby endeavoring to prolong the conversation.

(8) Every unusual event in the life of children seems to provoke a step forward in their general development, and in particular, in the development of their ability to speak.

Holidays, performances of trained animals, trips to the country, and so forth invariably give rise to a tremendous step forward in the children's development, in the development of their speech.

(9) Finally, special training must be given and special exercises performed to develop the children's speech.

EXERCISES TO IMPROVE PHYSICAL SKILLS

The teacher-nurse gives the children practice in walking, running, crawling, riding, throwing balls, etc. Two or three times a week she leads the children in special calisthenics and fast-moving games. The calisthenics to be used are prescribed by the preschool institution's doctor, taking into consideration the individual characteristics and the ages of the children. If these exercises are made interesting and the children participate actively, they derive considerable pleasure from them.

The number of participants varies from two to four, or six to nine, depending on the children's age and size, the level to which their physical skills have developed, and the nature of a given exercise.

In order to teach children from 15 to 16 months old to raise their feet when walking and not to drag them on the floor, have them step over a stick, a colored line (rope) or building material piled up on the floor. Playing a game to the accompaniment of some musical instrument or singing helps the children to develop an even step in walking.

Children must be given practice in keeping their balance while they walk. This can be done by having them perform some action, such as, for example, clapping their hands while walking. The same thing can be achieved by having the children walk on a plank (25 centimeters wide) which is placed on the floor or raised 10 to 20 centimeters at one end.

Children learn to climb up on a low bench or a box turned upside down. The height should be 10 centimeters for children 1 year and 5 to 6 months old, and 15 centimeters for those 1 year and 7 to 8 months old.

Exercises in crawling are also conducted using low furniture or a climber. It is absolutely necessary that the assistant watch carefully during such activities.

With children of 2 years of age (after 1 year 6 months), the active game called "Collect the Balls" may be played. The nurse shows the children a basket containing brightly colored balls of various sizes, puts them out on the floor and says to the children to pick them up and to put them back in the basket. "Quickly, gather all the balls," says the nurse cheerfully. "Come on, look for the balls," she goes on. When all the balls are gathered, the game starts all over again.

Simple games involving running can also be played, such as "You Can't Catch Me." These games may be alternated. In the course of the first game, the nurse says "Catch me," and slowly runs away from the children. Children try to move faster in order to catch up with the nurse. In the second game the nurse pretends she wants to catch the children and they run away from her. Usually, children express their joy very loudly, together with some fear at being caught.

Much interest is aroused by a game called "Catch the Birdie." At the end of a rope, tied to a small stick, a celluloid or cutout paper bird is attached. Shaking the rope, the nurse makes the bird "fly." "The birdie flew away and landed on top of the children's heads," says the nurse, touching the head of some child. The name of the child can be called out. When children try to catch the "bird," it flies up higher than the outstretched hands of the child. During this game, children make all sorts of movements, raise themselves on tiptoe, and crouch, trying to jump up and stretch out their arms. Children enjoy this game immensely.

When children are 1 year 6-months-old they can play the game "Let's Stretch Our Arms," based on the imitation of motions made by adults. Children sit in a semicircle in such a way that all of them can see the nurse who sits in front of them. As she performs various exercises, the nurse accompanies them with appropriate words: "We raise our arms, we lower our arms." Repeating the movements and words a number of times, the nurse gets the children to imitate the movements. At first the children do not pay attention to the words accompanying the movements. But little by little a given word gets associated in their minds with the movement it illustrates, and the children begin to obey the spoken commands of the nurse. As a result, their arm and leg movements become more varied. Imitating the nurse, the children wave their hands, make little circles with their hands, clap hands and tap with their feet.

The nurse accompanies all the children's movements with words pronounced softly and gently; she also hums or sings in time to the rhythm of the given movements. When the children are making movements with their hands (waving, clapping, turning their wrists), the nurse might say, for example: "Look at our hands. See how well they clap, clap, clap, one two, one two," and so forth.

PRACTICE IN MANIPULATING OBJECTS

In order to teach children to perform certain actions involving objects, activities should be carried on in small groups. For children of 1 year to 18 months, these activities are conducted five to six times every day; with older children four to five times.

For these activities small building material must be provided: cubes, boxes with lids, etc. The nurse teaches the children to perform a number of actions with these toys: to take rings off a rod and put them back again, to close and open a given object. Gradually, these exercises become more complicated; at the beginning of the year a baby is given a rod with three rings, then five, and when the baby reaches two years, rods containing six to eight rings are given to him.

During these exercises the children also learn to perform more than one action with a single type of material: for example, to take cubes out of a box, set them up on top of each other, construct something with them, imitate a simple structure made by an adult (a tower, a train, a fence) and afterwards, put the cubes back in the box.

In the course of these exercises, the nurse directs the attention of the older children to the size of objects used (big, small) and their shape (cube, circle, sphere), and indicates the color of the objects. Showing the biggest, then the smallest toy, the nurse stresses the difference in size.

The same concepts are developed in playing with rings and a rod. The nurse teaches the baby to put the rings which he is taking off the rod on the table in their proper order. Putting the rings on the rod, the child should start with the biggest, as is stressed by the nurse and demonstrated to all the children. A similar game can be played with various sized cubes and *matreshki.*

A good device for table activities is a box containing a set of small objects: small bobbins, tiny china animals, and colored bits of material. Children take them out of the box, name them, then put them back.

If children have acquired various skills in handling objects and have perfected them during independent activities, then by the age of 2, they will know how to put together two or three-part toys, to build simple structures with cubes, and to name both the objects and actions.

When children are 2 years old, they may be given pencil and paper, but these are given mainly to help develop manual dexterity. The teacher-nurse must see to it that children use pencils properly, "drawing" on paper and not on inappropriate objects (walls, tables, chairs, floors) and that they do not bang their pencils on the tables or roll them on the floor.

During activities of this kind, the nurse must tell the children: "This is a pencil. We will draw with it. And this is paper. People draw (or write) on paper. Look, how beautiful!"

In summer with children over 18 months old, play with sand and water may be organized, but only under the watchful eye of the nurse. The sand for the children to play with must be clean and slightly damp, and the sandboxes sufficiently spacious and equipped with seats. Playing with the children, the nurse turns their attention to the qualities of sand, shows what can be done with it, sprinkles some of it into molds and boxes with a little shovel, makes pies, mounds, holes, canals.

For playing with water, children must wear waterproof aprons; the water is poured in bowls or larger containers specially designed for this purpose. The nurse shows the children how they can play with water. She pours some into containers of thick glass, and, using a funnel, pours the water from one container into another and puts floating toys on the water. The children always enjoy these activities.

While the children are playing, the assistant watches to make sure that children do not put sand or water in their mouth, do not throw sand at each other, and do not splash water about.

During the game, the teacher-nurse names the things she herself does and also the actions of the children. She sings songs about water, and so forth.

MUSICAL EXERCISES

The nurse continues to do musical exercises with the children during their second year. The children usually derive great pleasure from them, and the exercises contribute to the development of their speech and dexterity. The children learn to listen to songs or nursery rhymes which are very simple in their content and melody. The nurse's singing must be soft and melodious. If the child can hear the words of the song, it is easier for him to understand its meaning. He will start to sing separate syllables, and later whole words.

To keep the children attentive, one may use toys which correspond to the words of the song. For example, before singing the song "Rover" the nurse may show a toy dog which the children will "feed" and stroke. Then they will listen with interest to the song, remembering from previous exercises how the dog barks. The children's attention cannot be held for any length of time; thus the exercises must be short and based on varied material.

For example, while putting a doll to bed the nurse sings a lullaby, the older children humming or singing along. Then the doll "wakes up" and, using a cheerful tune, the children begin dancing along with the nurse. She demonstrates how leg and arm movements must be alternated in dancing, and the children imitate her. The nurse takes by the hand the children who seem to be the shyest or most sluggish and disinterested. But this should be gone about carefully, and should the child refuse to participate in the general happy mood, he must be left alone. The older children can do dance movements without prompting. To give the children an opportunity to listen to music, it is convenient to use a record player. Stores have records for sale designed for special purposes, such as recordings of short musical works arranged for children of preschool age.

When children are listening to music, they must sit quietly without bothering each other. Those who disturb the quiet atmosphere must be spoken to and persuaded to calm down.

The nurse must prepare in advance for musical acitivities, know the songs she will sing, listen to the phonograph recording, and rehearse the dance movements she will show the children. Besides a record player, the nurse may use some child's musical instrument, such as a triangle.

Not only during these exercises but also during play time, the nurse sings nursery rhymes and attracts the children's attention to them.

STRENGTHENING THE CHILD'S ORGANISM

The building up process begun in the first months of a child's life is continued under appropriate conditions and utilizing special procedures (see directions in corresponding passage for infants in their first year).

Just as in the previous period of their life, children continue to sleep out of doors. For children 1 year old and over, appropriate covering for sleeping out of doors consists of pajamas and padded sleeping bags. In cold weather, a warm blanket may be placed on top of sleeping bags.

The children also spend two periods out of doors during their waking time: five to six hours when the temperature is not lower than $-15°$. In the summer the entire life of the children is organized outside. Clothing and footwear must correspond to the time of year and the weather, and to the size of the child so as not to impair his movements.

In cold weather, "airbaths" (exposure to air) are taken indoors. The room must be thoroughly ventilated in advance, gradually bringing the temperature to $18°$. Clothing must be shed gradually and with the utmost care. First, a long sleeved shirt is replaced by an undershirt. When children are used to this change, their stockings can be removed, leaving the children in their undergarments and finally in just their underpants.

During an airbath, children must be kept active, and airbathing is therefore combined with active games. On cool or rainy days, airbaths are taken on the open veranda or in a room with open windows.

With the purpose of strengthening a child's organism, certain procedures involving water are also carried on, such as rubbing and showering.

Systematic wet rubs for periods of two to three months condition children over 1 year of age to showers during the summer time. Wet rubbing begins with a water temperature of $+34$ to $33°$, and every two to three days the temperature is lowered by one degree centigrade until it reaches $+26°$ in the winter or $+24°$ in the summer. The water treatment is administered after the children's outside play period.

Older children who have spent several days playing in partially shaded areas can be brought out under the direct rays of the sun for some relaxed play. The doctor will determine which of the children should not be exposed to the sun because of the state of their health. For the first few days, exposure to the sun must be limited to five or six minutes, and overexposure (reddening of the face, perspiration) should not be permitted. As soon as a tan appears, exposure to the sun may be increased up to eight or ten minutes for two or three times a day. Sunbathing is permitted only under the strict control of the medical staff.

CLOTHING FOR CHILDREN IN THEIR FIRST AND SECOND YEAR OF LIFE

The kind of clothing children wear has a strong influence on their health. The clothing must fulfill its basic purpose: to preserve body warmth and not to allow overheating, which may be the cause of a child's falling sick.

The clothing should be comfortable, light and attractive, and must correspond to the child's body measurements. It should be easy to put on and take off, not hindering the child's movements and not making breathing or blood circulation difficult. Clothing for infants is made out of easily washable material and should have a soft texture so as not to provoke itching and skin irritations.

The infant's first clothing is a nightie and a jacket. The nightie is made out of thin cotton material without buttons or trimming. The edges of the nightie come together in the back, one over the other. The jacket is made out of woolen material, has long sleeves and fastens in the front. There is no need of collars on either of these garments.

At a normal room temperature it is not necessary to cover the baby's head with a cap or bonnet. This not only makes the baby "soft" but may cause the growth of various crusts on the baby's head.

To cover up the lower part of the body, two diapers or sheets are put one on top of the other, one of wool and the other on top of lighter material. Another kind of diaper usually made out of muslin is folded in a triangular fashion. One point of the triangle goes in between the baby's legs and the two other ends are caught up under his buttocks, and the whole thing is fastened on the stomach. Small children are wrapped up all the way to the armpits but in such a way as not to make them uncomfortable (the baby should be able to move his legs). If it is cool in the room, the baby must be covered with a woolen blanket. At normal room temperature, it is better not to cover the baby with a quilted blanket as he may get too hot.

After two months of life, the baby's movements become more energetic and varied. The swaddling clothes in which the baby is wrapped up hinder to a certain extent the development of necessary movements. Therefore, it is desirable that children at this age wear, instead of swaddling clothes, a type of panties with booties attached called "diaper-pants."

This garment allows the baby to move its legs freely and to turn over on its side.

From the sixth month on when children know how to sit properly and are beginning to crawl and stand up, the type of clothing worn previously is no longer comfortable and convenient. All children, both boys and girls, wear an undershirt, a jacket or blouse, long overalls and light shoes with leather soles. In the course of the second year when the children know how to walk, girls may be dressed in dresses and boys in playsuits.

Keeping this clothing clean is very important to the well-being of the child as well as for his health. Damp, wet or soiled clothing must be changed immediately, as it not only provokes in the children unpleasant sensations as well as skin irritations, but it also brings on chills. A child who has been trained to be clean gets very upset if ideal conditions of cleanliness are not maintained. This serves as a signal that his diapers, undershirt, etc. must be changed.

When changing the baby the nurse should talk to him, naming objects and actions associated with dressing. 9- to 10-month-old babies have usually learned by this time how to respond with actions to the nurse's gentle commands ("raise your legs," "sit down," and so on).

The choice of material and style for children's clothing must correspond to the time of year and the temperature of the surrounding air. Bundling up the children excessively causes overheating, abundant perspiration, skin irritation and rashes. It is also one of the causes of stomach troubles.

Clothing for small children must be sufficiently loose so as not to hinder their movements or make them feel awkward when they walk. In making children's clothing, one must allow for the size of the head so that when a shirt, a blouse or underwear is being put on the child, it does not provoke unpleasant sensations in the child. If garments have straps, they must be sewn in such a way that they do not keep falling off the child's shoulders and irritating him. If such straps have several buttonholes, this will enable one to change their length as the child grows larger.

In the summer when it is warm, children go out in shorts, light shoes and a little straw hat. On cooler days children wear either dresses or suits, but when it is windy or the temperature drops, they wear either a light coat or a wool sweater.

In winter children wear padded coats, long trousers, overshoes of a medium height and a wool cap. Mittens must be provided for their hands, and they are attached with either an elastic or tape long enough that the child can easily move his hands. In damp weather, high overshoes or galoshes must be provided.

The long scarves in which parents wrap up their children only hinder their movements. These can successfully be exchanged for small sized scarves which can be worn under the coat.

Suggested Distribution of Duties between the Nurse and Her Assistant for the Groups of Infants in Their Second Year of Life

TIME OF DAY	HEAD NURSE	ASSISTANT
7:00–8:00 A.M.	Receives children, checks them, watches over children who are playing.	Supervises children, changes clothing of children received by the nurse.
7:30–8:30 A.M.	Washes children's hands, gives breakfast (first of all to those who arrived earliest).	Gets everything ready for breakfast. Helps the nurse, washes children's hands, feeds them.
8:30–9:10 A.M.	Leads activities with younger and older subgroups.	Clears dishes off the tables. Supervises children who are playing.
9:10–9:30 A.M.	Helps assistant to put younger children to bed, supervises older children at play.	Takes younger children to the bathroom and puts them to bed.
9:30–11:00 A.M.	Dresses older children for outside and spends time with them on the playground.	Takes older children to bathroom, dresses them for play outside. Washes dishes and tidies up.
11:00–11:30 A.M.	Returns from outside, undresses older children, washes hands.	First assistant takes in and undresses children, takes them to bathroom and washes their hands. Second assistant gets the dinner.
11:30–12:00 P.M.	Gives dinner to older children.	Second assistant serves food, helps feed children. First assistant lifts younger subgroup of children out of bed and takes them to bathroom.
12:00–1:00 P.M.	Washes hands of younger children, feeds them, watches over older children at play. Helps assistant to put older children to bed.	Washes hands of younger children, feeds them. Puts older children to bed.
1:00–3:00 P.M.	Leads activities with younger children, supervises their play and keeps watch over children who are sleeping. Gets younger children ready for bed and settles them down.	Washes dishes, cleans room. Watches after sleeping children. Takes younger children to bathroom and puts them to bed (second nap).

Suggested Distribution of Duties between the Nurse and Her
Assistant for the Groups of Infants in Their Second Year of Life

TIME OF DAY	HEAD NURSE	ASSISTANT
3:00–4:30 P.M.	Takes older children out of bed, directs body strengthening procedures; washes hands, feeds, leads activities, supervises the sleeping children.	Takes older children out of bed and takes them to bathroom, helps with body strengthening procedures, feeds children, brings food for younger subgroup.
4:30 P.M.	Takes younger children out of bed, washes their hands, feeds them, leads activities. Plays with children, supervises games, gives children over to the parents.	Takes younger children out of bed, puts them on toilets, helps feed them. Washes dishes, tidies up the place.

Note: Toward 11:00 A.M. the assistant nurse of the second shift arrives, and for two hours they both work together.

PLANNING CARE AND UPBRINGING

The care and upbringing of the infant groups is a directed purposeful process, and therefore planning is imperative. The planning helps in distributing the work in a regular ordered manner, forces the teacher to think through the educational methods and approaches and to prepare in advance the equipment and toys which will render the objectives attainable.

A plan is drawn up for each age group based on "The Program of Instruction in the Kindergarten" but taking into consideration concrete conditions, the distribution of the ages of children in a given group, the children's physical, neuro-psychological development and their individual characteristics.

The plan for a given period of time must anticipate to provide for:

(1) Educational objectives for children in each age subgroup
(2) Changes in the living conditions of the group or the makeup of the group, the introduction of new equipment, devices, accessories, toys, etc.
(3) Work with parents (getting acquainted with home conditions, talks and consultations)

On the basis of planned objectives, concrete measures are set down regarding the organization and carrying out of proposed schedules: sleep, feeding, developing health habits, cleanliness, and independence; and the organization, contents and proper ordering of activities, and play for each age subgroup must be envisaged.

The plan of work for the group of infants in their first year of life is made out for one month in advance. This plan reflects the general, overall work with the group (or subgroup) as a whole, but also devotes attention to individual children. Projected activities are spread out over the days of the week, with each acitivity to be repeated two to three times a week. Activities are changed as the children assimilate their contents or upon observing a decrease in interest on the part of the children.

For the group of children in their second year, the instructional work and care is planned for one week in advance and must correspond with the objectives already set for the entire month. Again, as with the younger children, provisions must be included relating to individual children.

Activities are spread out over the week in the following manner: activities and exercises in speech development and in familiarizing the children with their environment—four to five times a week (including time for observation by the children during outside play); development of physical skills (play)—three times; gymnastics or calisthenics—two to three times; manual dexterity (children 12 to 17 months)—three to four times; (after 17 months)—three to five times; musical activities and games (children from 12 to 17 months)—three times; (older than 17 months)—two times. While constantly repeating activities, the nurse gradually makes them more challenging. For example, planning activities involving the handling of objects, the nurse first gives the child a rod from which he must remove a ring, and then later she teaches him how to put it back on the rod.

When some game or activity is being performed for the first time, it is important to discover the best method for directing it. When the game or activity is later repeated, one can rely on the plan worked out the preceding time. Before making a plan, the teacher and the nurse evaluate the educational level of the group, the children's progress in assimilating habits, their behavior, general health and well-being.

The conclusions drawn from this consultation will help to properly formulate the contents of further work, the degree of complexity, the amount of repetition desirable, and various individual approaches to the children.

The monthly plan is evaluated in a meeting attended by the administrator in charge of the school as well as by the doctor.

Educative work with the children must not only be planned, but also evaluated. An evaluation helps to measure the value of educative work done with the children, brings out the achievements as well as failings and helps to indicate the direction in which future work should proceed. Daily the nurse makes brief notes in the notebook prepared for that purpose as to what games and activities took place on a given day, what has been achieved by the children, whether they became interested in the games and activities, what obstacles were met. There is no need to make a list of games and activities, as they have already been indicated in the plan.

It is desirable to make an evaluation of particular methods and approaches used with the whole group and with individual children. This will help to improve the quality of subsequent work.

PERSONALITY OF THE TEACHER–NURSE

Cultured and well-educated people who are devoted to the cause of communism are needed for the proper education of the new generation. They must love and fully understand their job, they must know how to be creative in applying their knowledge to their work, and they must constantly strive to improve their skills.

The teacher-nurse is called upon to fulfill an important function for society: to be the first educator of children in their infancy. Great responsibilities and complicated problems confront her. She must safeguard the life and the health of children, insure proper care for each child, and create conditions in which the children will remain cheerful and enjoy life. She must help them to acquire physical and good health habits, acquaint them with the surrounding world, develop their speech, and teach them to play and occupy themselves without bothering others.

The fulfillment of these many objectives requires of the teacher-nurse a basic knowledge of medicine as well as pedagogical knowledge. She must be thoroughly acquainted with the special characteristics of very young children, the ways of caring for them properly, the contents and methods of educative work with the very young. The study and assimilation of *The Program of Instruction in the Kindergarten* is an obligation of every nurse.

After starting work, the nurse continues to improve upon her qualifications: she reads professional literature, takes part in seminars, and gets acquainted with the experiences of her co-workers and colleagues.

The education and upbringing of young children is greatly influenced by the personal qualities of the teacher-nurse, her character and behavior. A nurse must possess the highest moral qualities, be a model for surrounding adults and children, maintain friendly relations in the community, and know how to evaluate her own and her colleagues' actions. All her work with the infants demands from the nurse love not only for the work with which she has been entrusted, but also for the children. She must endeavor to do everything encompassed by her job in such a way to insure that the children grow and develop in a normal manner.

Love and concern must be shown for each child. Therefore it is not permissible for either the nurse or her assistant to be swayed by personal feelings and spend more time and devote more attention to attractive or well-behaved children than to others. It is important, however, for more love and care to be given to those children who seem to need it particularly: either the newly arrived or those who are physically less strong than the other children.

Children are very sensitive to a change of conditions. Shifting from home conditions to those in the kindergarten, their whole schedule changes and children tend to shy away from adults, notwithstanding the fact that the need for adult attention and care remains unsatisfied. Therefore, a newly arrived child needs more attention and kindness on the part of the teacher.

The nurse must without fail be very patient and not easily upset or depressed when obstacles are met in the course of fulfilling planned objectives (a child not getting used to the new way of life, not assimilating new habits, frequently being difficult to handle, and so on). A baby's training is a long process, and rapid and easy success must not be expected. However, this must not lead to a decrease in the energy and persistence of the nurse in fulfilling the planned objectives.

The nurse constantly observes each child, tries to notice any change that may occur in the physical or psychological countenance of the child, and tries to strengthen and develop everything of a positive nature that appears in the child. At the same time, she endeavors to discover what causes the appearance of negative elements (lethargy, overexcitement, crying and whimpering, and so on) in order that she may take steps to eliminate anything disturbing the correct growth and development of the child.

The nurse must be close to the children, know how to play with them and to have a good time. To this the children respond with love and attachment.

Throughout her contacts with the children, there must be no sharpness, no irritability. This can only make the work of the staff more complicated and will not improve the children's behavior. Constant restraint and the knowledge of how to control one's feelings must become inalienable characteristics of each nurse.

The nurse is in contact with the children in the course of a whole day. The children sense her deft and soft gestures when she changes their clothing, they hear her calm gentle voice during feeding time or when she is putting them to bed, as well as her cheerful talk during play and activities.

Even the very small children who do not understand the meaning of words are very sensitive to the quality of adult speech (friendly, exasperated) as well as timbre of the voice (sharp, loud, calm). In response to unhurried speech spoken in a voice pleasant to the ear, the little baby smiles and begins to gesticulate with his hands and feet to express his pleasure. A loud, sharp voice frightens small children, while older children try to imitate it.

The quality of the teacher's speech and her tone of voice, not only when she is dealing with a baby but also in her conversations with adults, do not escape the attention of the children.

The nurse explains to the parents those problems which are difficult for them to understand, and she does this tactfully without insisting or patronizing; she convinces them of what is sensible and good for the correct upbringing of the baby, while not allowing herself to adopt a didactic tone of voice.

Talks with parents can only have positive results when friendly in nature and full of good will, even if the parents are not always right. Reserve, modesty, and good manners are qualities indispensable to the teacher-nurse.

Whereas the nurse in attending the very young babies must wear such clothing as is customary in general nursing establishments, there is no need for the teacher attending children in their second year of life to do the same. She can replace the white uniform with a short-sleeved dress made of colored cotton. On top of the dress, a colored apron may be worn.

A dress of pleasant appearance (color, design) attracts the children's attention, evokes pleasant feelings, brings liveliness into the child's environment, and serves to prevent any similarity to hospital conditions.

The teacher-nurse trains her assistant very thoroughly, since she is her closest helper in the care of small children. She helps the assistant to acquire the preliminary information regarding child care and upbringing, she gives her advice and directions aimed at improving her work, and checks whether the assistant has followed them. The nurse encourages attentiveness and a concern for the children on the part of her assistant.

While preserving her authority, the nurse maintains a friendly relationship with the assistant, striving to attain the best results through a friendly working atmosphere.

V

The Care and Instruction of Children in their Third Year of Life

OBJECTIVES

In a unified preschool institution, children at the beginning of their third year are transferred from the infant group to the first preschool group. This transfer takes place in the month of September. If, at that time, some children have not quite reached the age of 2 (are short by one or two months) but their physical and mental development is good, these children should not be held back in the infant group.

The transfer into the new group, even though this takes place within one given institution, nevertheless represents for all the children an important event, and one which is associated with various well-known difficulties. The staff in charge of children in their third year must be specially prepared from the medical and teaching viewpoint.

The children are met by a new teacher, sometimes even by a new assistant. They find themselves in a new homeroom where the setting is somewhat different and the objects used by the child are placed differently. In order for the children to get used to the new conditions more rapidly and with greater ease, the teacher must get acquainted in advance with the children who are to be in her charge, observe their games and the way they act with each other, observe their emotional attitudes, and talk with them. It is also important for the teacher-nurse of the forthcoming group to be told of the special characteristics of each child, and for the teaching staff who are receiving the new group to be given written descriptions and pertinent data regarding the development of the children.

It is very desirable for the teaching staff to find time toward the beginning of the year to visit the families of their future pupils. This will fill out significantly their initial impressions of the child, his parents, and the living conditions of the family, and will help to establish indispensable mutual cooperation and a unity in the influence of teacher and parents on the child.

As she begins her work with the children, the teacher or teacher-nurse must already be well acquainted with the objectives which it is her job to fulfill, as well as with the special characteristics of children in their third year. A knowledge of the characteristics of this age will help in properly organizing the children's life and making it meaningful and happy, in organizing varied and useful activities, and, finally, in directing the life of children toward the goals of the program of instruction.

Compared with the second year of life, the third year finds the child becoming physically stronger, more resistant, and capable of greater exertion. During this year, his weight increases by 2 to 2.8 kilometers and he grows approximately 7 to 8 centimeters. The central nervous system of the child improves significantly and its efficiency is increased. The very first goal of the teacher of this group is to protect and strengthen the child's health and to concern herself with the physical development of the child.

The children, to an extent greater than that at the previous level, are capable of concentrating on a given activity, controlling their desires and restraining themselves. They still, however, tire quickly and become overexcited. The increasing capacity of the child's nervous system and his greater mastery of speech help him to grasp easily very elementary relationships, contribute to the process of orienting himself to his environment, and form good habits. Therefore, it is very important to select carefully as models for the child's imitation those verbal expressions which are rapidly assimilated by a child. Any change in habits or basic physical movements will be effected slowly and require great efforts.

The teacher must also bear in mind the still considerable vulnerability of a child's organism at this age, and the need for building it up systematically and thereby increasing the resistance of the organism to colds and infectious diseases. The physical development of the child and the building up of his organism must be carried out under the systematic observation and control of the doctor.

One of the most important characteristics of children in their third year is the fact that they are capable of greatly improving their physical skills, of developing greater balance in basic movements (running, walking, crawling) and greater manual dexterity, even though the children are fairly well coordinated with their hands and have learned to use them with a certain skill.

The teacher must make sure that the child is constantly clean, that tidiness is maintained in the main room, and that the schedule is strictly observed. It is her duty to protect the child from excessive excitement, noise or exhaustion, and to be concerned about his general well-being.

Correct physical training is closely related to the training of children in self-reliance. The urge to act independently is a need of any growing, developing organism; it must be strengthened and fortified by all available means, thus guiding the children's activities in the right direction. In working toward these goals it is extremely important to train the children to be self-reliant. This involves training them to have good health habits and to be responsible for doing simple tasks (putting a toy in its place, putting on socks, etc.). When a certain level of self-sufficiency has been attained, the children can be taught more successfully to help each other.

Children develop friendly and conciliatory attitudes toward adults and children which manifest themselves in their everyday relationships, and when they are playing together. Children are taught to play together, to greet adults and children of the same age group, to perform and obey commands or requests from the adults, to ask politely for whatever they need, and to say "thank you." These very elementary habits and behavior patterns, as well as the positive emotions which accompany them, will help in the future formation of patterns of social behavior.

With correct training, contact between children begun in the earlier stages increases and develops. This reveals itself in the fact that the children communicate more frequently with each other, with the teacher, and with the assistant during play time, and in the fact that in the daily course of life they are more willing to join together in various forms of free activity.

Children show a noticeable increase of interest in each other. There appears also a selectivity in their relationships; imitation is expressed more vividly; the children are capable of actively showing sympathy and doing something for somebody else, especially for someone younger: they will console a crying child, give him a toy, try to put a cap on the head of a baby getting ready to go outside, and so forth.

However, among children of this age group, conflicts and quarrels frequently occur. They find it difficult to give in to each other or to wait for their turn (excessive emotionality, weak development of restraining processes); this especially occurs with certain children who are more excitable or more spoiled.

Constant attention must be given to the children's conduct and their interrelationships. In working successfully in this area, good contacts between parents and teachers are particularly important.

Under favorable conditions the children's speech develops rapidly during this period, and this exerts a strong positive influence on the whole psychological development of the child. According to data from the research of N. M. Aksarina, the vocabulary of children reaches 1200-1500 words by the end of their third year. Children begin to use fluently various grammatical structures characteristic of conversational speech, and their pronunciation of words and sounds improves. As a whole, their speech becomes more understandable and distinct. All this contributes to a noticeable increase in their oral communication with surrounding people. An increasing role is played by the spoken word in the regulation of the children's behavior and in the whole educational instructional process.

However, the group may contain children with poorly developed speech. They avoid contact with adults and children alike and do not ask any questions. The speech of these children is indistinct and they use babbling words: *koko, bobo, bye-bye,* etc., and one-word sentences. The cause of this condition lies most frequently in one of the following: insufficient contact between children and adults, sickness, or a low level of teaching and training.

The development of speech in all its aspects is set as a goal for the group of children in their third year. This goal cannot be separated from that of broadening their orientation to the surroundings and that of the formation of concepts of objects, events and their corresponding qualities. With children who are retarded in speech development, the teacher must have more frequent contact, and she must motivate them to speech in games and activities.

The life of children in their third year must be enriched with esthetic impressions. One must develop their visual and auditory perception and their physical sensitivity; develop an interest and love for music, singing and verse; and foster the corresponding skills and abilities which give these qualities a chance to appear and develop in artistic activities: humming, dramatizing in musical games typical movements of some of the characters, and so on. At this age it is particularly important to develop sensory impressions as a basis for mental development and esthetic training (recognizing and differentiating colors, shapes and sounds). If these aspects of child development are given sufficient attention, then this will have a positive effect both on the esthetic and overall development of the children.

Children in their third year are capable of enjoying a melodious tune or a bright picture, and of noticing what is beautiful in nature (falling snow, a beautiful sweet-smelling flower). The teacher fosters a positive emotional attitude toward the surrounding life, closely associating this goal with the esthetic and moral experiences of the children.

The all-around development of a child is realized in the process of varied activities. Hence the teacher's responsibilities consist in being constantly concerned about the organization of interesting and meaningful games, activities and observations, as well as active participation in an everyday routine.

ORGANIZING THE LIFE OF THE GROUP AND EDUCATING THE CHILDREN THROUGH THE ROUTINE OF DAILY LIFE

The normal physical development of the child, as well as his orderly behavior, depends to a great extent on the clear organization of life and the strict observance of the schedule. Any violation of the schedule invariably affects the children. Therefore, both the institution staff and the parents must, through common efforts, attempt to observe the schedule strictly.

The kindergarten schedule for children in their third year is established on the basis of generally accepted norms concerning the most important physiological characteristics of children of this age group.

Periods of time elapsing between feeding times must not exceed four hours. The length of time children of 2 ½ to 3 years must sleep within a span of 24 hours must be equal to twelve or twelve and a half hours, out of which children sleep for about two and a half hours during the day (only once during the day).

The schedule of the children's life also provides for the proper variation of the different forms of children's activities. Active games alternate with quiet games and activities; an activity requiring greater concentration alternates with one requiring little concentration.

Daily Schedule for Children from 2 to 3 Years of Age
(Day Attendance)

FALL-WINTER PERIOD

AT HOME

Rising, morning toilet	6:30–7:30 A.M.

AT THE KINDERGARTEN

Receiving the children, inspection, play	7:00–8:00 A.M.
Preparation for breakfast, breakfast	7:50–8:35 A.M.
Play and activities (in subgroups)	8:35–9:15, 9:30 A.M.
Preparation for outdoor play, play (children in first subgroup)	9:15–11:15 A.M.

AT THE KINDERGARTEN

Preparation for outdoor play, play (children in second subgroup)	9:30–11:30 A.M.
Gradual (in subgroups) return from outdoor play, undressing, play	11:15–11:30, 11:40 A.M.
Preparation for dinner, dinner	11:40 A.M.–12:00 N., 12:30 P.M.
Preparation for nap, outside nap	12:40–3:00, 3:30 P.M.
Taking the children out of bed as they awake, air baths and water procedures, games	3:00–3:30, 4:00 P.M.
Preparation for afternoon snack, snack	4:00–4:30 P.M.
Play, activities (in subgroup)	4:30–5:00 P.M.
Play, departure of children for home	5:00–7:00 P.M.

AT HOME

Play	Up to 7:20 P.M.
Preparation for supper, supper	7:20–8:15 P.M.
Getting ready for bed	8:15–8:30 P.M.
Night sleep	8:30 P.M.–6:30, 7:00 A.M.

Daily Schedule for Children from 2 to 3 Years of Age
(Children Boarding at School)

FALL-WINTER PERIOD

Getting the children out of bed as they awake, morning toilet, inspection, air baths and water procedures, play.	6:30–7:00 A.M., 8:00 A.M.
Preparation for breakfast, breakfast	7:50–8:35 A.M.
Play, activities (in subgroups)	8:35–9:15 A.M., 9:30 A.M.
Preparation for outdoor play, play (for first subgroup)	9:15–11:15 A.M.
Preparation for outdoor play, play (for second subgroup)	9:30–11:30 A.M.
Gradual return from play, undressing, play	11:15–11:30, 11:40 A.M.
Preparation for dinner, dinner	11:40–12:30 P.M.
Preparation for nap, nap outside	12:30–3:00, 3:30 P.M.
Taking children out of bed as they awake, air baths and water procedures, play	3:00–3:30, 4:00 P.M.
Preparation for snack, snack	4:00–4:30 P.M.
Play, activities (in subgroups)	4:30–5:00 P.M.
Preparation for outdoor play, play (for first group)	5:00–6:25 P.M.
Preparation for outdoor play, play (for second group)	5:15–6:40 P.M.
Return from play (gradually, in subgroups), undressing, games	6:25–7:20 P.M.
Preparation for supper, supper	7:20–8:00 P.M.
Play, evening toilet, preparation for night sleep	8:00–8:30 P.M.
Night sleep	8:30–6:30, 7:00 P.M.

A single schedule is established for the children in their third year, even if there are some children only about two years old, since the distribution of time for sleep, the waking period and feeding in the course of a whole day is the same for all children of this age group. At the same time, the condition of health of each child and his special characteristics must be taken into account. For children who need more sleep (for example, the smallest and those who take a long time falling asleep) or for those who are either excessively active or weak, it is recommended that they be put to bed earlier and awakened later than the others. In other cases, for example for children who need more time for eating than most children, it is only sensible to serve them food earlier than the others so that they may go to sleep at the same time as the others.

Much attention must be given to those children who were recently admitted to the kindergarten or to those who have been absent from it for any length of time regardless of the reason. The teacher must find out what kind of schedule the child had at home, and gradually make him accustomed to the kindergarten schedule.

It is possible, for example, to alter the schedule slightly: to ask the children to come to the table later than the others and put them to bed somewhat later than the others; not to insist upon the participation of these children in activities during the first days if these activities did not take place at home; and so forth. Understanding and kindness on the part of the teacher and the assistant towards the children, and commendation for even small successes in carrying out the requests of adults and in various other things, will help to get these children to conform willingly to the pattern of life of the kindergarten.

The parents must be acquainted with the schedule set up for the group, and they must be counseled as to the best means of coordinating the home and school life of their child. When put to bed at the proper time (not later than 9 P.M.) the child wakes up more easily in the morning and arrives at the kindergarten in a happy frame of mind. Provided he had a good night sleep, he will be active for a period of five or six hours.

First morning breakfast must be eaten by the child no later than one to one and a half hours after he wakes up. If the length of time between waking and breakfasting does not exceed one and a half hours, he should not be given food at home. Thus, he will eat with great appetite when he breakfasts at the kindergarten. In other cases, we recommend that the parents give the child a cup of kefir (yogurt made with mare's milk which is very popular in the Balkans and the East), an apple, a carrot, or some kind of juice.

FURNITURE AND ARRANGEMENT
IN THE MAIN ROOM

A prerequisite for the proper functioning of the schedule is a well-thought-out arrangement of all furniture and items in the common room and all attached areas. The arrangement must correspond to educational needs and be suitable and sensible. For example, keeping in mind that it is difficult for small children of this age to play in large groups, the staff must spread out the toys in various areas of the room and give some thought as to the best way they should be arranged, so that it is convenient for the children to play with them in various positions, such as standing or sitting, and so that the children may easily pick up a toy and put it back in place. A space must be provided where a child may pull a truck or build something. Others should be able to play quietly at some distance. Tables must be placed where the light is best and in such a way that the light falls from the left. . . .

When choosing furniture, the age and size of the children must be kept in mind. If the group contains some children who are smaller than the others, it is desirable that these children be provided with furniture of reduced dimensions; thus for children 75 to 84 centimeters tall the height of the table top, as measured from the floor, should equal 37 centimeters, and the seat height above the floor level should be 19 centimeters. In other cases, when some children in the group are taller than 100 centimeters (100–109), they must be provided with furniture of a larger size: the height of the table top above floor level should be 47 centimeters, and the height of the chair seat 27 centimeters.

We recommend that the color of the walls and furniture be light, well-matched, and pleasing to the eye. For wall decoration, artistic pictures must be chosen, such as prints and artistic reproductions with subjects understandable to children. Photographs representing life in the institution can also be used (enlargements framed under glass). In order that the pictures may be closer to the child and may attract his attention as well as make sense to him, they must be hung rather low, a little higher than a child's height. There is no need to stick the children's own art works on the walls, put paper flowers in vases, tape animal or people cutouts on the windows, or block off the light with a large quantity of indoor plants or hanging curtains.

Much attention must be given to tidiness and order in the main living room and to a pleasing toy display. Care must be taken to see that no needless things are lying around on the teacher's table, windowsills, and closets.

Measurements for Basic Children's Furniture
(in centimeters)

		85–94 CM.	95–99 CM.
	CHILDREN'S HEIGHT		
TABLES	Distance between table top and chair seat	19	19
	Height of top above floor level	41	43
	Width	40	40
CHAIRS	Height of seat above floor level	22	24
	Depth of seat	20	21
	Height of back	22	24
BEDS	Length	120	120
	Width	56	60

RECEIVING THE CHILDREN

In the morning the teacher receives and greets each child and talks with him, thus indicating her own cheerfulness. Children are very sensitive to the tone of voice and words of the teacher. The teacher, seeing a little boy entering the school with his father says "Look, Boris has come. What nice red cheeks! I bet he walked very fast with his Daddy!" In such a sentence, spoken gently, there is much pleasure for the boy; he feels that the teacher was waiting for him and was pleased that he was able to walk fast like his father. Boris smiles, answers the teacher's greeting cheerfully, calmly says "good-bye" to his father and runs toward the group.

During these brief morning encounters with the parents, the teacher may discuss minor details about the child. She finds out, for example, how he slept, what he did the previous evening, in what mood he got ready for the kindergarten, or how he played with other children. Deeper problems concerning both parents and teacher should not, as a rule, be discussed during this short time. To talk these over, a better setting is needed, as well as more time.

Up to 8 o'clock the children play on their own. These morning games are very meaningful for establishing a calm but at the same time happy disposition in the children; in this lies one of the most important objectives of the morning period. Therefore the toys must be placed in such a manner as to attract the children and remind them of their slight but real experience in handling these toys (dolls and cars, building materials).

Some children may enjoy participating in watering plants, setting the breakfast table, and so on. The time when the group is assembling must be used for talking to the children. This is all the more feasible in that the child arrives in the morning with a set of new impressions. Some child saw a new kind of truck in the street, another a flag on a house, and so forth. "It was a red flag," points out the teacher, "tomorrow is May First."

There is great value in keeping the conversation going, in reinforcing the interest shown by the children, and in inducing a child to converse. The teacher asks, for example, who bought Mary such a beautiful kerchief or who cut Kolya's hair. Children readily respond to such questions, and the teacher should use their answers to prolong the conversation. Mary, aged 2 years and 8 months, explains: "Mommy bought me this kerchief." The teacher examines the pattern on the kerchief and says, "How beautiful; take care of it." Such talks are of extreme value in establishing close contact between the teacher and child as well as in developing the child's speech. Without noticing it, the child gets accustomed to such contact, which pleases him and soon becomes indispensable.

Sometimes, however, things turn out quite differently. Olya enters, happy and smiling. She expects everybody, especially the teacher, to notice her new bow. But no one notices anything. Then Olya comes near the teacher and tries to attract her attention. But the teacher does not understand her mood. Pushing Olya aside, she fixes Slavya's pants. Olya stops smiling, but does not go away from the teacher and says in a low voice, "I have a new bow; I have a new bow." "I see your bow," says the teacher indifferently, not looking at the little girl. "Go and play." Olya is hurt and upset. Not only must the teacher be attentive, but she must actively encourage the children to welcome a new arrival or a child who has been absent on account of illness, to approach and greet him, to take him by the hand to where the toys are, to show him a picture or give him a toy.

If a number of children from the older group are present during the period when the children are received at the kindergarten, the above-mentioned simple rules of conduct are more easily assimilated by the younger children. But hints must be given by the teacher, upon which the older children will put rules of conduct into use and become natural helpers to the teacher. The group's teacher must carefully evaluate whether the morning reception of children is performed satisfactorily, whether it has established the proper atmosphere for the whole day, and whether it has benefited the children.

An important place in the day's schedule is given to such operations as washing, toilet routine, feeding of children, putting them to bed, and dressing. The correct organization and methodical application of these procedures is important for the health and normal physical development of small children. All these tasks must be performed at a specific time and in a planned sequence; the teacher and her assistant must watch to see that the child is kept warm, that he is fed at the appropriate time and in suitable quality, and that he sleeps the necessary length of time—that is, that all the child's needs are met. Then the child will be contented, healthy, and organized.

The principle of gradation must guide the everyday routine. This can be achieved by establishing the correct order within one activity and by relating one procedure to another, thus excluding unnecessary waste of time, effort, and energy of each child in waiting to be washed, to receive food, or to be given a chance to play. This very important principle is based on the research by the department of education and development of the Institute of Pediatrics AMN (N. M. Aksarina, N. M. Schelovanov). Its methods are thoroughly learned by workers in institutions dealing with young children. Their experience must be utilized especially by teachers working with children of younger preschool age.

At feeding time, when getting the child ready for bed, or when dressing him, it is essential to get the cooperation of the child, to train him to act independently, and to teach him to observe the established rules of conduct. Creating contact between adults and children, asking the children questions, having them perform little errands, and answering the children's questions—all contribute to the establishment of close contacts and to the development of the children's speaking ability.

All this is significantly easier to achieve when there is understanding and cooperation between the teacher and her assistant. The teacher acquaints her assistant with the kinds of things expected of children in their third year and explains in what way they must be given help. It sometimes happens that the assistant, hurrying to attend to her domestic duties, begins to dress or wash the child herself, without taking time to teach him to do this on his own. To avoid this, the teacher, in establishing the schedule, must note where and when her assistance will be most needed.

If the children have been taught to carry out the activities mentioned above, by the age of 1 year and 8 months they are quite willing to obey the directions given by the teacher; they go to wash, sit at the table, and so forth. Nevertheless, one must always keep trying to arrange things in such a way that a transition from play or an activity in which the child is absorbed is not sudden and unexpected and will not rudely interrupt the child's activity.

WASHING UP

Washing is an important part of good health habits. Children in their third year attempt to participate actively in washing and can go through the necessary gestures by themselves, provided they have been taught previously to act independently. For this reason, children who have just moved up from the second year of the kindergarten can wash up more easily and faster than those children who did not attend the institution. They are already developing a certain association between the process of washing up and a given moment in the daily routine (the assistant is setting the table for dinner, some of the children begin to tidy up toys, others are going toward the bathroom, and so forth).

The teacher and her assistant teach the children to wash their hands and faces by themselves and to dry themselves. They also teach them the necessary cleanliness habits: wash hands before meals and whenever they are dirty, wash in the morning when waking up and in the evening before going to bed, use only one's own towel. The process of washing up should also be used for speech development and orientation to the surroundings.

To insure that the washing operation is not carried on simultaneously by all the children, the teacher, without interrupting the play of all children present (that is, before breakfast or before dinner), guides a number of children toward the bathroom (the number depending upon the number of faucets available). First go those who eat most slowly or have a poor appetite and those who are already prepared to go and wash.

Helping the children, the teacher and her assistant roll up their sleeves, check the flow of water, encourage neatness and a businesslike atmosphere, and sometimes hurry along those who love to play with water. Although the children come into the washroom in small groups, some children will nevertheless have to wait their turn. They must be taught to wait patiently until their turn comes, that is, until others have finished. They must do this without shoving the other children. Two to three minutes of waiting not only will do no harm to the child, but may turn out to be useful to his training, teaching him patience and some restraint. Those children who seem to indicate the need of using the toilet are directed by the teacher or assistant toward the toilet before washing. The teacher and her assistant must be certain that there is no draft by the toilet (in cold weather) so that the children are not chilled. Special attention must be given to those with low resistance and those who have recently been sick.

In order for a child to learn to find his own towel rapidly and to use only his own, bright pictures should be picked out and put near the towels as marks. Each one of them should be examined with the children and talked about. When things are set up in this way, the child remembers the object illustrated in the picture and learns to name it accurately. The teacher must still be sure that the child is using only his own towel. The child who painstakingly washes himself feels very pleased when he receives the approval of an adult.

In some cases the singing and use of an appropriate nursery rhyme or song may stimulate the desire to wash, although the rhyme should not be repeated daily. An example:

> *Water, water, wash my face*
> *So my eyes shine and my cheeks are rosy.*

or

> *One has to wash in the morning and the evening*
> *Shame, shame on the dirty chimney sweeps.*

FEEDING OF CHILDREN

Children who are brought up in a unified preschool institution learn early in life to be independent and self-sufficient. Therefore, eating habits greatly improve in the course of their third year. They are already eating comparatively quickly but without neatness, as their movements are still uncoordinated. Daily exercises, with adults encouraging self-reliance, give excellent results. By the age of 3, the child learns to eat more quickly, more neatly, and with more assurance. Most children by then know how to hold a spoon properly, but some of them keep on in the old way.

Almost always, in any given group, there are children who are less self-reliant than others. These are the ones who joined the kindergarten later than the others or who were often sick. They must be helped while eating and even be spoonfed. It is more difficult to get children who, at home, were kept for a long time on liquid or fine-ground food, thinly cooked cereals, or bouillon to accept the food in the school's diet. These children do not know how to chew properly and often refuse the food to which they are not accustomed. New requirements must be presented to these children gradually, without provoking negative reactions in them, using every means to encourage the child, even if it is with little success.

There is no doubt that the pleasant appearance of the dinner table, of the carefully set dishes, and of the food itself, will exert a favorable influence on the appetite of the children. If the table is covered with an oilcloth with cheerful-looking patterns or with various kinds of plastic materials, such a pleasant appearance can be achieved very easily. It is harder to maintain the required state of cleanliness if a tablecloth is used. Therefore, there is no need to hurry with the introduction of tablecloths. One should not be excessively severe and unreasonably demanding toward small children should they spill soup by accident or scatter crumbs. In trying to achieve a situation where every child eats the portion he has been given, each child's general condition must be carefully watched. He may be not quite healthy, overly tired, not accustomed to a given dish, or deeply upset by something. In such cases one should not insist that he eat everything, as this may even be harmful.

Here are some examples of feeding norms: 150 grams of soup, (the plate not filled to the top); a small hamburger or cutlet or portion of fish—70–80 grams; vegetables—100 grams; a cup of fruit compote (stewed fruits)—150 grams. A dessert spoon is recommended for eating soup, along with a small, very stable cup. Bread must be cut in small thin slices.

Children sit down at the table one by one as they finish playing and washing up. Ten to fifteen minutes before the meal must be devoted to quiet relaxed play. The child should receive his food as soon as he sits at the table. The teacher names the dishes placed in front of the children, stimulating positive attitudes toward the food served. For example, she says "Today we have nice and tasty *kasha*," or "Look what nice red apples we are given for lunch." She praises the children who try to eat neatly and who sit quietly, noticing the achievements of individual children. For the most part, she does not address herself to all the children at once (in order not to distract them) but to small groups or to an individual child, and in a low voice.

Cloth napkins are essential for children in their third year. These are attached under the chin and tucked inside the opening of the shirt or dress, or else tied up behind the neck. The napkin protects the child's clothing and trains him in cleanliness. In the second half of the year the napkin need not be tied up behind the neck, but is placed next to the child, as children by then know how to eat neatly. Such an approach will stimulate the child to observe neatness during meals. Many small children, by the end of their third year of life, can use paper napkins properly. Cloth napkins must be washed without waiting for the general change of linen.

SLEEP

The day sleep or nap provides indispensable rest for small children. When children have finished eating, they are sent to play; care is taken that they do not get excited. They then go in turns to the toilet. Putting the children on the toilets and washing their hands is performed under adult supervision, after which the children can again return to their toys.

Children are settled in bed only when the majority of them have used the toilet. Such sequence insures proper control over children, normal preparation for going to bed and for the nap itself, and also the creation of a quiet atmosphere in the bedroom.

Children undress with the help of adults. Whenever they are undressing or dressing, it is important that from the very first children be taught tidiness and perseverance. One helps the child first to remove his outer clothing, then shoes, then underwear and stockings or socks.

Some children, more self sufficient than others, know how to take off a shirt, for example, and even how to fold it neatly. The teachers praise such actions and make other children aware of them. Children 2 years old need, of course, a significant amount of help on the part of adults, but this help must only be available to those who really need it. Sometimes even an older child seems to need help. This might be a child who, for some reason or other, hasn't mastered the operations of undressing and dressing. It may simply be that he is tired or in a bad mood. In such cases, the teacher and the assistant may undress or dress a child, but this does not mean that the child is to be completely passive. He must participate in some aspects of the operation ("put on the chest band, please" or "pull up your socks").

As a rule, children of this age group fall asleep quickly, but the more active ones may turn about in their beds for a fairly long time. It is good to sit for a while near such a child, to stroke his head, or to say a few soothing words to him. If sleeping takes place on the veranda, then it is particularly important that the child, as soon as he is put in his sleeping bag in the warmth of the room, be taken out to the veranda. It is well known that sleeping in the open is particularly healthy. Children not only fall asleep quickly but sleep calmly and peacefully. In the sleeping area (veranda) it is absolutely necessary for an adult to keep watch over the children.

Children wake up gradually. They must be taken out of bed just as gradually. Those children who are dressed after sleep may go and play.

OUTDOOR PLAY

The time spent outside, as indicated by the planned schedule for the day, is vital to the health and the development of the children and for the realization of various educational objectives.

The meaning of outdoor play is not always sufficiently appreciated by the teacher. Sometimes, under the pretext that the weather is either too cold or too windy, the teacher deprives children of fresh air or shortens the outdoor play and does not take the children out in the second half of the day. Actually, nothing exerts such a positive influence on the health and well being of a child than well organized outdoor play and games in the fresh air.

Outside play should help to enrich the children with interesting and valuable impressions about nature and surrounding life. Besides, outside play gives children necessary exercise. The child can run about, crawl, and play in the playground with the type of toys which cannot be used easily indoors. To derive the full benefit of outdoor playtime, to take full advantage of its educative content, is one of the most important objectives of the teacher.

Dressing for outdoors, particularly in winter time, is one of the most complicated processes for both children and adults alike. Therefore, this operation must be organized very efficiently. Children are made ready and divided into two groups in preparing them for outdoors. Before dressing, they are directed to the bathroom. The teacher and her assistant help the first group to get dressed. At the same time, the teacher keeps an eye on those children who are still playing in the room. The small children are dressed with the help of available adults. It is also good to encourage older children to help with the little ones, but their help must be supervised to stop them from giving unnecessary help and preventing the little children from using their initiative.

It is important to use this brief period of time to promote the establishment of good relationships among children of the same age group and children of various ages. An attentive teacher will accomplish this naturally, because common activities in themselves stimulate a feeling of reciprocal friendship in both the younger and older children. Volodya, who has been helping for some days to dress Dima, informs the teacher with a feeling of pride, "Dima has already learned to put on his pants. I just helped to pull them up a wee bit." The teacher immediately announces to all the children, "You know what? Volodya taught Dima to put on his pants."

Dressing for outside must be done in a certain order. We will indicate the most convenient order as borne out by experience for the fall-winter period of the year. Children go to the closets, take their leggings and snowboots, and sit on a bench placed as near as possible to the place where the clothing is kept. Having dressed by themselves or with the help of adults, they take their hats and sweaters, which are then put on them by adults. After this, it only remains to put on a coat and mittens and tie up the scarves.

In the course of the year, children are taught to dress more and more on their own. The teacher and her assistant must check carefully to make sure everything necessary is put on the child. Perhaps he did not take his galoshes out of the closet and it is muddy and cold outside. He may have forgotten to put on underpants under his trousers (they may have been removed because the child wet his pants). Perhaps it is relatively warm outside, whereas the child has dressed for very cold weather. The staff must decide exactly what the child should wear.

While the children are dressing for outdoor playtime, the teacher takes advantage of any appropriate moment to talk with the children, getting them acquainted with various objects and widening their interests. She teaches them to say correctly the names of various items of clothing and some of their qualities (fur coat, blue scarf). This teaches them to use essential words, to talk about the weather and the games they will play, or what they will see, during playtime. The teacher supervises the correct pronunciation of words and sounds.

Contact with children during dressing time provides ideal natural conditions for training them in good manners such as politely making a request, saying "thank you," and passing someone peacefully without hurrying and without shoving. In the contact between the teacher and the child, room should be found for a cheerful joke, a verse, a clever saying or proverb.

In children's poetry, as well as in the national folklore, the description of the ordinary life of a child—washing, dressing, combing hair—occupies a large place. Some of these nursery rhymes, jingles, or verses are already familiar to the children, and when they are said by the teacher at an appropriate moment make a strong impression and are easily remembered.

When the children are finally dressed, they go out with either the assistant or the teacher (according to an agreement between the two on this point). Then the remaining younger children get dressed. The children return indoors in the same order—by subgroups. The teacher takes care that those who went out first come in first.

During outdoor playtime the individual play of the children occupies a large place. The teacher also organizes daily some active game, such as a ring game, and leads gymnastic exercises (walking on a log, running down a hill, crawling down and through something). During the time set aside for outdoor playtime, children can be taken to the nearest park or square[1]. Here there is always an opportunity to utilize the natural conditions for the development of physical skills, such as stepping over a ditch or a puddle or running down a hill.

When the children leave the building to go to the playground or to the garden, they feel strongly the change of setting and conditions: the fresh-

---

[1]Square is understood in the English sense—a quiet square with little traffic and a large garden, with trees and lawns in the center.

ness of the air, the brightness of the sun, the wind. They get a great sense of joy at the sight of falling snow, or opening leaves, or green grass. This stimulates them to lively activities; they want to dig the snow, gather flowers, catch insects, and so forth. In a child of 3 there begins to develop a consciousness of his surroundings, which is promoted mainly by the observations made by the children and the responses given by adults to questions formulated by the little ones. On this basis, such an important quality as curiosity begins to develop in the children. The children may themselves notice ... how a fence is painted, how a house is renovated, the way school children plant bushes, and how the streets become clean and beautiful. The interest aroused in objects and events of the surrounding life is useful not only in broadening the child's outlook but also in developing his feelings and sensitivity and his general behavior.

During the time he spends outside, the child encounters a wider range of phenomena than when he is inside the building. This fact must be taken into account when planning observations provided for in the program, but the teacher should not simply pass by anything else interesting or important which may occur unexpectedly.

During the period spent outside, the most favorable conditions for contact between young children and older ones exist. Children are brought together in games and are persuaded to offer help to the older children in their tasks. The 2- or 3-year-old may participate to a certain extent in the work of the teacher and of the older children in attending to the garden or the playground—picking up stones, raking leaves and transporting them in small wheelbarrows, gathering vegetables, etc. During the outdoor play time there is also an opportunity to arrange meetings between children in their third year and the younger groups attending the kindergarten. This is a valuable experience for the 2- to 3-year-old children, as they begin to feel grown up and capable. They are quite willing to play with the 2-year-old children and lead them about by the hand.

In taking care of the children's health and continuing to work for the establishment of hygienic habits and good manners, the teacher takes careful note of the children's appearance—an untied scarf, mittens taken off, a dirty nose or hands. She trains the child to use a handkerchief on his own and to turn to the teacher when help is needed. She must check to make sure a given child is neither cold nor too hot.

During the time spent outside, it is particularly important to regulate the activities of each child. Some must be encouraged to take part in active games, whereas others must be kept from becoming overexcited. Still others must be helped to play together without getting in each other's way.

In the evening when parents come to take the children home, the teacher tells them how the child feels, how he acted during the day, how he played, what his activities were, and what kind of relationship he has with children of his own age. The teacher advises the parents not to let the child take part in games that may excite him before the night sleep, and not to tell him new fairy tales (toward the evening, the child is already tired and no new demands must be made of him). Schedules of children spending the night in kindergartens must also take these requirements into account.

THE PLAY OF CHILDREN
IN THEIR THIRD YEAR

The whole life of a child is inextricably tied up with playing. The smaller the child, the more time must be devoted to play.

Toward the beginning of his third year of life the child's play becomes relatively stable and varied, provided that in the previous age group attention was given to proper supervision of play. In the course of the year, the children must make tremendous progress in their general development, particularly in the development of play activity, and the educative influence of adults in all of this will be decisive. The contact of smaller and bigger children in the course of their play is also of great significance. The teacher must have a clear understanding of the educational objectives which are to be realized through guidance in the children's play.

It is important to create in the children a cheerful, happy mood, to spur them to active behavior and to improve their physical skills; to teach the children to play with toys, to use them with care, and to notice their attractive appearance. The children must also be taught how to select a game or toy, must be encouraged and taught how to play in groups, and must develop friendly attitudes toward each other. While play is in progress, the teacher develops the children's speech, acquaints them with the names of objects and with the way to use them, with their purpose and with some related qualities, deepening and refining the children's conception of the surroundings (near and within reach of their understanding) and encouraging inquisitiveness.

It is up to the teacher to make sure that the games of the children in their third year are sufficiently varied, that the contents of the games are gradually enriched, and that in the process of playing, positive relationships grow up among the children. This will insure the most successful fulfillment of the educational objectives in play, and will permit the children's life as a whole to be organized around play.

The teacher must consider it important to observe the children at play and their behavior during play. This will help the teacher to make a better study of the child, to see his individual characteristics, and to pinpoint concrete educational problems not only in play but in other activity in the routine life.

Organization of Playtime

In the *Program of Instruction in the Kindergarten* it has been stated that to create happy and educationally valuable playtime, children must have at their disposal various toys and equipment. The teacher must make it his concern to see that at all times not devoted to routine procedures and activities, the children have the opportunity to use their imagination and initiative in play. Conditions must be such that each child can, whenever he wishes, choose the toy or game of his choice. At the same time, bearing in mind the limited life experience of 3-year-old children, the teacher guides their play and assists in varying the games and in changing the children's activities. For this purpose she alternates quiet and fast-moving games, removes some toys and brings others in, attracts the children's attention to them, advises them to play with some particular toy or other, and plays with the children herself.

In organizing children's games, the teacher must take into account the time of day. Morning games must create in the children a calm, happy, and at the same time active condition. The children are presented with familiar toys. The teacher supervises and sees that each child has found a game for himself. Sometimes in the morning when there are very few children in the group or on the premises, a new toy can be brought in. It must be shown to the children and given to them to play with, and the children must be shown various ways of using it. For example, the teacher should demonstrate how to sit on a big rocking horse and how to rock, what the other children may do at the same time (rocking together), how to get off the horse carefully, and how to give it water. Later on, it is best to take the toy out of circulation at the proper time. As the teacher is mainly occupied in the morning with receiving children, all toys that need constant watching (mosaics, cutout pictures), as well as large moving toys which make noise and excite the children, should also be quietly removed.

The group must be provided with a sufficient number of toys and they must be spread around conveniently. This will help a child, even the one who finds it difficult to find his bearings in new surroundings, to see the toy and to take an interest in it.

Toys which naturally lead the children to perform familiar actions and lead to the development of simple "thematic" games are useful in introducing organization into the children's play. Such toys are usually placed in play corners—dolls which may be put in pushcarts or carriages, in cars, or on a chair. There may be kitchen accessories and tea sets, toy equipment for washing and ironing, etc. Even at the beginning of the year, these toys bring children together, although they do not necessarily require any cooperative activity on the children's part.

Building material spread out on a number of tables attracts the children in morning play. With this in mind, the teacher might build some simple structure out of large or small building pieces, thus directing the children toward a specific type of play: for example, making large gates through which children begin to roll cars, or a fence as an enclosure for animals, or a bridge on which dolls may stand.

When they arrive in the morning the children are given for independent play some toy from among the educational toys with which they are familiar. The moving toys selected should, if possible, be noiseless ones—wooden carts, cars, rolling wheels. Play with these toys stimulates the children to energetic action and gives them pleasure.

Some teachers, especially at the beginning of the year, use successfully for the reception time the simplest forms of entertainment—funny toys, tricks, nursery rhyme games, funny looking dolls, clowns. This form of play or entertainment is most applicable in working with children of a younger age. But even here they are not out of place as they are much enjoyed by the little ones because of their dynamics and unusual features. A newly arrived child, or a child who is just plain mischievous, will as a rule quickly forget his troubles, join the game voluntarily, and start communicating with the teacher.

For example, the teacher takes the child's hands into his own and plays with his fingers, bending them to the accompaniment of such words as, "This finger is a granddad, this one a daddy, that one a mommy, and this one is our little boy. His name is Kolya." Children love when nursery rhymes are dramatized in this way.

Before the day sleeping period and before outdoor playtime are the best times for organizing children's games. The teacher and the assistant help the children who have awakened to dress, and then suggest a game. The attention of specific children must be attracted to the toys available to the group. This approach is particularly advisable for children who have not been in the group very long or are not very lively. After sleeping, they are sluggish and do not know how to occupy themselves.

Toward the time when the children are waking up, children of the older group (one to four children) may be invited in. They will help the younger ones to dress, then will play with them for a while, using their own initiative or following the teacher's instructions.

In the second half of the day the teacher adds to the available toys some new ones with which the children are not as yet able to play. For example, the educator winds up a big new top, and the children watch with delight the way it goes round and listen to the sounds it makes. Then the children learn to play with it themselves, or the teacher asks one or two of the children to bring up a toy and name it. Other children come up and all together they inspect the toy, talk about it, tell what it is called, and discuss the various ways it can be used. . . .

From the moment when the children wake up until the time they are prepared for outdoor play, there is approximately a one-and-a-half-hour interval. During this time the teacher assists in the development of the children's independent play and directs a second activity. In the period before the beginning of the first activity (in the morning), as well as before the second, the children's play must be directed in such a way that their games do not resemble in their nature the activities to come. For example, children who are busy with active games should be diverted from them if the activity is to be centered on physical development.

In the second half of the day games and entertainment may be organized; amusing toys, shadow plays, puppet shows, and slides may be shown. In the kindergartens where children board, this is especially important in making the children happier. For children who spend the night at the kindergarten, quiet games of various kinds must be organized before the children are put to bed for the night.

In the instructional program the various types of children's play applicable to the three-year-olds are indicated.

Active and Role-playing Games and Building

In the independent activity of 2-year-old children, active games—when the little ones roll or push various carts, cars, and wheels, or simply run around—occupy an important place. At first, even the character toys (dolls representing people or animals) are used only as something to move about, carry, or load.

The teacher encourages active games while at the same time taking care that the children do not become overtired and do not remain for any length of time in a single position. Movable toys should be given most often to apathetic children, to those who spend too much time just sitting, playing with dolls, animals, etc. It is important to utilize extensively in active games the basic physical skills and the toys particularly suited to the purpose of developing such skills. This development plays a great role in the general upbringing of the child, in his neuropsychological growth, and in the formation of positive character traits.

Toward the end of the second and the beginning of their third year, themes begin to appear in the children's play. They reproduce with the help of toys a set of interrelated, familiar, and sequential actions, borrowing from their immediate surroundings. For example, they feed a doll, wipe her mouth with a napkin, and put her to bed. Or they prepare food for the doll, feed it, and walk it or drive it around in a carriage. A cart is loaded with small stones or pine cones, the load is taken to some imaginary place where the cart is unloaded, and then the entire process is repeated.

In conditions prevailing in places where children are brought up and educated together, they start to form into groups of two or three at an early age, although they do not always share a single conception of the intent or contents of the game. That is, properly speaking, [they play] games "side by side." This is very natural among such small children. Games "side by side" must be encouraged as they give the teacher an added opportunity to train the children to take notice of each other's games and even to take into consideration the interests of the other participants in the game. For example, two children are sitting on a bench. The teacher explains that Kostya is driving a car and that Valya is rocking a doll. The teacher asks Kostya to drive more carefully and not to toot the horn too loudly because the dolly (Valya's daughter!) is going to sleep. Gradually, through the acquisition of new knowledge and experience in cooperating with others, and through the influence of the teacher's advice, the children begin to coordinate their actions in play to a certain extent.

When the children are about 3, thematic role-playing games start to develop. Preschool children begin to take on certain roles (daddy, mommy, the doctor, a driver), and they imitate these figures in their play. The game assumes a simple structure. "I am the daddy and you are the mommy," says Vitya (2 years and 11 months), turning to Olya (2 years and 10 months). "It's time for us to go to work." Taking each other by the hand, the children walk about the room, then sit down again on the bench. Vitya "drives," rocking from side to side. This ends the game.

In their play the children do not limit themselves to what they see in everyday life at home and in the school, but include new facts and events of interest to them—a child goes somewhere in a train, repairs a car, or imitates the barber.

The imagination of the child emerges and develops in such thematic role-playing games. Illustrating in their play some kind of life situation, the children not only imitate what they have observed but alter it to a certain extent, thus expressing their own feelings and indicating their own interpretations.

If children in their third year are supplied with the simplest form of building material (blocks) and are taught the rudiments of construction, they will play building games with enthusiasm.

As the third year progresses, the child, under the teacher's influence, progresses from simple manipulation of materials and extremely simple objectives (for example, putting one block on top of another) to individual "construction." He is delighted when he notices some likeness with familiar things: "I made a bridge! I made a bridge!" Toward the end of the year, sometimes earlier, children announce ahead of time what they intend to build or give a definite answer to some adult question: They say, "I will build a house," and, in fact, achieve their project.

This is actually a new and important step in the evolution of their play. It will occur within a reasonable time providing the teachers guide the children's construction games and show them how they must build. Building skills acquired by the children while in the previous age group are, of course, very significant in this regard.

In building a structure herself, the teacher tells the children what she is going to build and accompanies the construction itself with comments: "Let's build a hill. First, we must put a big block here, and here, a plank. Give me the plank, Vera. This is the way we are going to lay the plank. And now, the car is going to go down the hill!" Should the child build something on his own, it is important to encourage him and to ask what he is doing and find some likeness in whatever he is building. Whenever necessary, a hint must be given as to what is missing: "And where is the roof of the house? The rain is going to come in and make everything soaking wet."

If the children can only build in a very primitive way, it is better not to rush them by asking questions intended to make the building process more complicated. Even the thing the child has made will seem like an achievement to him.

In guiding the building games of a child during the time scheduled for play, the teacher, observing how individual children go about it, reminds them of the particular structures built during the activity period. For instance, she gives the child a doll and asks him to remember the way he built a fence around it. The main objective of the adult is to teach the child not only to copy the adult's structure but to build something definite by himself (a house, a bridge, a couch, and so forth).

Right from the beginning of the year, the teachers organize the children into fast-moving games. First they include small groups, but toward the end of the year practically all of the children in the group take part in the fast-moving games, obeying certain simple rules.

In the evolution of their play and in the organization of the children's life, much significance must be placed not only on the choice of toys, but also on their convenient arrangement. For independent active games, carts, carriages, platforms on wheels, two-wheeled rolling toys, balls of various sizes, and hoops must be provided. Tricycles help in developing various physical skills and dexterity.

Character toys are chosen in such a way as to remind the children of familiar people and animals and to make more distinct the impressions they have received from looking at pictures or listening to adults talking. For example, it may be that a child never saw a rabbit, but he knows this animal well from favorite fairy tales or pictures. With the help of toys, a child may become acquainted with objects which he has never seen before.

Favorite thematic toys for children are dolls (male and female) of various sizes. Soft toys are good, especially if they have celluloid head and hands. Dolls made of polyethylene are pleasant to handle because of their elasticity—they wash easily, and parts of their body are moveable. A doll's clothing must correspond to educational and instructional aims. It must be easy to put on and take off, have a simple pattern, fasten and unfasten; the doll must have a change of underwear. Practice in dressing and undressing dolls during play is a proven way of instilling self-sufficiency and neatness in the children.

The 3-year-old group of children is also provided with a so-called "fun toy." Frequently it will make some sort of noise: a bird that pecks, a clown that beats a drum. Usually, the teacher herself shows how this toy works and is to be used, as children are not likely to find out on their own how the thing works and may only succeed in breaking it.

It is good to select objects that can be strung together—rings, beads, spools, wheels. In selecting these, it must be kept in mind that the size of the aperture or hole should be small, such as in spools, so as to present certain difficulties for the child to try to overcome. A string or tape with a metal tip may be used for stringing. This kind of activity contributes to the development of manual dexterity and coordination, and trains the child to concentrate and be attentive.

The teacher must see to it that a number of toys, especially those which are the children's favorites, are similar in nature, for instance, a number of dolls of the same size dressed alike. Small children of this age are inclined to be imitative and frequently a child, seeing a toy in the hands of some other child, will want to have exactly the same toy. The toys must be spread out in the various areas of the room in such a way that the children can play with them peacefully, without disturbing each other. A child of 2 or 3, because of the nature of his nervous system, gets tired and excited very easily; therefore relative peace and quiet during play and during some activities is absolutely essential. Such an atmosphere is also valuable in that it gives the child an opportunity to listen to a great number of "small" sounds, for example, the sound of one block being placed on another or sounds produced by metallic objects clanging against each other. This aids his sensory development.

In numerous children's institutions extra available rooms are used either for games or activities with groups of children. These are the places where the children are allowed to play independently, provided that they remain within view of the teacher.

In the common room there may be a large carpet on the floor on which various toys are placed (the carpet must be kept clean at all times). In the winter children like to sit on such a carpet and listen to a story. Various rides and ball games in these areas may be organized. However, bearing in mind that toys should be spread around in various areas of the room, an additional one or two small carpets for games must be provided. In this way, some of the toys are on the carpet, some on shelves, and others in the closet or on specially installed shelves.

One corner of the room may be provided for play related to housework. Here there may be washbowls, a little iron, small rags, etc. Children enjoy pretending to wash, press, and hang clothes on a line. Doll furniture should be rather large, so that the child himself can sit on the doll stool during playtime. Not infrequently, two or three small children are seen sitting thus and feeding dolls or teddy bears.

In some institutions various large toys for housework games are made available to the children. These are sometimes made by the parents. They are good in that they correspond to the size of the children, as for example a stove of such size that a child can stand and "cook" at it or a washbasin with a real faucet so that the children can "wash" themselves or their dolls.

Among the various toys for children of this age, there must be a number of animals—a dog, a cat, a rooster, a hen with chickens, a rabbit, a teddy bear—as well as various cars and trucks. Toward the end of the year an excavator or dump truck may be added. The interest of present day children in such toys is easily understandable; even the very small children see such machines constantly and, naturally, are fascinated by their dynamic quality.

. . . . Many colored and white bits of material of various sizes should be provided. Children like to wrap up their dolls in these.

It is useful to have some discarded material around or else material specifically acquired for the purpose of dressing up. While playing, the children put on kerchiefs, aprons, and animal costumes. Such basic costumes for dressing up are suitable in the second half of the year. The children will have used these in their play previously, but in the transition from one group to the next they discover new toys with which they must first become familiar. Therefore, the costumes used in dressing up can be more varied for this new group, as the children's fantasy is more developed and their experience in playing is broader.

To organize construction games, it is important to provide a variety of building material (about three boxes per group). The most suitable materials for children of 2 to 3 years are blocks and the table set of *Agapova*. To go along with the building material, a number of small toys must be provided, such as small dolls that stand up as well as various animals. For construction games, a separate table must be provided.

It is also good to have large building materials for playing on the floor and out of doors. For games on the playground, plywood boxes of various sizes can be used with success, as well as smooth boards.

Toys are brought in gradually: first come the most familiar, then those requiring more experience and know-how, for example, an iron for pressing, a pick-up truck, games with cutout pictures of six parts instead of only four.

Some of the toys must be kept by the teacher, who, once or twice a month, changes them around. A toy that has not been seen by the child for a while will again seem new and delight him. Moreover, caring for the toys in this way will help train the children to be careful and neat. A toy display is not advisable. Most toys are taken out of the closets by the teacher and the children at playtime and later put back under the teacher's supervision.

When bringing a toy to the group, the teacher should first attract their attention to it. If it is a new toy, the teacher, in showing it to the children, asks whether they know what it is called and how one can play with it. In general, at the beginning of the year, the teacher herself explains or tells the children about the toys. Later on she relies on the experience of the children, leads them into conversations, and makes their previous impressions more vivid. For example, showing a rooster and a hen, she reminds the children that not long ago they actually saw in the yard hens and a rooster and that they were busy pecking grain. The teacher lets the child hold the toy and play a little with it, and then reminds him that it must be passed on to someone else. It is good for the teacher to have two or three spare toys of the same kind so that they can be distributed simultaneously to several children.

From time to time the teacher goes about the room with a group of children to take stock with them of all available toys and to remind them of where they are kept. This is best done either in the morning before breakfast, or else in the evening.

A child should have a chance to use the toys available to the group at any time when he is free. The teacher participates actively in the play activity of the children 2 to 3 years old, trying not to limit her participation to the bringing in of the various toys.

While supervising the children, the teacher sometimes also takes part in the game started either through her or the children's initiative. Adult participation may take various forms. For example, a child pulls an empty cart and does not think of putting a doll or a teddy bear in it. The teacher suggests: "Put the teddy bear in the carriage and give him a ride." (The next time, the child himself will put a teddy bear in the cart.) If the toy falls out of the cart without the child noticing it, the teacher picks it up and strokes it, indicating that the animal or doll is hurt. Or again the teacher may build a stove, make a present of it to the children and say that now they can cook *kasha* or soup, or boil water or milk. It is good to remind the children about what they have observed—mother cooking food on a stove, a cat drinking milk. "You ought to give some milk to your cat," suggests the teacher to the child who is holding a toy cat in his hands.

The teacher supplies hints, or advises the children while they are playing, as to various other ways a given game can be played, referring to their experience and their previously acquired knowledge. For example, a number of 2 ½-year-old children are sitting in a "car," which has already on several occasions been "built" for them out of benches. They hold dolls in their hands with which they talk. The teacher sits with the children and says: "Let's go, children, into the woods to gather berries which you will give to your dolls." Thus, the children have a goal to apply to their games. Together with the teacher, the children get out of the "car," gather "berries" imitating the teacher, and give them to the dolls; then they "drive" on. Suggesting such a game is justified by the fact that many of the children have actually been in the woods and gathered berries.

In suggesting to children the contents of a game (without actually naming it), the teacher contributes to the development of independent thematic games and to the development of the children's initiative. A question asked by the teacher or a discussion of the game brings about the particular change in the structure of the game necessary for achieving educational goals. "Did you already bathe your doll? No, not yet? Let's do it then." Or: "Where do the dolls live? Don't they have a home? Let's build a home for them." If the child cannot manage to put together some kind of building on his own, the teacher helps him or calls one of the other children to help.

From the very beginning of the year, the teacher organizes play activity during which the children are taught how to play with toys, how to handle and use them correctly. The game will consist mainly in the imitation of adults. In play activity, actions are centered upon the favorite toys of the children: dolls, cars, blocks. In such games, the child is expected to show concern and affection toward the doll: the doll, Masha, is fed so that she will no longer be hungry, and she is dressed so that she will not catch cold.

Repeated play activities reinforce the better instincts of the children and their incipient morality; this process also helps to link together two or three characters in a series of sequential acts. For example, when children gradually come together in a group in the morning (or in the second half of the day) at playtime, the teacher shows to three or four children how a fence, a chair, or a bench may be constructed out of blocks; then she takes a doll and sits it on a chair or leads it about the garden, as if they were taking a walk. Children look at the game with interest and start to repeat the teacher's actions. From day to day, the children are shown how to put away the blocks in the toybox, and this induces the children either to pass the blocks on to someone else or to place them back neatly in the box. Under such guidance, children learn not to simply pile the pieces up at random, not to throw them about, and not to bang the blocks on the floor or against other objects.

Although the children were taught at the previous age level to clean up building material and to arrange it neatly, this training must be continued systematically so as to breed habits of tidiness and care with toys. In other cases, the teacher takes a doll, carefully wraps it up in a blanket, puts it down in a carriage and suggests that someone give it a ride; she teaches the children how to roll balls to one another (for a distance of one half to one meter), how to throw them gently, how to roll them through gates, how to roll them to hit some large object (for example, a large block or a box).

In play organized by adults, the children must be encouraged to exchange toys, give them to each other, and to yield to someone else's wishes. For example, Katya wraps up a doll and passes it on to Kolya so that he may put the doll in a carriage; Kolya then passes on the carriage to Sacha who will wake up the sleeping doll, Zina. The repetition of such play activity will help to make the children more sociable also in the games which they initiate themselves.

In supervising their play, the teacher must constantly check to make sure that the children do not take toys away from one another, but rather become accustomed to surrendering or sharing them. To make these habits endure, the following play activity is recommended for the second half of the year, to make children willingly distribute their toys among their friends. The teacher calls up four or five children, suggests that they all sit on stools or on the carpet and examine the toys placed in a basket or a box. Then a child is chosen to hand out toys to the other children. When the children receive the toys, they play for a while, then exchange them as they please. Then all the toys are collected again and another child is asked to redistribute them. Coaxed by the teacher, the child asks all the others which toy they wish to receive. It is very important that the smallest child of the group be given the opportunity of distributing the toys. This participation assumes added meaning in that by giving pleasure to many children each child learns not only to receive but to give. It is even better when a child from the older group, who is well known to the little ones, is asked to take part in the group game and demonstrates how things should be relinquished without regret.

.   .   .

Games of this kind may be organized in the morning before breakfast or after the daytime sleep. In each case, a suitable time must be selected. A convenient number for such groups is three to five children.

The teacher attracts the children into games as yet unknown to them while keeping in mind the experience and the interests of the children in her care. At first, initiative regarding the choice of game and the evolution of its contents rests with the teacher. For example, she tells the children that she is going to be a doctor and will be taking care of their doll-children. Children bring their dolls and the teacher goes through the motions of an examination, talking with the children all the while.

Or else, having prepared in advance a few boards, the teacher makes a kind of primitive airplane. Some children help to set the boards in a given way—that is, to build. When the airplane is "ready," the teacher invites the children to "fly." The invitation will be enthusiastically accepted. The children may be reminded of the appropriate verse by A. Barto about building a plane:

> *We ourselves will build a plane*
> *We will soar over the woods*
> *We will soar over the woods*
> *And then return to mommy.*

The children repeat some of the words and smile happily.

If the children are lively and happy in games organized by an adult, if they begin to bring to it something personal (taking some doll on the plane and talking to it, or getting off the plane and back into it again) this means that the teacher has aroused feelings in the children without crushing their independent action by her initial suggestion of the game.

It is very useful to introduce some artistic element, such as a beautiful sentence or singing, into individual and group games, because this contributes to the positive emotions of the child. Moreover, his speech will improve and he will acquire the ability to sing simple children's songs or nursery rhymes. For instance, a little boy is riding a toy horse. The teacher sings a song about a horse. The same method would be used when a child is using some other toy. It will be observed that soon afterwards, whenever playing with similar toys, the child will try to hum or sing the song he has heard previously.

When children reach the age of 2 ½ years, the teacher introduces something new in directing the children's playtime. She draws more from the experience and knowledge previously acquired by the children up to that time and endeavors to develop their own initiative. In connection with this, the oral method, the use of the spoken word, acquires a greater significance. Now much less frequently, and even then only to some children, is it necessary for her to demonstrate how to use or handle a doll, a cart, etc. It is important to keep in mind what the child is capable of doing, and in relation to this, the child can be asked to think of something to do, and the teacher should set concrete goals, and if necessary, give him hints as to how to attain them. "Make a bridge," says the teacher, "on which you can roll a car. Let's see what you need. Take this, that, etc."

Educational and active games, as well as little dramatizations with table-theaters, will increase the educational significance of thematic role-playing games. Games with set rules and dramatizations which are on a suitable level for the children and are dynamic in nature produce emotional experiences. They include concrete acts and therefore they are frequently and very naturally reflected in one of the various forms of thematic role-playing games.

The teacher contributes to this process in various ways. For example, she shows a table-theater dramatization of a fairy tale or popular story several times, then talks with the children about the various characters and suggests that the children take part in the older children's games, for example, by playing the role of a mouse. Or the teacher makes a pair of rabbit ears and the children hop around like rabbits. One of the children might pretend to be a sick rabbit and lie down on the floor (on the carpet); some other child covers him up with a doll blanket.

A positive influence is also exerted by the children's books, which should be easily understood, dynamic in structure, and illustrated with bright pictures. For example, the teacher reads a well known story, after which there is a discussion. Toys are given the names of the characters in the book. The teacher, playing with a small group of children, dramatizes various episodes from the story. Then some of the children also begin to act.

The better the subject matter of the book, the better it organizes the children and the more valuable it is for the purpose of education. However, the teacher should not be overanxious to develop the acting ability of the child nor to impose her own wishes upon him. It is essential to guide the children's play actively, while still permitting the children freedom and a chance to be relatively self-reliant.

Games with Educational Toys

Play with educational toys takes place just as much during the activity periods, once or twice a week, as during the specifically scheduled time for children's play. These games occupy a special place in the instructional process of children in their third year. They are directed toward the sensory development of the child, that is, the development of sensations which are the source of our knowledge. Play with educational toys serves also to develop the children's speech, to broaden their horizons, and to develop their ability to differentiate such qualities as size, color, sound, special relations, texture, and so forth.

At this time the planned development of sensations is very important, because through this the children form correct impressions of their surroundings, and the impressions thus assimilated are richer and more exact.

E. I. Tikheeva, the most distinguished of the Russian educators, found the training of sensory perceptions to be of exceptional importance. She discovered that each new sensation acquired by the child becomes clearer and more precise in proportion to the number of sensory objects used in this process. Therefore, actions with objects, examination, comparison and contrasting (based on touch and visual perception) found wide application in her practice.

In independent activities, children often use educational games. But before giving these to the children, the teacher must show them how to play with them. At first it is sometimes necessary to organize special games or activities, gradually including all the children. Otherwise, children would aimlessly handle the toys and throw them around. For play activity with educational toys we recommend that small groups of eight to twelve children be formed.

Rods or poles with plain or many colored rings (five or six), wooden dolls (*matreshki*), colored balls, blocks, and multiple toys are recommended for children in their third year. Almost every one of these toys may be used to achieve the programmed objectives: the differentiation of color and size, the development of small movements, and a feeling for shapes. One must start with the simplest. For example, the children roll small colored balls from a toy slide. They feel the properties of the ball: it is smooth and rolls well; but however one tries, it is impossible to put balls in a pile, for they roll away. Later, children may place the colored balls (for lack of anything better, made out of clay and painted) in boxes of the same color.

Children may be asked to collect together the rods or poles of one color, with corresponding rings. It must not be required that these rods or poles be of the same size. Any errors are corrected by the teacher, who attracts the children's attention to the fact that some rings are smaller and others bigger. It is only toward the end of the year that children will learn how to put together a rod with the appropriate rings.

The teacher shows how to differentiate small and large wooden (two-part) dolls, then strengthens the knowledge and skill acquired by the children by challenging them to differentiate.

During the games, it is indispensable to talk to the children, thus promoting concept formation such as, "Let's see which one of the wheels is the biggest!" In order to have the children master a particular educational goal, the teacher employs a variety of approaches. For example, the children are asked to find the missing part of a toy, so as to make sure it is the right size; or else to gather a number of marbles of exactly the same shape or color. It is important that the child should not only see the model object but also hold it in his hands, handle it, and compare it with others.

For table games with printed matter, the most suitable are: lotto, puzzles or two-part pictures, cutouts of two or three parts, and pictures as indicated in the *Program of Instruction in the Kindergarten.* First, the teacher examines these various pictures with individual children or with small groups, explains the pictures, makes sure the children recognize the subject matter, and teaches how to put together the cutouts. Toward the age of 2½, many children can put together cutout pictures and know how to put toys together by themselves; lotto may be played with children of 6 to 7 years of age without the immediate participation of the teacher.

Games aimed toward the development of hearing and acquaintance with the surroundings must be systematically planned. "Say what makes the following sound" (bell, drum). "What am I doing?" and so forth.

Attention must be given to see that all children use a variety of educational material in the course of a game.

Play with Water and Sand

Sand, snow, and water are natural materials which are favorites of children of all ages. The children are attracted to these because they offer the possibility for varied and lively activity: to pour in and out of some container, to dig, and to build. Numerous pleasant sensations are experienced in the course of such games. Children love to bury their hands in warm sand or water, make shapes out of damp sand or snow and play in sand boxes. Playing with sand never bores a child.

Outstanding pedagogical leaders such as E. I. Tikheeva, L. I. Tchulitzkaya, and L. K. Schleger evaluated very highly play with natural materials: The Soviet approach to education for early childhood and preschool age places much emphasis on such play, inasmuch as it adds to the development of sensations, and to the ability to differentiate the quality of materials (sand runs, water flows, etc.). These materials should be widely used with children in their third year.

The sand is kept in specially made sandboxes with smooth enclosures. There the children can sit for some time to make "pies." For this purpose children are given spades in assorted shapes. The sand must be clean and not too dry. Together with this it is good to have some dry sand available. Children love to pour dry sand in some containers using funnels. This allows them to feel the sifting quality of the sand.

The teacher plays with the children, shows them how to rake sand, pat it, pour it from one container into another, how to use shapes and the resulting patterns, and makes sure that each child is kept active. Through contact with the children, the teacher focuses their attention on new words: *dry, damp, sand, pour, cold, warm, heavy.* Words used with immediate actions and sensations enter easily into children's speech and contribute to the enrichment of impressions.

Playing with children, the teacher herself makes for them a house with a yard, a bridge, a garden, using natural materials (pine cones, pebbles). It is useful to attract older children into playing with sand. They add their inventiveness and the little children strive to imitate the older ones.

Care must be taken not to let children put sand in their mouths or pour it on each other, but to use it carefully. If the area where children play is not shaded, care must be taken that the children do not get too hot; they should wear something on their heads.

In the summer, play with water is organized in the playground. Sometimes it is combined with other games: the children dig a hole, pour water in it, mix it all up, prepare "meals" for dolls or make animals drink.

For play with water, it is desirable that suitable containers be provided. These should be attached on supports at a height of about fifty centimeters. The children play standing up. It is good to have a variety of toys to play with in water: small plastic or rubber dolls, fish, ducks, boats. Children love to bathe dolls and wash toys.

Children have much fun splashing and playing in natural ponds, in very shallow areas, or else in specially designed wading pools. During play with water, care must be taken that the water and air temperature remain sufficiently warm.

ACTIVITIES WITH CHILDREN
IN THEIR THIRD YEAR

The program of education in kindergarten develops a limited circle of skills and knowledge, of the kind that is most successfully assimilated by children in the course of their activities: for example, pronouncing correctly sounds in their native language, knowing how to answer questions in the presence of other children, listening together with all the others to a story told by the teacher, acquiring some knowledge regarding surrounding objects and events, and getting used to talking (babbling), drawing and singing.

Activities with children of this age and the methods of conducting them are varied. Many of them are performed through educational games which enable the easier assimilation of skills. This is very important, since the teacher, relying on the strict attention of the children, stimulates their interest and at the same time broadens their horizons, helps to formulate certain concepts and to develop essential skills. For example, with the help of some educational game, the teacher teaches children to name toys (ball, car, doll, plane), develops their sense of observation and their attention.

Activities with children in their third year are conducted in turn with both subgroups. Such an organization of activities allows the teacher to see each child better, have contact with him, give him sufficient attention, and insure his participation. When activities are performed with small groups of children, the children will be able to hear the teacher better, gradually to get used to cooperating with other children, and to learn to wait a little until the adult is ready to address him.

It is very important that children of various stages and levels of development enter into these games. This gives those who develop more slowly an opportunity to model themselves on worthy examples. But all children may be included in one single group whenever a song is to be heard or whenever performances of the toy-theater are shown.

According to the ability of the children to take part in common activities and to the extent of their attention span, the teacher begins to include the whole group in such activities as speech exercises, drawing, and music (toward the middle of the year). Division into small groups is nevertheless maintained in all cases when individual contact with each child is necessary or whenever the kind of activity requires a long wait on the part of children, as is the case with some educational games, playing with toys with multiple parts, and looking at pictures.

When the teacher is busy with a group of children, the assistant supervises the others. It is very important for the children not to bother each other; therefore, one of the bedrooms or a distant corner of the common room divided by a curtain or a movable screen should be used for special activities for small groups.

The schedule includes two activities a day—one in the morning and the other in the second half of the day. The activities conducted with small children are simple and on the appropriate level for this age group; they last about seven to ten minutes. Success depends to a significant extent upon the preparation of the teacher. Everything that is conducted by the teacher herself must be thoroughly assimilated by her, presented in a lively manner and with ease, but at a slower speed in comparison with the activities with children of older groups.

For activities with small children, all available visible materials are used: pieces of surrounding equipment and furniture, pictures, toys, as well as artistic forms—a song, a proverb, or a line of verse. This increases emotional perception and contributes to understanding and memory.

The children's restlessness must be taken into account, as well as their spontaneity and ability to imitate. It does happen that these traits are mistaken by the teacher for naughtiness. For example, during speech exercises, Dima (2 years and 2 months) picks up a marble which he just rolled and announces in a loud voice, "I have a marble." Immediately Lara raises her work and says, "I have a drum." These examples are followed by Kolya, Sasha, and so forth. The teacher is displeased and reprimands the children because they disturb the quiet atmosphere. However, the teacher in this case is quite wrong.

The choice of visual material must depend upon the corresponding educational goals and esthetic considerations: not every toy or picture may be used as a device. For example, if the objective is to acquaint the children with colors, colors in the selected items must be "pure" and true. If educational games are planned with dolls, the knowledge of all items of clothing must be thoroughly known to insure sequential dressing and neatness in dressing. Also, not only must all clothing be easy to remove, but it must also be clean.

While talking to the children during activities, asking questions or explaining something, the teacher must be extremely careful about what she says: she must use correct names and simple sentence structure. Nevertheless, she should speak expressively in a lively manner, and endeavor to expand the children's vocabulary by introducing new words and forms of speech. It is important to remember that a child is most impressed by speech directed to him personally.

At the beginning of the year, the teacher can rely only to a very limited extent on the participation of the children, particularly in speech development exercises. She must sing by herself, relate something, and act out sketches with the help of toys, attempting to retain, even if it is only for a short while, the attention of children who are rather passive at this point. An example of such an exercise may be the reading of a poem for children the subject of which is animals. The reading may be accompanied by showing such animals in toy form. The participation of children may be limited to the imitation of animal cries.

As the children's ability to listen, speak, and perform some actions develops (helped by the guidance, examples and explanations of the teacher), a basis gradually appears upon which the children advance towards more active participation, such as answering questions or performing commands.

For example, for one given activity, an educational game called "Find the Toy" is used. It consists of finding a number of various familiar toys which have been placed visibly in different areas of the room. The child called by the teacher is asked to go and find a particular toy. "Kolya, go and find the big teddy bear." The child faces a challenge—to understand and to remember what he is expected to do, as requested by the teacher. The child must walk by a number of other toys, take and bring back the teddy bear, show it to the children and name it. At the same time, this game requires the participation of the whole group, as the children must look at how Kolya goes about finding the teddy bear and check whether he brings back the right toy.

The teacher must be careful that there is progress in the child's speech, physical activity and orientation within the environment. She takes into account the child's growing capacities, and uses these as a basis for further development. For example, in a group of children 2 ½-years old the teacher must not be satisfied with a child who calls an egg "*ko-ko*," a car "*bi-bi*," or who answers a question such as whether he wants to play by shaking his head. It is expected that a child use the proper names of things or people and answer questions by using words.

In the course of these activities, the children acquire certain new abilities: attention, memory, the ability to listen and act according to instructions given by the teacher, and the ability to listen to other children.

DEVELOPMENT OF SPEECH, BROADENING
THE CHILDREN'S HORIZONS, AND
ORIENTING THEM IN THEIR ENVIRONMENT

The development of speech is the main objective of the teacher and is to be achieved not only during such time as the teacher is in contact with the children in the everyday routine, out of doors, and in play, but in all activities conducted in this group.

Whether the teacher is teaching the children sounds, playing some active game with them, or conducting games using educational toys, she must constantly give special attention to the children's understanding of the spoken word, as well as to increasing their vocabulary and their use of proper grammatical structure. Nevertheless, a number of special exercises are planned for the children in their third year, directed toward expanding the children's orientation to the objects and events of life surrounding them, expanding their active vocabulary, developing their ability to answer questions and to ask questions themselves, teaching correct pronunciation of words and sounds, and developing intonation for expressive speech.

The approach to be adopted in the above activities may be varied. It may be the telling of a story, a reading performed by an adult, educational games, games in rings, looking at pictures, excursions, observations, artistic performances or spectacles.

It has been mentioned above that contact with the children in the everyday routine and during excursions to play is very significant in the process of acquiring fluency in the native language. Attention must be given to the development of proper usage in the course of activity periods: The teacher must include children in conversations, ask them questions, answer their questions, help them to express their thoughts more clearly, attract their attention to what is being said by others.

Another objective of no less importance to be achieved in the course of activities is the training of children to listen to and understand artistic forms of speech: a story, a fairy tale, a poem. This is not always given sufficient attention. Sometimes children are read random stories and tales which are inappropriate either because of their subject matter or because they are written in a boring uninteresting style. These do not create any reactions or feelings, and therefore cannot contribute to the development of esthetic sensitivity. The selection of literary works which may help children learn their native tongue, its structure, rhythm, and richness must be made with utmost care.

In the body of Russian poetry created specifically for educational purposes, there are many highly artistic selections which are specially intended for children in early childhood and of preschool age. Small children are attracted to popular Russian nursery rhymes and jingles mainly because of their rhythm and musicality as well as by included fun elements (clapping, etc.). Children are always willing to listen to adults and to repeat many times in a row the words of a song. The love of small children for the play of sounds, for popular folk tunes and dance rhythms has been repeatedly stressed by K. I. Tchukovskii, the most important research worker in the field of child speech.

For reading to children of 2 to 2 ½ years, popular nursery rhymes or jingles are selected which the children can understand and from which they will derive pleasant sensations. The fact that an occasional word, rarely used in present day speech, will not be understood by the child should not disturb the teacher. What is important is that the children get the general meaning.

In order for the reading not to leave the children indifferent, it is important that the song chosen should sound light and melodious when sung by the teacher, thus stimulating the children's desire to remember and repeat it. Distorted words and incorrect stress, which alter the rhythm of the verse, are inexcusable.

Listening to popular children's songs or verse performed expressively by adults (or sometimes by older children) does have an influence on the development of expression in speech, as children not only listen but often repeat what they hear and catch on the intonation of verse. Listening to very simple children's verses not only satisfies the need in children for the diversion of sounds, but is very useful for their assimilation of correct pronunciation—which is still lacking in some children—and development of rhythm in their speech. First children remember only the sound pattern, then later, when they are about 2 ½ years old, they repeat the whole tune.

The reading of rhymes and jingles is also useful in that the children go on to evolve games which include the use of words, rhythmic sounds and rhythmic phrases, all of which delight the children, although they do not always penetrate their meaning. Children's games involving sounds and words indicate their sensitiveness to the aural aspect of their native tongue. The presence of such games in children's institutions is considered a positive factor in education.

The program of activities also includes listening to fairy tales and children's stories. Russian fairy tales and children's stories represent perfect models of the national language, combined with valuable ethical content. They endear themselves extremely quickly to the children's hearts, and stimulate their desire to reproduce separate expressions, rhythmical phrases, and melodies. To tell a story to the children in an easy-flowing and expressive way is not a simple thing. The slightest deviation from the proper rhythm or the replacement of a single word by another will inevitably ruin the effect. Therefore, to tell a story requires preparation: memorization of the text, mastery of the rhythm and the proper mode of expressive delivery, and the development of skill in establishing real contact with the children. For children 2 to 2 ½ years old, many wonderful Russian stories are still difficult to understand, but there are nevertheless certain ones which, although extremely simple and understandable for the children, are yet highly artistic. Among these are "The Speckled Hen," "The Giant Turnip," and, toward the end of the year, "Teremok" and "Kolobok" or "The Doughnut." Of course even these children's stories will be much more fully understood by the children later, for 2- to 2 ½-year-old children are mainly interested in the sound aspect of these stories. Just the same, the children enjoy the over-all theme and the happy ending of these stories. Words expressing images, characteristic in fairy tales, are remembered by children, enter their speech, and widen their vocabulary.

Children are not able at this age to tell a story in its proper order. Starting to tell a story, they very often forget what is most important, but they willingly finish sentences started by adults, remember small details, and notice whenever something has been missed or forgotten when someone tells the story over again.

At the beginning of the year, stories are recited during the activity periods in two shifts, in subgroups. Such organization creates better conditions for contact between the teacher and the children as it provides an opportunity of giving special attention to each child. But the story, jingle, or song must not be heard only during an activity period, but also at any suitable time in the course of the day.

Sometimes the telling of a story is accompanied by the showing of pictures, illustrations of the characters in the fairy tales, or performances of "magic lantern." The inclusion of visual impressions contributes greatly to the children's enjoyment and to their better understanding of the fairy tales, but it is important to remember that it must not be used to the exclusion of simple storytelling and listening, which is more helpful in developing the children's imagination.

Whenever pictures or little statuettes are shown, this should be done without hurrying, but rather giving the children ample time to examine them. Looking at pictures or statuettes is used to encourage active and partial repetition of stories. Gradually, the children will remember the story; nevertheless, during activity period, the stories should not be recited by the children themselves, especially not by a number of them. Listening to imperfect speech will tire and bore the other children, and it must be remembered that their span of attention is very limited. Therefore, stories should be recited when the teacher is working individually with a child or with a small group of children. As the need arises, the teacher takes part in storytelling, helps the child to remember the sequence of events in the story, and develops the child's confidence in his ability to express himself.

Valuable literary materials which will make an impression on small children are usually short tales, with subject matter appropriate to this age level and language which is simple and understandable. Such are the short stories by Y. Taitz, N. Kalinina, and U. Shabad.

In the book "Block on Block," Y. Taitz tells about the life of children in kindergartens. These stories are very short, but each one reflects the warm relationship between the author and children and there is much of interest for them. The story "Holiday" is quite within the children's reach of understanding, as well as "Ahead of Everybody" or "The Train." The children also easily assimilate the stories of N. Kalinina. This writer, using linguistic means, describes scenes from children's lives. The story "How the Kids Built a House" tells about children's games. This story should not be read, but told, changing the text to bring it closer to listeners (by changing names in the story to names of children present). This heightens the children's interest in the story, helps to establish valuable contact between the children and the storyteller, and creates an animated atmosphere.

After the story has been told, the children are shown a number of pictures corresponding to the story and talk about them with the teacher. This type of conversation attracts the children's attention to the pictures and develops this active speech.

For storytelling, another book may be recommended: "In the Summer," by N. Kalinina (it is better to acquaint children with this book in the summer time). Each story has an interesting plot. Some details should be left out whenever telling the story. . . . After the book has been read, it should be given to the children for examination, for them to use freely, watching only to make sure that the children use the book carefully. After use, it should be put back in its place.

Pictures greatly help the comprehension of the events which have been described. Looking at them, children will more easily understand what has been read to them. The examination of pictures is used to increase vocabulary and activate speech, and also to teach the children to notice relationships between events which are very basic in ordinary life, and to be able to express themselves more fluently on a wider range of subjects, using in some cases quite complicated sentences. This will contribute to the development of thought and speech in the children.

Small children have to be active and are very fond of imitating. Suitable moments for this may be found even when examining pictures. For instance, in the story "How Vassya Caught Fish" it is related how he unclenched his fist but there were no fish in his hand. Clenching and unclenching their fists gleefully is an excellent exercise for the children to do, and at the same time it helps them fully to understand the story. The children also willingly imitate animal cries, thus exercising their vocal cords and getting practice in aural perception. In the course of the whole year, whenever pictures are being shown, the children must be divided into small groups, as it is only under these conditions that they will be able to inspect the pictures adequately.

A number of poetic works are appropriate for children of this age; short poems and little books of verse are enjoyed by the children for their rhythm, imagination, and melodiousness. Verse may be either recited from memory or read, but in either case one must not permit any distortion of the artistic form.

Listed in the program for children in their third year are the verses by Barto: "The Bunny," "The Ball," "The Horse," and "The Plane." These verses are of a poetic nature, fit in closely with children's games, and stimulate good feelings. Children sympathize with the rabbit left on a bench in the rain, and listen with a smile of approval to the tale about the horse.

Children at this age are very spontaneous; therefore, if they like some poetry, they will repeat it with great emotion. Attention must be given to the fact that children should not hurry, should not swallow the ends of words, and should speak distinctly.

Of the stories in verse published for this age, the following are particularly recommended: "My Teddy Bear" by Alexandrova and "Masha Is Having Dinner" by Kaputikian. These works are closely tied in with children's play and the main characters are favorite children's toys. The books are written in verse in language that is musical and rhythmic. The reading of these books requires a lively and bright intonation because the text contains onomatopoeic qualities, exclamations, and questions, all of which attract the child's attention and encourage his speech activity. Children can remember the text with ease, and, while looking at the pictures, they repeat it and acquire as they go along some information about objects, animals, and so on.

The subject matter of some of these children's books is recommended for dramatization by children of the older group, who will be able to act out a whole story for the benefit of the younger group. Particularly recommended in this respect is the fairy tale "The Frog by the Well" which has in it the elements of a children's game. The book is richly and abundantly illustrated. Children listen to the reading with interest and look at the accompanying illustrations. The children then answer questions and discuss themselves what is in the illustrations, remembering the various phases of the story.

Apart from the reading and reciting of artistic literary works, a significant role is played by stories composed by the teachers themselves on the theme of the children's lives. These home-made stories can by no means replace original artistic works. However, they do help to provide a bridge between the children and the artistic work, to sharpen their conception, to interest them in particular events and phenomena, and to develop their understanding of the various episodes of a story when the events, although ordinary, may never have actually been observed by the children. After such stories, it is easy to get the children to talk. For example, in the evening the teacher tells the children the following: "Once upon a time children were getting ready for a walk. Suddenly, I see that Irene cannot find her gloves. They are neither on the hanger nor in the coat. Where can they be? Irene begins to cry—'How can I go for a walk without gloves?'—but Dima says 'Here are your gloves, they have been found. It seems that they were drying on the line.' How did this happen?" Children will tell in a lively manner that the gloves were put there by Irene's mother, or that Irene on her way to school picked up some snow, and so on.

Another time, the teacher could tell the children a story about how a few days ago they fed pigeons in the street, how they saw a beautiful red star which had been put up to decorate a house for some holiday, or how nicely some children were playing with dolls. Children do not remain indifferent to such stories; they express their feelings, ask questions. This is why it is important to choose as a subject for these stories events or facts children have actually observed for themselves. These bring out positive reactions and have educative value.

To broaden the children's outlook, to train their powers of observation, and to develop high moral qualities, specific excursions are organized. For example, somewhere near the school, a new bridge is being built or flowers are being planted in the square. While the children are observing something, the teacher's brief but lively explanations and her impressions help the children to notice the things that are most important and noteworthy. The teacher must know in advance what is going to be shown to the children and prepare questions as well as facts worth mentioning to the children.

The subjects for these observations will be determined by the plan for the development of speech and the orientation of the children in their environment. Thus, to give an example, if the desired goal is to give the children accurate impressions of a hen and chicken, a "trip" is organized to take the children to a place where a hen and a chicken can be found (provided there is such a place very near). The children will be able to see how a real hen scratches the ground or calls to her chickens. The children will notice by themselves that the hen is large but the chickens are small and squeak. As for the fact that chickens are yellow and fluffy and that the mother hen calls them in order to give them each a worm, this must be clarified by the teacher herself. For a few minutes, the children watch the chickens, talk about them, and ask questions.

On the following day all these things should be brought into the conversation to remind the children about what they have seen, to help them make impressions more vivid, and to re-experience the feelings aroused in them by the interesting observations of the previous day. Children get used to answering such questions as: "Where did we go?" "What did we see?" "What kind of hen was it?" "What did the chicken do?" "What were they like?" Looking at pictures (the series "Domestic Animals") representing a rooster, hen, chickens, and so forth will intensify the impressions received and will provide the children with additional enjoyment.

In the summer, a walk may be organized in a vegetable garden which is cared for by children of the older groups. It is useful to show the children the vegetables that have been grown, such as cucumbers (large and quite small). Children of the older groups should tell the little ones how they took care of their garden, how they watered it and pulled out the weeds.

Walks in the streets are very interesting to the children, especially at holiday time. Organizing walks along festive streets, the teacher attracts the children's attention to the decorated buildings, portraits of V. I. Lenin, red flags, and bright electric bulbs.

In any kind of guided observation with small children, the emotional reaction is of prime importance. What gives pleasure is remembered by the children, and it is this that they like to talk about and ask questions about. But care must be taken to limit the number of impressions so that the children will not be overwhelmed and fatigued by their abundance and so that they will not have to look at too many things at the same time.

The interest of the children in what is being observed is greatly increased if the observation is accompanied by some clever word or phrase, a line of verse, a lively expression, or a question, particularly if the teacher's own interest is manifest in the tone of her voice. At the same time, it is important to take notice of the child's own observations, to stimulate him whenever he makes a remark on some detail, and to attract the attention of other children to a remark made by one of them. Whenever observations are being made, it is important to train the children in the proper attitude toward what is being observed. Thus the teacher can, by the tone of her voice or by the expression on her face, create in the children an excited state of mind when they are admiring festively decorated buildings. Respect for the labor of those who participated in the construction must be felt by the children when they are observing a new house. All this is very significant for the esthetic education of the children and the development of their interest in all events of the life around them.

Large pictures which can be studied by ten or twelve children at a time are valuable equipment for teaching the native language and for enlarging and refining children's impressions. The use of pictures to develop and enrich the speech of children was highly regarded in his time by K. D. Ushinskii, who considered pictures to be the best means of stimulating a child to speak. Children perceive the meaning of the picture in an emotional manner; they name the objects represented on it and experience a sense of joy. It is with great pleasure that they listen to the adult telling about the picture, especially if this is done with the use of imagery along with concreteness, and if the teacher speaks expressively.

In order that they may acquire a number of impressions about domestic animals, the children are shown such pictures as "The Cat and the Kittens" and "The Rooster and the Hen." Talking with the children about what is portrayed in the picture, the teacher teaches them to see things correctly, to name the animals illustrated in the picture, to say what the animals do and what kind of animals they are. The children get used to the correct names and learn the pronunciation of new words.

From the series "Pictures for Kindergarten," the picture "Holiday" is quite suitable for understanding of children of this age group. This picture should be shown soon after the First of May celebration. The artistic images of this picture are familiar to the children and stimulate in them the desire to tell what they spontaneously feel about the pleasant experiences they associate with this great Soviet holiday.

Comments and answers to questions put by the teacher help the children to examine the picture in detail as well as to increase their interest: "What a good looking, elegant little boy! Let's have a look at what he has in his hands." And the children answer "Yes, it is Kolya. He has a little flag in his hands, a red flag. You were right!" After such a talk, it is good if the children can recall some festive poems and sing together with the teacher some appropriate song.

Besides large pictures, children must be shown smaller artistic pictures for the purpose of making observations. Each child holds a picture in his hands and tells the others what is illustrated in it. Of course, this does not yet represent a story. Sometimes it is simply naming the objects illustrated in the picture: chicken, doll, little boy. But if the picture represents a simple but interesting action, the comments given by the child are longer and include one or two sentences of a few words each: "The little girl is holding the doll"; "The towel is hanging here."

Pictures may be of all kinds. The choice should depend on the artistic values, the clarity, the realism and the lack of unnecessary details, and, of course, on the subject matter which must be within the experience of the children.

For activities with individual pictures, some of the pictures from the album by O. I. Solovieva, "Speak Correctly," are very suitable. Naming the objects represented, as well as their properties and any actions involved, the children not only acquire new words, but get accustomed in their speech to the use of various grammatical structures.

In order to develop perception, aural orientation, and the acquisition of correct pronunciation, a number of games such as "Guess Who Called," "Say What Is Making This Sound" or "What Am I Doing?", specially devised for their educational value, are widely used. The teacher hides behind a short curtain and moves in her hands a variety of things which make a characteristic sound or noise: she rattles a rattle, rings a little bell, squeezes a "talking toy," etc. If this game is being played for the first time, or if the given toys are seldom used by the children, these must be shown to the children at the beginning of the game and the corresponding noises or sounds made. But if the game has been played before, then the children will be able to guess what is going on behind the curtain without any preliminary demonstration. Children may even recognize other sounds, such as when one of the children from the older group plays with a ball, pulls a cart, or claps his hands.

Games involving the imitation of sounds are useful for training the vocal cords, for the development of aural attention, and to help overcome the tendency in children to soften the hard consonants of the language. Among such games are the lotto game of V. Fedaevskaya, "Who cries like this?" and some fast moving games, for example, the train game, the favorite of all children.

In the second half of the year, the educational games played with 3-year-olds, such as "Knock-knock, Who's There" and "The Geese," may be used.

It is very useful to get the participation of children from the older preschool age in these educational games. Older children significantly facilitate the organization of the games and offer models of pure and correct speech. The children in their third year imitate the older ones and gradually remember the rules of the game. In active games involving verbal refrains, the older children pronounce the words distinctly and expressively, help the teacher to regulate the younger children's movements, organize a circle, put together the cars of the "train," and so forth.

CHILDREN'S PHYSICAL EDUCATION

The physical development of children is mainly based on fast-moving games. In such games, the children are called upon to run, walk in a definite direction, crawl, jump, and so forth to produce the basic movements so essential to their normal physical development.

These movements have already been acquired and learned to a certain extent, and therefore the goal to be attained by children in their third year is further development and greater coordination. The children are required to perform such movements as they are able to do, and greater precision and agility is demanded: for example, they are urged not just to throw a ball, but to attempt to impel it in a definite direction, that is, roll it through a nearby gate which is relatively wide.

Special equipment will be very influential in the children's development. It should be widely used both during independent play and during definite activity periods. The children practice climbing on various types of ladders or on a climbing wall specially designed for gymnastics, crawl through gates, go up and down wooden climbers, and do exercises for balance walking on boards of various widths and lengths. Equipment for children's physical activity must be provided both in the playground and in the children's room.

Well planned and regularly performed games and gymnastics are exceptionally important for the child's vulnerable organism. They insure timely physical development and proper respiration and circulation, as well as providing the children with happy experiences. Daily exercises designated by the doctor are performed according to the prescribed pattern. Guided by information provided in special literature on the subject, the teacher also conducts other activities aimed at the physical development of the children.

Fast-moving games are conducted daily during the times scheduled for activities and outdoor play, and also during the second half of the day. Games requiring considerable moving about demand a great deal of energy on the part of the children, and hence they usually take place during the time assigned for outdoor play, that is, when the children may be lightly clothed. For example, the game "Run Up to Me" may be played at the beginning of the third year of life with subgroups of children (eight to ten people), either outside in the playground or inside the building. In this very simple but absorbing game, the whole action consists in the children running up to the teacher only when the words "Come to me" are said. In the course of the game, the teacher moves on several occasions to the other side of either the room or the playground, and the game starts all over again, with the children facing in the opposite direction. This game may be made somewhat more complicated by asking each child to return to his own place. When this variant is used, children must use more skill in finding their bearings in the area.

The teacher's tone of voice during the play must be cheerful and lively but not excited, as all fast-moving games always excite children to a certain extent. It may happen that the children will push or shove each other, or, seeing a free chair, will try to sit down simultaneously on the same chair. The teacher must keep in mind the possibility of such "collisions" and come to the help of children in time; also, she must encourage even the slightest attempt by a child to be considerate to others by trying to go around another child or even to let him pass.

Among the fast-moving games is one called "You Can't Catch Me." The children must catch the teacher when she calls out. This game requires the observance of very few rules by the children, but its value still depends very much on the teacher's performance. The teacher must run lightly without making any sharp movements or changing direction, as this excites the children and demands from them an orientation and agility they have not yet acquired.

The teacher must know what games are appropriate for the children and alternate games requiring more or less movement. She must also notice any sign of weariness. If the child becomes breathless, perspires or begins to show signs of overexcitement, this must be taken as a sign that he needs to rest. At the same time, those children who avoid fast movements and prefer sitting games should not be overlooked.

For general physical development and the development of rhythm, the teacher plays various ring games with the children, especially out in the open. These favorite games arouse in the children the desire to reproduce the gestures and movements involved at the same time as all the other children, and thereby to follow the rhythm of the game.

For each group of children in their third year, there should be small equipment such as balls, jumping ropes, marbles, and flags. The use of bicycles or swings also contributes to the improvement of the physical skills of the children.

DRAWING AND MODELING

Interest in drawing and modeling appears in the child before he is even 2 years old. In the course of the third year this interest increases, especially when adults draw in the presence of children, give them pencils to use, and show them how to hold them. All research scholars and educators agree on the significant role of drawing and modeling in many aspects of the development of young children. In the process of drawing and modeling, the child's perceptiveness, memory, and thought processes develop greatly. He begins to compare and contrast various objects according to their general outlines, dimensions, shape, and color. Also, drawing and modeling contribute in a natural way to increased manual dexterity, which is so important to the development of a child of 3.

Children like drawing, the act itself as well as the traces on the paper. At the beginning of the year the movement of the hand is poorly controlled by the child's vision; this is characteristic of drawing at this age. These so-called doodles are very important in the evolution of imaginative creative work; they precede the emergence of powers of imagination. Gradually, in relation to the acquisition of muscular control, appear the first likenesses of somewhat recognizable shapes. Having drawn something vaguely oval stretched to one side, the child says, "duck"; and a ring with lines going away from it makes the child announce "the sun."

Such specialists as N. P. Sakulina stress the importance of an encouraging attitude toward these drawings and attempts to find likenesses between the drawings and some real objects. It is proper for the teacher herself to help the child to see some kind of resemblance in what he has drawn. While urging independent efforts on the part of the children in drawing and modeling, the teacher adopts some special techniques of teaching them. Thus, E. A. Flerina is making a serious study of the appearance of images in drawings and has worked out a series of exercise games for the purpose of developing manual dexterity and the contents and shapes in children's drawings. As a result of such exercises, the movements of the child's hands while holding the pencil become more energetic and varied. The child can then intentionally perform and repeat certain definite movements. Following the instructions and demonstration of an adult, he draws a number of dots representing either snow or rain; he makes circular movements, drawing smoke rings, balls and marbles; he makes so-called unidirectional movements, either horizontals (paths, rulers) or verticals (sticks). So that the child can master the corresponding movements in the actual drawing, it is advisable to have him perform them first in the air.

Such exercises, which are somewhat in the nature of a game, are conducted during activity periods. Having learned this or that aspect of drawing (for example, having learned to make circular lines), the children are glad to have the opportunity to reproduce this particular form. During activities in drawing and modeling, the teacher demonstrates other approaches. For example, she shows the children how to draw a road or how to roll clay. It must be kept in mind that no less than half of all activities, including drawing and modeling, must be kept for independent work by the children. Constructive participation of the teacher (when she models herself or draws simply shaped objects—an apple, a cucumber—and shows her work to the children) is very significant.

Toward the end of the third year, when the child is drawing he will often announce what he has drawn and even sometimes announce in advance his intention: "I will draw a ball."

Drawing is associated with visual perception and, to a certain extent, involves a stationary position. Therefore, suitable conditions must be arranged with care. It must be remembered, for instance, that drawing requires good lighting of the tables at which the children are busy (light must come from the left). These activities must be conducted in the morning hours. Care must be taken that the child does not lean his head down too close to the table and does not lean with his chest on the table edge.

A child must be taught to hold his pencil in his right hand—first in his fist, then correctly. Care must also be exercised to see that the child always holds his pencil with the writing end down.

Colored pencils from ordinary children's sets are used for drawing. Children in their third year are given pencils of one or more different colors. The children gradually remember and differentiate four colors: red, blue, yellow, and green. These colors leave a bright trace on the paper and bring out associations: green for grass or trees, and so forth. It is not desirable to give the children light blue, light green or similar colors. The size of the paper to be used should be the same as used in the school notebooks for drawing.

The best way to do modeling is to give children some clay, as this is the material easiest to handle and is suited to the none-too-strong hands of children. Nevertheless, it may be changed for plasticene, which should be kept in some warm place.

Modeling with clay gives the child tremendous pleasure as this material lends itself well to creativity. It is perceived by the child through touch and sight. The child succeeds faster than in drawing in representing particular objects, although the first things made out of clay or plastic material bear the same shapeless character. At this age, the child simply tears off small pieces of clay from a large lump, without attempting to shape anything.

After some time, the teacher shows the children the way to work with clay: to tear off a piece and roll the clay, how to give it this or that shape—a ball, a sausage, a pancake.

At first the child cares little for the results of his work and often makes a lump out of what he has just finished. It is up to the teacher to teach the children to care for what they have succeeded in making. Praising their work, encouraging a child's intentions ("I'll make an apple"), and including his work in some play situation will arouse in the child the desire to preserve what he has just accomplished. In modeling, just as in drawing, the child notices a likeness to an object only by association after he has finished. For example, having rolled some clay, he suddenly exclaims, "Sausage!" The teacher praises the child and advises him to make a few more sausages. It is only slowly and after much repetition of particular actions that a child begins to show signs of intention, more often than not arising as the modeling is progressing.

The imitation of adults and older children is very important in modeling, as in this medium models are easier to perceive and lend themselves more readily to being reproduced. Having noticed that an older child has made a snowman out of three lumps of clay, a younger child of some 2 ½ years also puts together two, still rather shapeless, balls of clay, announcing: "A snowman!" The teacher sometimes shapes before the children an apple, a carrot, a sheep, or a rabbit, suggesting that the children try to recognize what she has made.

In all cases, such items as have been made by the children (even if their work was not entirely their own) are kept for some time in the group or are exhibited so that the parents can see them. A valuable educational approach is to use objects made by the children out of clay for games (for feeding dolls, and so forth).

The teacher at all times encourages comments made by children who are in the process of modeling and any appearance of initiative or the smallest amount of success achieved by children. Here, the animated, precise, and enthusiastic talk of the teacher takes on great significance. It is a helpful factor in the speech development of the children, their thinking and their esthetic feelings. At a given point the teacher may say: "Look, children, what a nice mushroom this turned out to be. Natasha made it. It has a strong stem and a round cap. Let's put it here on the shelf." Interest shown by the teacher in the imaginative work of small children heightens their desire to model, draw, and examine their works.

At the beginning of the year, activities are conducted with groups of four to six children. Then, the number of children may be increased to include half of the group, and toward the end of the year all the group may be included in this activity. At the time scheduled for drawing and modeling, the teacher teaches the children to obey certain rules: to draw only on paper or on the blackboard, not to bang with their pencils, not to wrinkle paper, and not to throw clay around.

ACTIVITIES WITH BUILDING MATERIALS

Activities conducted using building materials and presented as play acquaint the children with a new and absorbing interest, building or construction, which is very important for the development of children.

Independent attempts to construct by children of 2 to 2 ½ years are relatively rare, and without the active participation of teachers the children would not attempt to build anything for quite a long time. Not knowing how to build, the children to whom building material is made available take separate pieces out of boxes, move them along the table pretending they are cars, or just throw them about, making out of the set of building material a shapeless heap. But when guidance is offered in the use of construction toys, and the children are shown the various aspects of building, and when teachers play with the children making definite models, construction becomes differentiated from other play and gradually becomes a meaningful form of activity, giving the children much satisfaction and happiness.

The development of interest in construction games is greatly and beneficially influenced by the observation of the older children (5 ½ to 6 years). Children of 3 watch with great pleasure the process of construction performed by older children, and if the older child shows a kind disposition to the little one, he will eagerly join in the play. Common play and activity add much to the enrichment of small children's speech as well as helping the smaller children to learn some aspects of construction as it is carried on by older children.

At the beginning of the year, having organized a group of six to eight children, the teacher builds in their presence not a huge but an interesting structure—a house, a bridge, or a tower—calls upon the children to participate to a certain extent, and organizes games centered upon the construction. For example, she rolls a car over the bridge, puts a doll in the house, talks about what she is doing, and asks the children questions to include them in the conversation. During the time devoted to construction, the children acquire many words and combinations of words, including the names of objects, actions and qualities (a tall tower, a wide road, etc.). Buildings and other structures must be simple but solid (they should not fall apart at the slightest push), and the color combinations should be pleasing to the eye. Selected small *matreshki,* small cars, and toy animals should also be brought into these activities.

Including games will heighten the interest of children in construction activities and will lead to more individual attempts to use building material for a somewhat more definite purpose. The children begin to pick up blocks more often, set them on the floor or the table, and try to build something. Thus the children develop their ability to hold something with their hands and the corresponding coordination, which is greatly helped by the numerous repetition of the same movements. The teacher must encourage the children's attempts to build something (a bench, a wall, a house), turning the children's attention to the size and color of the blocks and other building materials. Occasionally, the child is asked to line up in a row the pieces which are identical in color, shape, or size. The visual comparison helps the child learn to better differentiate colors, sizes, and shapes, and this is important for the development of the sensory faculties of the child. This also helps him to learn the correct names for shapes (a block, a brick) and also for colors and sizes.

With the purpose of developing building skills in children, certain activities are conducted in the course of which the teacher shows how, for example, a tower can be built from three or four blocks and a flag fixed to the top of it; or else how gates may be constructed out of three to five pieces through which a doll or a car will pass. Such activities may be conducted with a small group one or two months after the beginning of the year.

Building pieces are distributed to children in the quantities needed for given projects. After a demonstration and explanations, the teacher suggests that the children start building something. The children will do the building rather quickly and then play with it.

In demonstrating various ways of building, it is important to combine skillfully verbal instructions with the demonstration. The words focus the children's attention, help them to remember specific actions, and activate their thinking. "Now I will build a tower; it will be tall and steady. I will put one block on top of another, and then another one. Look how well the blocks stay in place! On top we will put a roof. Here we are, it's done!"

In the second half of the year, the following approach may be used: Before the children have arrived, the teacher builds a number of small houses for various toy animals (dogs, cats, pigs). When the children come, she suggests that they build houses for other animals (rabbits, mice) and place these animals in the right houses. The teacher should select ahead of time the particular materials needed for these structures. Independent attempts on the part of the children to build something must be encouraged; in case a child encounters difficulties, help must be available.

It is important that the goals of construction should be set in the form of a game on the level of the children's understanding. A concrete goal within the range of understanding of the children—for example, building a fence for animals or a ramp down which cars may roll—will be better grasped and comprehended by the children.

The teacher carefully examines constructions made by the children and encourages their initiative. After activities, the children help the teacher to put the building materials away in the proper boxes.

Toward the end of the year, the children can make simple constructions such as those recommended for the younger kindergarten groups in the book by V. G. Nechaeva, *Constructions in the Kindergarten,* and in Z. V. Lischtvan's book *Games and Activities with Building Materials.*

SINGING AND MUSIC

In unified preschool institutions, as a rule, musical training is provided by a music teacher, with the help and participation of the regular teacher. In groups of children in their third year, regular musical activities are conducted twice a week, but in addition they should be supplemented daily by songs, circle dances and movements in time to the music.

Children in their third year have already been encouraged to a certain extent to be interested in music and to respond emotionally to music which is on their level. Children love to listen to singing, eagerly move and sway to the music, make dance movements, clap their hands, and try to hum or sing part or all of the tunes familiar to them.

Children's love and interest for music and singing must be encouraged and further developed. New goals are set: developing skill in listening to music and the ability to differentiate contrasting sound patterns, encouraging children to hum and sing along, teaching group movements to musical accompaniment, developing skill in acting out simple roles in musical games requiring a number of different characters.

At the beginning of the year, children hear the songs which were performed the year before in the preceding group. With pleasure they recognize the familiar words and melodies and begin singing along without prompting. The children listen with special enthusiasm to songs involving games and sounds they are able to recognize. Thus, if the song is about a cat, they are eager to "mew" at the proper places in the song.

At the beginning of the year, music activities are conducted with the children divided into two subgroups, but as their ability to remain attentive and to coordinate their singing and movements develops, the two subgroups may be combined.

The children must gradually be introduced to new songs and encouraged to hum and sing along. Of course, children at this age are still very limited in their ability to sing individually. Nevertheless, they are able to reproduce, even if imperfectly, the rhythm or the melody of certain children's songs. The teacher must be attentive to the quality of her own singing and that of the older children, since this will be imitated by the younger ones.

In order for the song to appeal to the children and to have them wish to sing it too, it is very important that the adults (teacher or music teacher) perform it in a beautiful manner. Singing must be pleasant to the ear and not too loud and the words must be heard clearly and distinctly. All the children must be able to see the face of the singer clearly.

The program provides a number of specially designed musical works intended for listening such as "The Little Horse" by M. Raukhverger, "Winter" by Karaseva, "The Cat" by V. Vitlina. Although these songs are quite easy as far as the melody goes, they require the full extent of the children's ability to perform them.

In the course of their third year, the children's physical development is greatly intensified; this is influenced to a significant extent by music activities. The children develop skill in adapting various movements to the contrasting musical sounds (marching and running, walking and dancing). Toward the end of the year children begin to dance better and more frequently when given instructions or a demonstration by the teacher, and they react fairly quickly to changes in the character of the music presented to them. It must be remembered, however, that the children easily become tired or overexcited. After each short "dancing" period they must be calmed down.

Whenever rhythmic movements are shown to the children, esthetic quality in the adult model performance must be assured. It is advantageous to show smaller children the performance of rhythmic movements by older children. Smooth movements performed by the older children give the little ones much pleasure and will provide excellent models for them to follow.

Almost all activities for children of this age bear a playful character. Nevertheless, besides these activities, the teacher should conduct other musical games having a more intricate pattern in which the children play a part commensurate with their ability and appropriate to the character of the music. For games with musical accompaniment, the following pieces may be used: "The Rabbit" by Grechaninov, "The Bear" by Rebikov, "A Festive Walk" by Alexandrova, "Lullaby" and "A Game" by Vitlin.

Games to the accompaniment of music are very significant in the development of a sense of rhythm and coordination. They also increase the children's love for music. The teacher and the music instructor, noticing the evolution of the children's receptiveness to music and of their self-assurance in their movements, challenge the children and express their pleasure in relation to the children's success. Toward the end of the year, the children can, with a reasonable amount of success, sing together the songs which are appropriate for them; also, they will know a few games, and their increased emotional receptiveness to good music familiar to them will be apparent.

VI

The Education of Children
from 3 to 7 Years Old

EDUCATIONAL OBJECTIVES

In line with the organizational principle in the new *Program of Instruction in the Kindergarten*, the material included in the program for the groups of children from age 3 to age 7 is divided up in accordance with the various types of activities: the so-called routine activity of everyday life, play, instruction during regular activity periods, and work training. In the new program the range of knowledge, skills, and habits which are to be acquired by the children during the course of planned activity periods is determined in a more precise and concrete manner.

The program includes a knowledge of surrounding reality: of the work of people in cities and on collective farms, of the life of people in the native region, of famous countrymen and those who gave their lives for the happiness of others. In addition the program includes a first introduction to animate and inanimate nature. Knowledge of the environment is of great significance for the general development of the child's mind, and for instilling in him a feeling of love for his country, good will toward his fellow men in other lands, and respect for work.

The program of broadening the child's conceptions and knowledge of surrounding life is closely tied in with the program of study in his native language. While the children are accumulating impressions of the material objects in the culture, of the occupations of people and of natural phenomena, the teacher continues to add to their vocabulary the correct and precise names of objects, actions, and the qualities of objects. She introduces into their active vocabulary words designating place, time, quantity, and size; she teaches them to understand the meaning and the beauty of the imagery encountered in riddles, fairy tales, and poetry. In activity periods the children are taught to express their thoughts in a concise and organized manner, to tell about their games, the observations they have made, and the events which occur in school and at home. The children are taught to understand and to love artistic literature, and to read poetry with feeling.

The newly revised program in arithmetic includes instruction in the arithmetic operations, familiarization with numbers, and instruction in the solution of addition and subtraction problems involving the digits.

The program devotes considerable attention to art education: drawing, modeling, cutting and pasting, and music. During the activity periods, the children develop esthetic appreciation, learn to use brushes and paints and to portray surrounding objects or events. They are also taught to sing and dance and to understand and love music.

The new element in the program of work for children in their seventh year of life is the preliminary instruction they receive in reading and writing: a pre-alphabet period of reading and writing instruction is included in the program of the kindergarten. This will create a favorable foundation for the children's successful assimilation of reading and writing skills in the first grade of school.

The desire to establish continuity between the preschool and school periods is reflected in the general objectives established for the group of children 6 years of age, which is called the preparatory group.

The nature of the instructional work to be carried on with the children outside of the regular activity periods is described: observations of people and nature in the course of walks or trips; a broadening of the scope of knowledge of household objects, plants, and animals in the nature corner; development of basic physical skills and the ability to manipulate objects; development of speech; improvement in the child's orientation to space and time; and so forth.

Thus, the new program is planned in such a way that the objectives of mental and esthetic education are achieved not only in the regular activity periods but also outside of them, where the objectives are attained by special approaches and methods differing from the instructional methods used during the regular activity periods and involving different ways of organizing the children.

The new approach to instructional work with children outside scheduled activity periods will require that the teacher be well organized and adequately trained, that she have the opportunity to work with each child and the ability to use every opportunity afforded by the environment to fulfill the educational objectives.

Close contact between the teacher and each individual child is needed, and this will lead to a greater diversity of teacher-child relationships. There are many occasions for such contact: when a new or favorite book is being read, when a particular act is being discussed, when the children are singing or listening to favorite pieces of music, observing natural phenomena. The initiative for establishing such rapport may come from either the teacher or the children. Moreover, the teacher must strive to develop the children's initiative in this respect.

The new program devotes considerably more attention to the actual process of instruction, in the strict sense of the word, than was the case in the *Manual*. This is apparent not only in the fact that objectives pertaining to the behavior and personal qualities of the children are defined in more detail, but also in the fact that provisions are made for a pedagogically oriented organization of the entire structure of the children's lives. In this organization of the children's lives, the central place is occupied by the children's play. Specific play periods are established in the daily schedule; specific types of games particularly adapted to the fulfillment of concrete educational objectives are recommended for definite times during the day.

These games have a variety of themes, reflecting not only the routine life of the kindergarten (medical examinations, vaccinations, and general health care, haircuts, baths, musical activities and going to bed), as is normal with 2-, 3-, and 4-year-old children, but also reflecting the occupations of people outside the kindergarten, and the vivid events in the life of the society. Games involving the dreams and aspirations of the children, their imagination and fantasies, serve to develop the moral qualities of the children, and to develop relationships and a collective spirit between them.

A definite place in the children's lives will be occupied by work training which is interesting in nature and appropriate to the children's stage of development. The program of work training is presented not only in the form of objectives, but also through an enumeration of concrete actions and assignments which are selected in accordance with the age differences among the children and the difference in their level of psychological and physical development. Some work activities are linked to a certain extent with games, or even serve as games: building various structures, making toys, washing doll clothing, and so forth. Others are directed at the fulfillment of basic living requirements: being on duty for a particular purpose and at a given time, taking care of the plants and animals, taking care of personal needs, making things for practical uses (little bags for flower seeds, book covers). In the course of work training, which begins in childhood, it is important to develop in the children not only the ability to perform definite little tasks, but also a feeling of enjoyment in the fulfillment of simple requests and obligations. For a healthy and normal human being, work is a need, and this is what must be kept in mind when we speak of work training as part of the educational process.

On an equal level with play, instruction, and work is the activity of the children which is directed at satisfying their basic needs: eating, sleeping, and self-care in the narrow sense of the word (washing, dressing, and so on). This activity is considered equal in significance because the teacher is responsible for developing the basic hygienic habits which in the long run must be considered as cultural habits: keeping clothes clean and tidy, knowing how to use the various utensils, being able to dress and undress rapidly, being able to behave properly at the table during meals, and helping others whenever help is needed.

ARRANGING THE GROUPS AND RECEIVING THE CHILDREN IN THE KINDERGARTEN

The transfer of the 7-year-old children to school completes the task of the kindergarten. At that time the directress is already preparing to receive new children in the younger groups and to fill vacancies left in the other groups.

In setting up the various groups in an institution which involves many different age groups, the following educational considerations must determine the selection process: (a) the groups must include children of approximately the same age; (b) the same teachers must remain responsible for groups of children who stay together from the age of 2 until they transfer to school.

One should never have certain children 5 or 6 years of age "repeat" the year, that is, be submitted to the same program for two years in a row. If children are not offered a program corresponding to their stage of development, they lose all interest in the kindergarten. Repeating can in itself be a good thing, but it is imperative that new problems and challenges be given to the children. Mechanical repetition of a year is dangerous not only because children do not receive the incentive needed for further development, but also because they acquire bad habits which are later difficult to break: aimlessness, a detached attitude toward activities and requirements presented by the teacher, indifference instead of lively curiosity.

Each new child is warmly welcomed by the director and the teacher; they introduce him to the other children, show him around the building, show him some of the toys, and tell him about a few of the rules of the kindergarten.

The first day spent by a child at the kindergarten is a day of great responsibility for the teachers. Everything must be done so that the child will feel welcome and at ease among a new group of adults and a large group of children of his own age. Kindness on the part of all, fascinating games and activities with the children, and interesting stories told by the teacher—all this promises the child happy new experiences of a kind he has never before experienced while at home.

Some youngsters of 2 to 4 years of age find it difficult to part with parents in the morning. They cannot imagine what lies ahead of them and have no conception of how long they will be separated from their families. How much warmth and kindness is needed on the part of the teacher in order to win the child's trust, to soothe him, and to make him wish to come to the kindergarten!

In September the teachers begin to work with their assigned groups according to the program planned for the approaching year of instruction and education.

In the middle, older and preparatory groups, it is desirable to stress the first day in such a way that it will be remembered as a happy day, a special occasion. For the first day of the kindergarten (usually about the middle of September) all the 3-, 4-, 5-, and 6-year-old children might be gathered in one very large room. The teachers congratulate the children on their promotion into the next group, and briefly (extremely briefly) tell about the main events of the forthcoming year. The directress also welcomes the children, and expresses her wish that they will grow up healthy, make friends, play together, work hard, and learn well. It is also desirable to bring in some presents, not for each child, but for the group as a whole. These presents may take the form of toys, equipment, or books, which will be used by the children for the first time in the new group. For example, the preparatory group might be given skates, skittles, or the book by B. Zhitkov, "What I Saw."

After initial greetings, which should not take more than eight or ten minutes, it is good either to show the children a puppet show or organize a concert. Facilities for this are always available. If the faculty of the kindergarten is unable to organize a concert using the local talent, then they should turn for assistance to a music school or Pioneer group. This should be a concert for the children and not a concert in which the children participate, as is the case for the Seventh of November and the First of May celebrations. Although restlessness is characteristic of children of preschool age and they may have the desire to perform, one should keep in mind that September is only the very beginning of the school year, and to organize a concert involving the participation of the children is not very practical at that time, because rehearsals would be needed. The need for active participation on the part of the children may be satisfied by giving them a chance to dance freely in accompaniment to music. Thus the new school year in the kindergarten is launched.

ORGANIZATION OF THE LIFE OF THE GROUP AND EDUCATION OF THE CHILDREN

The organization of the children's lives within the kindergarten setup requires first of all rational planning of routine activity: the furniture and equipment should be arranged so as to be convenient and comfortable; the meal schedule must be strictly observed by the kitchen help; the work schedule of the assistants in preparing for the children's meals and sleep, in administering water conditioning treatments, and in cleaning up the rooms must be carefully worked out. Full responsibility for the instructional organization of life in the kindergarten rests with the directress.

PHYSICAL EDUCATION

The basic objectives of physical education are: (1) strengthening the child's health and building up his body resistance; (2) promoting natural development; (3) developing the basic physical skills required in life; (4) developing physical attributes (speed, agility, endurance); (5) developing moral qualities and volitional character traits; (6) forming good health habits. All these objectives are pursued throughout the entire educational process in the kindergarten.

To work effectively, the teacher must obtain all the data concerning the medical history of children. It is advisable to have their physical condition (health condition, level of physical development, and posture) checked in the presence of the teacher, utilizing any assistance she may be able to offer. All this data, as well as information relating to the vision and hearing of the children, must be taken into consideration in the teacher's work.

Of special significance is the proper attention to the nervous system of each child. The work must be planned so that it does not lead to over-excitement and unstable behavior. At the same time the children must be given ample opportunity to satisfy their natural need for movement. The personal example the teacher gives is of great importance: it embodies calm self-assurance, composure, an even and expressive voice, and an attitude of fairness toward the children. A cheerful atmosphere must prevail in the kindergarten, and the children must be interested in their activities and be friendly toward each other.

Physical education is promoted by very careful control of conditions: providing a well-lighted, spacious room, a suitably planned and equipped playground, a good diet, and comfortable clothing.

In September, as soon as the groups are formed, each child must be provided with a table and a chair appropriate to his size. Each child's furniture should be marked so his place at the table can be assigned for the whole year.

Fulfilling the educational objectives will depend to a great extent on the planning of the children's lives and the observance of fixed schedules and diets. Children get accustomed to playing, studying, working, taking walks, eating and sleeping at definite times during the day. Correct observance of the schedules will depend on the proper organizing of the teacher's work and that of her assistant, as well as on the availability of proper equipment.

A comfortable routine helps to control the child's behavior, to stabilize his nervous system, and to regularize his activity. It helps to develop in the children hygienic habits of great value for their health. The teacher guides the daily routine without forcing the children to strain or hurry unnecessarily. The children must feel lighthearted and not experience a feeling of constraint. It is useless to keep the children waiting in line or for their turn, and in fact it can be harmful to them.

The formation of good personal health habits represents one of the most important objectives of physical education. The younger the child, the more he needs the care of adults. Regular washing, regular changes of underwear and clothing in general, and the care of the child's hair and teeth are the responsibilities of the family. If children board in the kindergarten, the responsibility for this care must be assumed by the teacher and the other personnel in the kindergarten.

The cleanliness and order in the children's environment, the precise adherence to schedules, and the proper care of the children in the kindergarten and at home will be decisive factors in their own training in personal cleanliness and neatness.

Developing the habit of keeping the body and clothing clean, dressing, undressing, eating by oneself, and maintaining cleanliness and neatness in general will give the children the opportunity to participate in looking after their own health and that of others. Being able to take care of his simple hygienic needs and to stay clean and neat increases the propriety of the child's behavior, develops his self-discipline, and accustoms him to cleanliness and order.

If good health habits are to be formed, the process of making new demands upon the children must be done gradually (as is provided for in the program). The children must be given the chance to observe the rules of personal hygiene without constant prompting.

Children are taught to wash their hands before meals and whenever they get dirty, such as when they are cleaning the play area, watering the flowers, modeling with clay, playing with sand, or using the toilet (children who board wash thoroughly before going to bed and in the morning).

In each group the necessary conditions must be created to make washing a comfortable and pleasant operation. The washstands must be installed in accordance with the children's heights. Each washstand must be provided with two soap boxes with small pieces of soap so that the children can hold them with ease. The towels should be of suitable length for children, that is, no more than 100 centimeters.

If the washroom is adjacent to the common room, the children enter the washroom in small groups and two children wash at each washstand. If the washroom is located some distance away from the common room, it usually is found to be more convenient to have the small children wash in their own common room. For this purpose, portable washstands can be used.

In training the children to wash by themselves eventually, the younger groups are helped to a certain extent by the teachers and her assistants. In the middle and older groups, care must be taken to insure that the children are not only washing thoroughly, but also are performing the operation rather quickly.

CONDITIONING

This is one of the means by which the health of the child is strengthened. In conditioning procedures, the individual characteristics of each child must be kept in mind, as well as the general condition of his health. Conditioning treatments must be applied gradually (gradual lowering of temperature, gradual removal of various pieces of clothing, gradual passage from localized to general procedures). Conditioning programs must be carried on systematically or else the type of body resistance being developed will break down.

Conditioning must become a part of the routine of the kindergarten and influence the whole life of the child. This is only possible when conditioning procedures are woven into the routine activities in the daily schedule.

During a conditioning process, the child must feel well. It is important to accustom the child to react sensibly to outside conditions: if it is cold, to move about; if it is hot, to play quietly or sit down for a while. Older children of preschool age should develop an understanding of the purpose behind the conditioning program, and should acquire a desire to be healthy and resistant.

Fresh, cool air should be widely used in the conditioning program. From the earliest years, children must accustom themselves to being in a room with partly opened windows, to spending three to four hours outdoors in any weather in the fall and in the winter. Only strong rain, wind, or frost should be considered valid reasons for having the children remain inside.

Children must be taught to wash with cool water from the faucet, to sleep with the windows partly open, and to sleep in bags with the windows open whenever a porch is available.

When it is warm outside, all aspects of the kindergarten life are moved outside. At this time the fullest possible benefit must be derived from the sunshine, with periods in the sun alternating with time spent in the shade.

Sensible clothing is important in building up resistance. Garments must be chosen according to the time of year and the weather. Clothing should be light, well ventilated and non-confining. The children must be able to play freely, even when this involves running, jumping, and so forth.

Special conditioning procedures—air baths, water treatments and sun baths—are applied under the strict supervision of a doctor or qualified nurse. In every kindergarten during the summer months, one type of water conditioning involving all the children must be conducted. This may take the form of sponging or bathing. In winter, however, water conditioning will only be carried on in the schools where appropriate facilities are available: a shower and bath room. General sponging may be replaced by wet rubs or by simply sponging the legs. . . .

MEALS

In the course of a nine to ten hour stay in the kindergarten, children are fed three times. If they remain for a period of twelve hours or for the whole 24-hour period, they are fed four times, with the meals spaced every three and a half to four hours. The meal schedules, whether at home or in the kindergarten, coincide in time and in the menu. With this aim in mind, the menus for the current day and for the following day are posted in the kindergarten for the parents to see.

The diet must be balanced in relation to calories and nutritional contents. Throughout the year the children must be given required daily amounts of dairy products and particular vegetables. Such food as is tasty and appealing to the eye is eaten by the children fairly quickly, without sitting for prolonged periods at the table.

Washing up before meals should not take much time. Gradually, as they finish whatever they were doing, the children go in groups of five or six toward the washroom, where the assistant is present. After washing their hands and without waiting for other children, those who are ready sit down at the table which has already been set. Through demonstration, example and reminding, the children are taught to hold their spoons in the correct way and use them properly. By the time they are four years old they learn to use a fork, and toward the age of five, to use both a fork and a knife.

DEVELOPMENT OF PHYSICAL SKILLS

Within the general area of physical education, an important place is occupied by physical development of movements. In view of the great significance of a sensible amount of mobility for the normal physical development of children and for the maintenance of good muscle tone, it is essential to insure that in the course of the day the children are able to satisfy their need for various physical activities, both on the playground and inside the building. The children must never remain in one position for any length of time, or remain motionless (sitting on chairs or on the carpet, standing in rows or in pairs).

Both indoor and outdoor areas should be provided with equipment and toys geared to develop a variety of movements (during prescribed activity periods and during free time). The teacher must make sure that children use on their own initiative the equipment related to climbing, throwing, and practicing balance. With the purpose of developing the children's physical skills through the routine of everyday life, the teacher gives them various tasks requiring speed, agility and coordination: bringing a certain object, putting it in a certain position, taking it away, etc. She takes notice of the fact that such movements should be natural and at the same time agile and graceful (not shoving each other, not dropping objects, not waving their arms about, sitting down quietly at the table, opening or closing a door without slamming it).

Throughout the day the teacher watches the posture of the children during play, activities, and meals. The children should hold themselves erect, but without strain; they should avoid stooping.

The physical development of children in kindergarten is promoted especially through various games. Both outdoor and indoor active games should be played extensively, especially games involving toys (balls, hoops, skip-ropes, quoits, skittles, bilboquet, and so forth) and games with rules. These games may be played either in small groups or with all the children at one time. (Small groups are better suited for exercise-type games involving climbing or jumping.) The teacher attempts to arouse interest in lively games, and teaches them to play familiar simple games by themselves.

Much of the outdoor recreation period must be devoted to games involving physical exercise and fun: during the winter, sledding down the hills, skiing and skating; in summer, riding bicycles, ball games, hoops, skittles (in accordance with the program). The choice of sports depends on the climatic conditions in the given area, as well as on the time of year and the local conditions of each kindergarten.

When the children are taking a walk in the country, natural obstacles such as small mounds, brooks, and dead trees, should be used to develop their basic physical skills. If in the vicinity of the kindergarten there is a reservoir, the 6-year-old children may be taught to swim.

MORNING EXERCISES

Morning exercises, which for all groups are conducted every day before breakfast, are very significant from an educational point of view, and are extremely healthful. But they will yield successful results only if the teacher devotes sufficient attention to both of these aspects. Unfortunately, far too few teachers show concern for the health factor in the morning exercises. They do not ventilate the building; their choice of exercises and exercise games, and the number of times each exercise is performed, are such that the children are not presented the requisite physiological demands.

Without forgetting about the organizational and educational aspects of morning exercises, the teachers must concentrate their attention particularly on the health objective. They must first of all insure proper ventilation of the building, clear everything as far as possible out of one area of the room (that is, push back tables and chairs), and remind the children that they must take off warm sweaters and put on lighter footwear.

Having arranged themselves (the little ones in a ring, and the 5- to 6-year-olds in three or four rows, one behind the other), the children perform from two to four familiar exercises for strengthening their shoulder muscles, expanding their chest cavity, strengthening the muscles of their backs and stomachs, and developing the muscles in their feet in order to prevent fallen arches (flat feet). Each exercise is repeated from two or three to eight times; (the most demanding exercise is performed by the children in the preparatory group. Exercises for the development of separate groups of muscles can be performed with objects (sticks, hoops, ropes). For correct posture, exercises performed while in a lying position are very useful.

After the exercises, the children run. They run one behind the other with large energetic steps, hugging the walls of the room. If there is not sufficient space for twenty-five or thirty children to run around the room, this drill may be conducted in smaller groups; or, even better, the running might be replaced by jumping in place. The morning exercises conclude with a period of quiet walking.

The children must be taught to breathe correctly during the exercises, and not to hold their breath. They should exhale at the point in the given exercise when their chests come in, and inhale when expanding their chests (for example, when their arms are stretched out, they inhale; when their arms are lowered, they exhale). When they are inhaling the children do not talk (they should breathe through the nose), but they should utter some word or sound when exhaling.

At the time of the morning exercises, the teacher reminds the children of the proper way to perform the exercises, and she supervises the proceedings, paying particular attention to the children's posture. Moreover, she accompanies some particular movements by playing on an instrument, piano, percussion, or string. A few times a week the music teacher plays on the piano as an accompaniment to the morning exercises.

In the winter the morning exercises are conducted inside with the vents open; in the warm months, they take place outside in the open air.

TRAINING IN MORALITY

The foundation of a completely moral personality is laid at an early age. The morality of a child is a combination of moral feelings and moral behavior. As the children develop and come into greater contact with the environment, their moral feelings increase. First there is simply love for parents and other members of the family; later come respect for and attachment to the teacher, friendly feelings toward children in the same age group (their classmates), friendliness and respect for the adults working the kindergarten, and respect for all older people, even those whom the children do not know personally. Children are taught to feel attachment and love for their home and for the national traditions, respect and love for V. I. Lenin, and respect and friendly feelings toward the peoples of other nations. In the formation of such feelings, adults play an enormous role. They influence children by their behavior and by their personal approach toward other people around them, toward traditions, and toward their homeland.

The moral feelings of children express themselves in moral conduct. Respect, love, and attachment for family and close friends must be expressed through generally accepted forms of attention and respect: greeting people properly and saying "good-bye," saying "thank you" after meals or after receiving a gift or some assistance, greeting everyone in the morning, saying "good night" before going to sleep for the night, giving special greetings on the holidays, letting older people pass or helping younger ones by picking up some object which they have dropped, offering a guest a seat, and knowing how to address people politely. The goal of the teacher consists in teaching the children in such a way that by the time they are 5 or 6 years old, they will act properly without special prompting or commands (the little ones, of course, must be reminded). The teacher must strive to make these habits of moral behavior so secure that the children will behave on all occasions in life in the way in which they were taught; that is, so that the children will greet people not only when they are entering the common room but whenever they meet adults in the hall, the vestibule, the playground, and so forth.

Certain things such as greeting classmates on the occasion of a holiday must become traditional in the kindergarten: children in the 4-, 5-, and 6-year-old groups should write letters to sick schoolmates or teachers (the teacher writes while the children dictate); they should write a letter of greeting on the occasion of either the Seventh of November, the New Year, or the First of May to some kindergarten in another republic; they should prepare presents for relatives and close friends on the occasion of the Eighth of March, and do the same for friends on their birthdays. Placing flowers at the Lenin Memorial, at monuments to heroes, and on the graves of those who gave their life for the freedom and happiness of the country should become a tradition among the children of the kindergarten.

Such personal moral qualities as humility, modesty, truthfulness, diligence, sociability, goodwill, cooperativeness, thoughtfulness, and cheerfulness form the foundation of a child's moral being. The evolution and development of these qualities is aided by the example set by the teacher, by the consistent and fair attitude she maintains toward all the children of the group, by her ability to understand the child's psychology and her ability to penetrate the motives of their actions. The teacher must remember that educating children requires perseverance and patience.

Children are rendered a disservice by those teachers and music instructors who always bring forward the same children (to perform in assemblies, to do interesting tasks) or who, in the presence of children, make comments about their abilities or their dispositions ("This is a very gifted little girl; she dances beautifully," or "This little boy hasn't the slightest ability in anything and behaves very poorly."). The praised children often become egotists and lose their sense of belonging in the group. Relating to egotists or individualists is always unpleasant for those who have to be with them. Even preschool children do not approve of the conduct of egotists. On the other hand, those children whose lot it is to receive only negative comments, indifference, and lack of attention frequently lose faith in their abilities or become bitter and attempt to irritate those around them by their actions.

Basically the foundation for moral behavior is more easily established through a reliance on the positive aspects in human beings, but in order for the teacher to be effective in this regard, each child must be accorded trust and love.

It is impossible to develop morality through words, lectures, and instructions alone. Kind feelings and proper moral conduct result from training and a very sincere example. Teachers must think ahead and plan good deeds for the group as a whole and for each child: showing sympathy for a sick comrade or teacher, soothing and comforting someone who has been hurt, defending someone who is weak, making presents with one's own hands so as to give pleasure to someone, helping adults within the range of what can be achieved by a child, and so on.

The stability of perseverance of a proper moral attitude depends on consistency and unity in adult demands. Both teachers of the group must agree to the very minutest details concerning what must be expected from the children. Nothing upsets a child's behavior more than discrepancy in the expectations of adults: one teacher allows a given action, another forbids it; one teacher has the habit of praising beyond measure the slightest achievement, while from another the child can never expect a kind word or praise for a real achievement. Of great significance in the method of moral training is the teacher's just evaluation of the child's behavior—the degree of approval or disapproval must depend on the personal qualities of the children.

SPEECH DEVELOPMENT AND BROADENING OF THE CHILD'S PERSPECTIVE

The daily activity of children is accompanied by spoken contact with adults and other children of the same age. To limit the oral contact among children (that is, to arrest the natural need to communicate through the spoken word, to exchange impressions and to ask questions), as is done by some educators and as is required by many school directors and to demand constant silence and order is simply doing harm to the children. The teacher's objective consists in training the children to talk among themselves in a friendly way (not yelling, calling others by insulting names or raising their voices), and to talk to adults in a pleasant and polite tone of voice and to answer questions willingly. Children must know when they are to be quiet, and where and when they must talk very softly (for example, in bedrooms at bedtime, or in the halls when other groups are busy at some activity).

It follows that in developing the children's spoken activity, the teacher must train them to converse in a cultured way; that is, she must teach them the cultural aspect of speech. If children are constantly required to observe silence in the common room and in the halls, then it cannot be expected that they will learn how to talk properly. Children must be trained to use speech actively, i.e., to learn how to speak and what to say in different conditions and circumstances.

What are the means of developing active and cultural speech in children? First of all, the examples supplied by the teachers: from their first meeting in the morning right up to the end of the work day, the teacher finds herself in contact with the children. In activity periods her speech is guided by the material in the program and by her plans, but during the remainder of the time the teacher talks freely, either with individual children or with small groups, even sometimes with the whole group. Subjects for such talks are determined by the daily routine activities of the children and by events in the surrounding life which happen to be of interest to the children.

The closer the teacher is to the children, the more readily she will find interesting and useful topics for conversation. Children are very sensitive to the teacher's attitude. They will never share their thoughts or impressions with a teacher who limits her relationship with the children to enforcing their observance of schedules and rules. When the time comes for washing up, such a teacher would say: "Go and wash up! Wash your hands very clean! Dry your hands thoroughly! Go and sit down at the table." When the time comes for outdoor recreation, the children hear the same kind of reminder; and so it goes from day to day. The teacher confines herself to giving instructions and commands. The children quickly get used to this and expect nothing more from such a teacher. The children have their own life, into which the teacher does not penetrate.

Such teachers can never have in their groups any "why" sessions, since children know that this particular teacher must not be asked any questions; she only demands quiet and order. Or else they learn the hard way that it is useless to turn to this teacher for anything as she does not know what interests them. The children seek answers from each other. They discuss what they heard on the radio or when adults were speaking, as well as what happened in their family or what they saw on the street.

Unfortunately, such situations are observed where the teacher stands alone on the sidelines for lengthy periods of time while the children derive excitement from their own lives. One is sorry for children who did not find in their teacher a friend as well as a guide and a participant in their games. One also feels sorry for the teacher who was not needed by a single little boy or girl—when there were as many as twenty-five to thirty children in the group! Part of the group plays independently, others talk and entertain themselves—all fine, but were there not two or three who would have liked simply to talk to the teacher, share their secrets and their joys? A very bad situation, indeed!

A true teacher is interested in everything that interests children. She will always find the necessary time and a suitable topic both for personal talk with each individual child and for general discussion with the whole group. Children would go to such a teacher with questions and stories and turn to her to settle their disputes, as they would know that they would always receive an answer and support. Some want to find out exactly what the score of their soccer game was; others how many puppies did Belka (the space dog) really have; a third group wants to know which is stronger, a lion or an elephant; and so forth.

Thus, the first requirement of a teacher is the ability to initiate and maintain meaningful conversations with children, while keeping in mind, of course, their age and resultant limitations. The younger the children, the simpler must be the contents of a conversation. With the 3-year-olds the teacher talks about what is going on at that very moment or what they see around them. As they grow up, the life experience of the children broadens. An expanding sphere of events comes within their vision and enlists their interest, and the topics of conversation are consequently enriched.

Observation of their surroundings during the recreation period and on their way to and from the kindergarten contributes to broadening the children's perspectives. The role of the teacher in broadening, ordering and refining the children's impressions is very great. During the time children spend in the kindergarten, the teacher purposely selects facts concerning the surrounding life which may be useful in developing the mind and the moral attitudes of the child. Thus, for example, in the course of a walk, she might have the children observe the work of builders, car drivers, gardeners, or store clerks, as well as various kinds of cars and various kinds of buildings and stores. Watching people at work should stimulate respect for working people and interest in materials, tools, techniques, and the end products of labor.

It is particularly important to bring to the children's attention worthy relationships between people, for example, a passerby explaining the way to someone who obviously does not know the area in great detail, or a schoolboy helping an invalid across the street. By the same token, the teacher must not remain indifferent to negative actions. The teacher must express her own feelings when someone breaks a rule, for example, a man jaywalks, litters the street, breaks branches off trees, ans so on. Criticizing such acts serves to develop in the children a corresponding attitude toward them.

Being systematically encouraged by the teacher to observe their surroundings, the children gradually become more alert and inquisitive. They tell the teacher about everything they saw outside the kindergarten, express their approval and criticism, ask questions, and discuss. Such talks between children and teachers serve to broaden the children's outlook, stimulate their interests and foster their sensitivity.

It must not be forgotten that, when the teacher makes systematic efforts to broaden the children's perspective, she also enriches their vocabulary. Bringing the children's attention to some new fact, she indicates the names of objects, actions, and qualities. Whenever necessary, she explains the meaning of words, corrects errors should the child use incorrect expressions, or helps whenever the child is groping for a particular word. It is such talks between children and teacher that contribute most to the expansion of the children's active vocabulary. In order to develop the apparatus of sound articulation and to work toward distinct pronunciation and phonemic discrimination, the teachers may utilize the tremendous opportunity afforded by playing educational games with the children.

A second prerequisite for teachers is that their own speech set an example for children in its tone quality, richness and purity of vocabulary, and grammatical correctness. The teacher must have a faultless knowledge of the children's native language. Toward this end, she must constantly work on improving her speech. The kindergarten must be provided with dictionaries of the Russian language, so that in case of difficulty information relating to a given word can be checked.

INSTILLING IN THE CHILDREN
A LOVE OF NATURE

The man who knows how to observe and relate sensitively to nature, who can perceive the variety of its forms, smells and beauty, will feel an active and very real love for nature. Such love would not allow that a bough be broken, that the bark be scratched with a knife, that birds be shot with a sling, that domestic animals be tormented or any living thing be senselessly destroyed. Those who from early childhood have been taught to look after house plants and care for domestic animals, those to whom adults have opened the first page of that fascinating book which is Nature itself, and who were taught to look and see, to listen and hear— those will become the true friends of nature. The example supplied by the great Lenin, who in the hardest years of the Soviet Union signed a law about the conservation of natural resources and the creation of governmental reservations (forests and so forth), cannot fail to inspire each teacher.

In the kindergarten conditions must be established by which the children are close to nature and have daily contact with it. This purpose is served by a cultivated plot of land somewhere on the premises and a nature corner in each groups's common room. What kind of plants must be selected for the common rooms? First of all, plants which grow rapidly, so that the process of plant growth and development can be observed by the children daily. Plants of this type include aspidistras, begonias, and fuchsia. It is imperative that in every common room plants are flowering almost year round. The following plants, transplanted from the ground outside into flower pots, will bloom in the fall: asters, chrysanthemums, stock, French marigolds, and phlox. In the winter, cyclamen and epiphyllum bloom; in the early spring come amaryllis, azaleas, tulips, narcissus, and lilies-of-the-valley. In the summer fuchsia bushes are covered with decorative blooms; geraniums, roses and many other indoor plants bloom. With such a selection of indoor plants, the children's interest in the plant life is constantly maintained.

Teachers must give some thought to the most sensible placement of the indoor plants from the point of view of educational values. Not all plants should be placed on window sills, as they would darken the room and the children unable to look out. On the window sills should go only a few relatively low plants. Those plants that grow best in the shade are placed in corners or between windows (philodendron, aspidistra). Small pots containing plants which thrive in the shade are placed on shelves and in closets, and some creepers are hung from baskets. All of this will also help to decorate the room (the plants kept on shelves must be looked after by the teacher herself). When plants are in bloom, they should be put low down so that the children can examine them.

The teacher must bring plants into the room systematically; in the fall, a collection of branches with beautiful leaves—birch with its pale yellow leaves, aspen with its red leaves, maple. In the winter the room is decorated with a few branches of pine or spruce. As soon as spring is in the air, branches of pussy willow, birch, and bird cherry are placed in water. The burgeoning green leaves, the inflorescence of the birch branches, and the flowers of the bird cherry tree all delight the children. Outside bushes and trees are naked; it is cold. But in the window there is a garden in bloom! Tiny bouquets made from the first spring flowers decorate the shelves and tables, bringing forth feelings of tenderness on the part of the children toward the wondrous shapes, colors, and fragrances of the flowers.

In summer it is nice to put modest field flowers or elegant garden flowers in the room. Do not put only huge bouquets! Let the children take care of the flowers in the garden and in the fields, but do not let them pick them in great quantities. The common room can be decorated with a single flower, or a simple branch, or a bouquet made from two or three plants.

In the nature corner it is advisable to have an aquarium with fish in it, a bird in a cage, a turtle, a hedgehog, or a squirrel. Outside it is good to have pigeons and a dog, in the summer perhaps a hen with chicks and a rabbit. An opportunity to temporarily house some animal in the nature corner should never be overlooked. Someone may have found a bird that fell from its nest. It could be looked after in the kindergarten, then let free again. Some hunter friend may bring in a baby fox, which becomes a temporary guest of the children, living in a cage outside and being fed and cared for by the children.

Training in the careful observation of nature begins in the younger group, with the teacher attracting the youngsters' attention to fish behavior in the aquarium or to the flowering plants indoors. The teacher suggests that the children watch the way flowers are watered, the way water is changed in the aquarium, and the way the fish and birds are fed. If the teacher, while performing these duties, gives some little tasks to the children, for example holding the watering can or putting a spoonful of grain in the birds' feedbox, the children will be delighted. They are proud of having helped the teacher. Gradually, the children take over all of this work under the guidance of the teacher.

In the 5- and 6-year-old groups care of plants and animals is assumed by children assigned to this particular duty for a given period of time. The children are taught to examine the plants carefully, to water or sprinkle them whenever this is necessary, to cultivate the earth in the pot carefully, and, as they do this, to notice any changes in the growth of the plant, communicating any such information to the teacher and to all the other children in the group. The children must grow up to be friends to the birds. What kind of birds do live on the kindergarten premises? Where are their nests? What are their habits? Answers to these and other questions are supplied as the birds are observed during walks and outdoor recreation periods. Unitl the children on duty in the nature corner have become completely proficient in their work, all of the children share the responsibility for seeing that the birds living on the premises are fed regularly. Gradually the children find out what type of food each kind of bird prefers, then in the summer and the fall the children gather and store up the food which will be needed by some of the birds during the winter (berries, grains, cones, etc.). When the birds gather at the feeding place, the children observe them. In the spring bird boxes are hung out and the children await the arrival of the first feathered guests. Later, they watch the birds as they feed their young.

During walks, the teacher also teaches the children to observe meterological phenomena: rain, snow, hail, wind, the shape and movements of clouds, the sun (noticing where the sun was when the children went out and where it is on their return), sunsets, rainbows, the moon and the stars. Also noted are seasonal changes—the melting of the snow, ice breaking, the falling of leaves, the migration of the birds, and so on. There are never two days as alike as two drops of water. The children develop the ability to point out even insignificant changes in the color of the sky or the clouds or the direction of the wind when they are under the close guidance of a teacher who loves nature. Graudally accumulating knowledge from their prolific observation of nature both animate and inanimate, the children 5 to 6 years of age get accustomed to recognizing various signs in nature: for example, a bright red sun just before it sets forecasts wind for the next day; whenever the swallows fly high it means dry weather; whenever the swallows fly low, there will be rain; when the ants hide in their hills, a storm is brewing; frogs croak before rain; spiders suspended on long threads mean good weather; if the smoke comes out of the chimneys straight during the winter, it means it is extremely cold. Watching nature must become habitual with the children.

BOOKS

Listening to good literature, looking at illustrations, reading aloud with expression and paraphrasing literature—all must find a place in the kindergarten, and not just in the regular activity periods. The artistry of the word reinforces other approaches to fulfilling the instructional objectives indicated in the program. It helps to introduce art into the children's lives and by doing so to reinforce the skills, knowledge and habits acquired by the children through the instruction they receive during the regular activity periods.

It is important to give preschool children, from a very young age, the opportunity during free time to look at and examine books, tell each other stories, recite favorite poems, tell riddles, and so on. At certain times, depending on the circumstances and not necessarily every day, the teacher herself will read a book or tell a story. Those children who wish to listen settle themselves comfortably on the carpet or around a small table, and the teacher finds for herself a place from which she can observe the group of children who are playing without breaking off her reading.

Books and readings must always provide happy occasions for each child. Therefore, the teacher should never simply read a book to fill up a spare minute; that is, while waiting for lunch or supper, she should never compel a child to leave an absorbing game in order to listen to a story from a book, and should never punish a child with a book ("You have been naughty. Sit down and listen to this story.").

Books to be used independently by the children must be kept in a fixed place (on the shelf, in a bookcase). Children must be taught to use books with care: to look at books only on tables, to handle them only with clean hands, to turn the pages carefully, and to put them back where they belong after they are finished. If the teacher constantly reminds the children that she expects them to comply with these rules, the children will develop a proper attitude toward the care of books.

In almost every kindergarten there is a library containing books suitable for all the different age groups. These books are usually kept in the director's office or in the faculty room. There should be several copies of each book, and all books should be kept in order. The teacher must bring children into these rooms and show them the books. It is important to teach the children to address the director politely whenever requesting a book for the whole group. It must also be explained to them that the given book must be returned to its proper place on the designated date.

DRAWING, PAINTING, MODELING, AND CUTTING AND PASTING

Since the creative activities of the children during playtime and during recreation periods is of a different nature than that which takes place during the regular activity periods, it is essential that the type of supervision also differ. Children who seem to show a particular interest in drawing and modeling must be provided with the opportunity of using various materials and working at places specially assigned for these purposes. Such opportunities will provide a favorable setting for developing the children's special talents.

While drawing, modeling, or doing cutting and pasting outside of the fixed activity periods, the children talk among themselves. When a child speaks, he thinks more clearly and his project takes shape in his mind.

Besides paper, paints, colored pencils and clay, other educational materials may be put at the children's disposal for the purpose of forming patterns (various kinds of mosaics), coloring albums, cutouts, and collages. Independent and precise use of these materials leading to successful results is of great educational significance. Outdoors, various types of play are suggested: making patterns out of small stones or pine cones, drawing in the sand, modeling with snow.

The teacher supervises the creative activity of individual children during play and recreation periods, taking into consideration primarily the educational objectives, but also the individual characteristics and abilities of each child. Under no circumstances should material covered during the activity periods be repeated.

The teacher may supply incentive by suggesting that the child might play a particular game which involves painting or cutting things out. Having gathered together a small group of interested children, she shows how the work is to be done, without overlooking the fact that children must be given the chance subsequently to perform independently. The teacher answers the questions of the children and, whenever necessary, assists them.

From time to time, 5- and six-year-old children help the teacher to make something which is useful or is particularly needed by the group. They prepare decorations for a special assembly, decorate invitation notes, and so on. Children are thus immediately involved in useful work in which the quality of performance is of real significance.

It is very important gradually to train the children to have a sense of responsibility in the care of materials used by the whole group, and to teach them to use these materials carefully, both during activity periods and during playtime. The children must develop a proper attitude toward the materials which they are using.

Whenever a child expresses the desire to do some individual work with materials during playtime, full responsibility for gathering the materials and cleaning up afterwards rests with the child. Cupboards and other installations used for storing such materials as paints and clay, and for washing out brushes and drying cloths, must all be very accessible to the children.

SINGING, LISTENING TO MUSIC, AND DANCING

The musical training of the children will not be successful if limited to scheduled activity periods. For proper child development, it is very important that songs, games and dancing be included in his everyday life. Various types of activities such as games, study and manual work give ample opportunity for the inclusion of music in various ways.

In role-playing games, a child can be given the chance to sing or dance in connection with the role he is performing and to express in the game the impressions he has received in the course of the musical activity periods.

During playtime, when the children occupy themselves with the activities they enjoy the most, music can and must play a certain role. On the teacher's suggestion, the children can gather to listen to records, to sing or to dance a little, or listen for a while as the teacher herself sings. It is very important that during playtime children should join in circle dances and games which involve singing. Teachers should be satisfied only when the children have begun to sing and play musical games on their own.

To develop in the children an ear for music and a sense of rhythm, musical toys (xylophone, bells, rattles, triangles, drums, tambourines) should be widely used.

Songs, circle dances, and games involving singing must all be carried on extensively during the recreation periods in warm weather. While going for a walk, the teacher may start a marching song. Children pick up the tune, walk more briskly and more cheerfully, and breathe more deeply. While the children are resting, songs of a calmer character should be played or sung; as they wish the children may join in circle dances and play games involving music, thus making the walk more interesting and more meaningful.

Music is included in morning exercises and other physical education activities, from time to time. The children walk, run and perform certain movements to the accompaniment of a piano, accordion, or records.

Music, singing and dancing play a large role in dramatizations. For "magic lantern" theater and puppet theater, singing serves to illustrate the action. Moreover, songs themselves may be dramatized. It is desirable for the kindergartens to establish a tradition of presenting concerts which do not require any preparation on the part of the children, but during which the children hear their favorite songs and instrumental works, play their favorite games, and perform their favorite dances. Music may also be used at other occasions, such as when stories are being read or as an accompaniment to storytelling.

On trips, it is perfectly suitable to recall and sing some appropriate song. This deepens and adds emotional beauty to the impressions of the children.

So that songs and music may penetrate deeper into the children's outlook on life, it is important that parents, too, learn some of the children's songs and circle dances and become familiar with their records and musical toys.

In the kindergarten the musical aspect of education is the responsibility of the music instructor and the teacher. The music instructor conducts activities, prepares the children for participation in special celebrations and assemblies, organizes children's concerts, accompanies the puppet theater performances, and remains at all times in close consultation with the teachers regarding music and singing. The teacher participates in musical activities, introduces the music instructor to the various age groups and to the individual characteristics of the children. She also consults with her regarding methods of meeting the educational objectives involved. During playtime, the teacher sings with children their favorite songs, plays familiar musical games with them, and leads circle dances. Moreover, if a music instructor is not available, she herself conducts musical activities; should she be unable to play some instrument, records are used. Both the music instructor and the teacher arrange a schedule of musical activities and a program of concerts.

WORK TRAINING

Work training is a most important goal of the communist education of the young generation.

The work training program must begin before the children attain school age; thus laying the proper foundation is the responsibility of the kindergarten. The program's objectives are to stimulate in the children an interest in and a love for labor, to develop elementary work habits and skills, and to introduce the children to the work occupations of adults and to encourage the children's respect for them.

The performance of work by the children is considered the most important means of achieving a communistic education as well as being an activity which will provide an outlet for the natural active nature of a child. Its role is particularly important in the moral aspect of the children's upbringing. Work unifies children and gives them the preliminary habits of performing collective work as well as the ability to communicate with each other, work together in a friendly atmosphere, and be of assistance to each other. Through work they are taught a proper attitude toward discipline, independence, and initiative. They acquire the ability to overcome difficulties, develop perseverance in seeing a task through to the very end, and strive to attain a high standard of quality in their work.

Along with active games and physical exercises, physical work which is appropriate to their state of development is a *sine qua non* for the normal physical growth of children. It increases the body's resistance and develops precision and coordination.

Properly organized physical work will be reflected favorably in the children's mental development. Work requires attention, understanding and initiative. While the children are performing physical work, the teacher gives the children information about specific objects, materials, and tools necessary for the work, and explains their functions and how to use them.

The special characteristic of the work of children, in comparison with that performed by adults, lies in the fact that tangible material results may not always be achieved. The main value of the work resides in its educational influence.

Work performed by children, especially in the initial phases, closely resembles play. Therefore, the first work responsibilities of the children must be linked by the teacher to play. After playing, toys may be cleared away, the closets and shelves must be put in order, and broken toys must be mended. Such are the first work assignments given to children. For children of a very young age, work activity is even more limited; it does not go beyond various types of self-sufficiency. And even then, the 3- to 4-year-old children think of this activity as play.

It is well known that small children love to play with water, soap, and bubbles while washing up. In the same way, the shoes they are putting on become cars, and the spoons they use for soup become boats. Tactfully, the children must be distracted from playing while attending to their personal needs, and must be reminded that they must wash, dress, and eat neatly.

Older children also weave into their work some play elements. For example, 5- and 6-year-old children help in cleaning the playground. They rake away dry leaves, gather up small branches and stones, and cart them away on wheelbarrows. But they pretend it is not a wheelbarrow they are using to remove the rubbish but a truck. One of the children is the driver and the others are janitors. In another case, the children and teacher build a snow ship, bringing the necessary snow and giving the mass the shape of a ship. Children imagine they are the builders of a powerful seagoing ship, still in the docks. Or again, gathering the harvest from the school garden, the 6- to 7-year-old children pretend they are collective farmers.

The link between games and work is expressed in the fact that occasionally in the course of games, the need arises to make some kind of toy: binoculars for the captain, a bag for the mailman, a cashbox for the box office. The opposite occurs also: a toy, made during an activity period, suggests a game to the children.

In discussing the relationship between play and work with regard to preschool children, one must keep in mind the emotions of the children. It is possible that work presented as a game might help the children to accomplish a particular job with interest. But it would not be right to transform work into play on every occasion. Gradually, the work performed by the children becomes differentiated from other activities and assumes the character of an independent activity, with its own specific objectives, contents and type of organization. The children must be taught to look upon work as something indispensable, useful and vitally important.

The program includes three kinds of physical work for children:

(1) Routine housework: looking after oneself, being on duty in the dining room, assisting in preparing for activities, participating to a certain extent in cleaning up the playground and the building, and assisting in a very elementary way in the preparation of food.

(2) Working with nature: caring for and cultivating the indoor plants and green vegetables (in the winter), working in the flower and vegetable gardens, caring for small domestic animals in the nature corner and outside on the grounds, feeding the birds daily and cultivating plants which will supply grain for the birds, gathering the various grains, and so on.

Working with nature is the best way to familiarize the children with nature. In performing the work [which must be appropriate to their strength and ability] the children acquire real knowledge of animate and inanimate nature, and the foundations for a materialistic outlook are thus firmly laid. The teacher must make it his concern to see that children do not develop superstitions and prejudices.

It is very important for children from the time they are very young to protect and respect the things in nature which they find around them, whether it be plants, domestic animals, or birds.

(3) So-called handiwork: making toys, fabricating things out of paper, cloth, wood (little bags to hold seeds, boxes to hold bits of paper).

The nature and exact types of work to be performed by the various groups is worked out in the program, with consideration given to the age and level of ability of the children. Thus, in both the younger and middle groups, the elementary type of household work, consisting of attending to one's own needs (being self-sufficient), is placed first in order of importance. Housework performed in the interest of the whole group and work in nature occupy only a limited place in the work program at this age because of the inability of the children to perform these tasks; this is due to the weakness of their bodies, their lack of coordination, and their insufficient development of habitual action.

In the presence of the children, the teacher herself sets the nature corner in order, prepares materials for the activities, lessons, and play, repairs toys, and mends books. Her work thus becomes a factor in the educational process. At first the teacher merely invites the children to watch her while she works, telling the children as she works what she is doing and why, then suggesting that they admire the results. After a certain time, depending upon the children's attention, she gives them the opportunity to take part in the work, bring things that are needed, and so forth. Approval and praise encourage the children to perform still other little chores. If such acts are systematically repeated, the children will then get used to the work.

In the older and middle groups, the physical abilities of the children increase, as do their strength and dexterity. The children begin to understand the social significance of work as the idea of collectives and of cooperative relationships starts to take on meaning. Therefore, in these groups considerable attention is given in the program to housework performed for the entire collective and for work in nature. Work performed by the children for the entire collective is of a great educational value, since every single child has an interest in the fulfillment of the objectives and the obtaining of results. Here all have a single goal, the efforts of one and all are aimed at obtaining certain specific results, and each child individually as well as all the children together must answer for the fulfillment of the work with which they were entrusted. Collective work unites the children through shared experiences, and the joys they share when the results of the work are good.

For children in the younger groups it is better to organize for work in small subgroups. They tidy up toys, wash house plants, clean the snow from the paths, plant onions, water the flower beds, and so on. The teacher guides the children, shows what needs to be done and how they should go about it. She herself takes part in the general work. Each child performs the same jobs as his neighbor. There is no division of responsibilities as yet.

The scope of collective work is extended and is more varied: cleaning and tidying up the common room and the grounds, working with the plants in the vegetable garden, gathering flowers and making bouquets, repairing books and various equipment, and building large devices and structures for the games on the playground. If several children are entrusted with the work, then the teacher must agree with them as to the best and quickest way to get it accomplished. She helps distribute duties, explains what each must do, and indicates the most convenient and economical methods the child should use. Explanations should be brief but accurate, and easily understood.

When the children get used to working together smoothly, they should be entrusted with organizing their own work: agreeing on the distribution of the various tasks involved, determining the order in which things should be done, and securing all the things needed for the work. For example, children might be assigned to clean up a closet containing tools and materials: one child should be given the task of sorting out the things used in drawing, another that of checking and repairing boxes containing the table games, and a third that of organizing the books.

When general work is performed by the whole group, it is most practical to divide the children into several subgroups and assign to each subgroup a definite aspect of the total job. For example, whenever the grounds are to be cleaned up, some students will rake the dry leaves, others gather branches, and still others take away the branches and leaves in wheelbarrows. If some have finished their work before others, it is best if they then help out the others. The various tasks should be redistributed from time to time: those who were gathering leaves now transport them, and vice versa.

Such a division of labor is possible among older children; they are no longer so easily distracted from their work because their neighbors are busy doing something else. When the work is completed, the performance of each group (or that of individual children in certain cases) must be evaluated and recognition should be accorded to those who work hardest, those who performed their work quickly and efficiently and then helped others. Attention should also be called to those who were lazy and hid behind the backs of others or only gave orders without actually taking part in the work.

It is important to consider carefully particular combinations of children in assigning them to small groups, so that the children with limited ability and those lacking self-confidence have the opportunity of working with the more able and better organized children. The wishes of the children themselves, their friendships, and their general interest should also be taken into account.

Certain types of work being assigned for the first time and involving the communication of new knowledge and skills to the children can be performed during regular activity periods. This applies particularly to work with nature: for example, the first time the children plant onions, sow seeds, transplant seedlings, or cultivate around trees. But much is learned also outside of the activity periods. This especially applies to household chores: cleaning the common room, washing doll's clothes, and repairing various pieces of equipment and books (whenever necessary). But when work is performed during the regular activity periods, it will require serious attention and careful supervision on the part of the teacher.

It must be stressed that the nature of the tasks assigned to the children and the corresponding skills they acquire will change in practice, according to the location of the kindergarten (city, country), the surrounding environment, and unique conditions of the kindergarten.

To bring about the success of the work-training program, the observance of the following educational principles is essential:

(1) First of all, the proper conditions must be established in which the children will be able to work: a place must be determined and time allotted in the daily schedule; equipment must be obtained which is suited to the strength and level of ability of the children; healthful conditions must be assured: cleanliness, fresh air, sufficient lighting in the building, work assignments which are appropriate to the physical strength of each group, correct posture, frequent changes of position, and adequate physical exercise.

(2) The development within the group of a happy working atmosphere, in which each child derives a sense of satisfaction from participating in work and seeing results.

6-year-old children must see for themselves where their help is required, get to work without being reminded, and bring the work to completion.

The work training of the children will be successful if they perform tasks systematically, not merely occasionally.

Some chores must be done daily (taking care of the house plants and the animals, feeding the birds), while other chores, although less frequently but just as systematically, should be done over the course of the whole year (washing doll's clothing, cleaning the closets and shelves where the toys and table games are stored, repairing toys and books).

In groups of 5- and 6-year-old children, the interesting tasks must alternate with others so that not a single week will go by without any general work activity.

Finally, there are seasonal things requiring varying amounts of time: for example, gathering flower seeds (sewing little seed bags, gathering seeds, sorting out the largest and healthiest, putting them away in bags, making appropriate labels with drawings), cultivating vegetables in the garden plots, and so forth.

(3) The general working atmosphere among the adult personnel of the kindergarten should be friendly, well-organized, and cooperative.

Special significance is attached to the example given by the teacher, her conscientious attitude toward her chosen profession, her embracing of the physical aspect of the work, and her respect for people working in other occupations.

ACTIVITIES

In the new program of instruction in the kindergarten, a definite part of the curriculum is scheduled to be covered in formal activity periods. The teachers communicate to the children new skills and knowledge, organize and to a certain extent systematize their life experiences, teach the children to relate stories, count, draw, model, sing, dance, listen to music, walk correctly, run, and jump. The children develop the ability to sit still for a considerable span of time and to be attentive. They are taught to observe and to listen, to answer questions, and to ask questions themselves.

The quality of work is determined by the results: to what extent have the children developed specific habits and skills; how are their drawings, their talks, their singing, and so on; how is their behavior, their discipline, their mental activity, and their willingness and desire to obey the instructions given by the teacher.

When planning and conducting activities, it is important to always bear in mind one of the most important objectives of learning: developing mental alertness, independent thinking, initiative, and the ability to apply in a practical way the skills and habits which have been acquired. If the children merely learn to obey the teacher's instructions mechanically, without understanding and without any emotional response on their part, then the instruction will not have any lasting effects on the child's development.

In order to encourage mental activity during the activity periods, the teacher must prepare questions which will require independent thinking, and not merely mechanical or stereotyped responses, and should seek full answers from the children rather than short, single-word responses. Teaching the children artifically contrived phrases with structures uncharacteristic of the standard spoken Russian language will have a detrimental effect on their learning of the native tongue and will impoverish their speech. It is important that children think, remember, compare, contrast, discuss what they have noticed and observed, and convey their thoughts in rich expressive language.

The children's mental activity must not be restricted by the use of a limited selection of materials and equipment, as vigorous thinking must be stimulated in the children if the goals set before them are to be attained. For example, suppose we are getting ready to teach the children to count up to five and familiarize the children with the digit five. We must prepare and distribute the appropriate educational materials, making certain that the number of objects of each kind exceeds five (seven rings, eight mushrooms). When a large pile of a given type of object lies before the child (he does not know how many) and he has to count off only five, then he actually counts and does not merely repeat the numbers automatically. Similar examples could be set forth concerning teaching the children about colors, shapes, plants, and so on.

For a more successful assimilation of knowledge of the human environment and nature, concrete materials and visual equipment must be utilized. In teaching children of preschool age, the following types of concrete materials and visual equipment are used: natural objects (household implements, branches, leaves, flowers, fruits of various plants), pictures, educational slides and films, drawings, and special educational materials. With the help of visual materials, the children acquire knowledge first-hand and not simply through verbal descriptions.

In their instruction, the teachers make frequent and extensive use of models and patterns which the children must follow very carefully. The teacher prepares a model drawing or structure or contrives a model story. Teaching with the help of models yields good results. However, for the various age groups, and at the various different stages in the process of assimilation of the program, the character of the models changes. If children are being presented a problem for the first time (for example, to make a decorative motif on a round napkin) then the children must be given a complete, finished model, and it must be analyzed with the children—which pattern is in the middle, how the pattern is done at the edge. As the children learn techniques and ways of performing the work and as their ability develops, it becomes less necessary to give a finished model or to indicate all the steps to follow from beginning to end. A verbal description might be adequate, or it might suffice simply to show a partly finished model or two or three models from which the children may make a selection.

The teacher's evaluation of the children's achievements must in no case be formal ("You did it right, but you didn't") or subjective ("I like this, but I don't like that"); it must be both educational and elucidating. The child must know what is good and what is not quite so good; conscientious efforts by the children must always be stressed.

The choice of activities must correspond to the special characteristics of the children's age. It must be remembered that children tire easily, that their attention span is limited, that they are emotional, that their experiences in life are not extensive, and that their ability to copy and reproduce things is only partially developed.

If the teacher's speech is dry or monotonous, if the tasks and approaches are too routine, if the character of the program materials is dull, and if the teacher lacks the knowledge and ability to link up the contents of the curriculum with the children's experiences and interests, then the general result will be boredom, a lowering of mental activity, and the failure of the children to acquire satisfactory skills and habits. To avoid this, the teacher must always keep in mind the level of knowledge and skills of the children in the particular group, and the materials selected for use in the program must be precisely suitable for them; this applies to instruction involving listening, answering questions, oral self-expression, handicrafts, educational games, and so forth. For example, in activities related to decorative painting, the children listen to the teacher, answer questions, examine samples of national art, and then paint.

Activities may include also poems, stories, and riddles which tie in closely with the contents of the program. Such things add interest and help the children to learn more thoroughly the skills and materials they are being taught.

Children develop rapidly in the preschool years. During this period, a difference of one year is of great importance. Even children of the same age range may differ significantly in their physical and mental progress. Hence, the same methods cannot be applied to children in the 3-, 4-, 5-, and 6-year-old groups.

The youngsters are not formally presented with the educational goals, especially since the instruction occurs most frequently in the form of play and games; at the end of an activity, no formal "analysis" is made scrutinizing the children's performance, nor does the teacher say, "Now let us draw conclusions and sum up what we have learned (in the manner of certain preschool teachers)." Teaching during activities is conducted without the children being aware of the process; the instruction should give them pleasure through the involvement of game elements and educational materials. The adoption of a dry, formal tone by the teacher when addressing the youngsters is completely unnecessary and to be avoided.

When conducting an activity for the entire group, certain sanitary requirements must be observed without fail: the room should be well aired, the tables should be suitably placed in relation to the windows, chairs and tables should be selected to be appropriate for the size of each child, and the children must be arranged so that they are all able to see and hear satisfactorily (that is, those with visual or hearing defects must be placed closer to the teacher).

The children must acquire the habit of sitting correctly at the table (holding their body, head and shoulders erect, not hunching over). Throughout the activity, the teacher should observe the position and posture of each child, reminding them of the correct position or, without speaking, carefully correcting a child's posture. It is advisable, when the children are drawing, constructing, doing appliqué work, or modeling, to suggest every fifteen minutes or so that they stand up and, without leaving the tables, straighten their backs and stretch, breathe deeply, and do a few arm exercises.

It is extremely important to insure adequate lighting in the class-

Suggested Schedule of Weekly Activities

FALL-WINTER SEMESTER

Activity	SECOND YOUNGER GROUP (3 TO 4 YEARS OF AGE)	MIDDLE GROUP (4 TO 5 YEARS OF AGE)
	Number of Times per Week	
Familiarization with environment: native language, literature	2	2
Arithmetic	1[a]	1
Drawing	1	1
Modeling	½[b]	½[b]
Appliqué work	½[b]	½[b]
Musical training	2	2
Exercises and active games	1	1

[a]In second semester.
[b]Scheduled only twice a month.

rooms. The kindergarten staff must insure that the children's eyesight does not become weaker during the time they spend at the kindergarten.

To assist the teacher, we will suggest a model schedule of activities for a one-week period.

In the indicated groups, daily activities are conducted after breakfast, for ten to fifteen minutes for the younger group and fifteen to twenty minutes for the middle group. Twice a week and as a supplement to the morning activity, an activity is held during the outdoor recreation period or after the afternoon nap.

It is not advisable to have the supplementary activities scheduled for exactly the same days throughout the school year. Depending upon the program and the time of year, the teacher will indicate on the calendar the particular activity which from the methodological point of view seems to be wisest for a given period; for example, a walk or an educational game to reinforce particular skills or knowledge. Moreover, during the outdoor recreation period exercises may be conducted to develop certain physical skills and time may be devoted to musical training.

In the school preparatory group there are 13 activity periods a week, each lasting 30 minutes; therefore one day a week there will be three activities. We recommend that the third activity be conducted outdoors; it may be a trip somewhere or a nature walk, a visit to the city, exercises, or active games.

From May to August inclusive, in all groups, there is one activity a day. Among the weekly activities are included:

Familiarization with the environment, native language, and artistic literature
Physical education
Musical training
Drawing and painting
Modeling
Construction

FAMILIARIZATION WITH THE ENVIRONMENT AND INSTRUCTION IN THE NATIVE LANGUAGE

Familiarizing the children with their environment is absolutely necessary for the psychological development of the children and for the development of their personalities. The teacher must enrich the child's perspective through knowledge of objects, people and their work, and animate and inanimate nature. This will enhance the development of the child's mental ability and lead to improved speech. An understanding of the environment is valuable when it is closely tied in with developing the child's sensitivity: love, sympathy, goodwill toward all, respect for workers in all occupations, pride in one's countrymen and the traditions of one's country, and the happiness derived from cooperative work. The process of becoming familiar with their environment must stimulate in the children a desire to discover and learn about new things and respect for the products of human labor.

The program outlines for the teachers the knowledge and skills to be taught to each age group. All objectives indicated in the plan have great significance in the mental and moral education of the children. Familiarization with these objectives will lead to an understanding of the most basic characteristics of our society and to an understanding of the role played by labor: All the objects around us are created by persistant conscientious work, all the comforts in our life are made possible by the work of people, and through the labor of many people nature is transformed. Any form of labor for the good of all must be thought of by the children as a joy, as an absorbing and indispensable life activity.

In the process of discovering their environment, the speech of the children evolves: they recognize objects, their properties, and the terms applied to them; they learn to express opinions, to ask and answer questions, and to describe what they see. In the programs planned for the

Suggested Schedule of Weekly Activities

FALL-WINTER SEMESTER

Activity	OLDER GROUP (5 TO 6 YEARS OLD)[a]	SCHOOL PREPARATORY GROUP (6 TO 7 YEARS OLD)
	Number of Times per Week	
Familiarization with environment: native language, literature	5	5
Arithmetic	1	1
Drawing	1	2
Modeling	1	½
Appliqué	½	½
Construction	½	1
Musical training	2	2
Exercises and active games	1	1

[a]For the older group: two activities a day, the first lasting 25–30 minutes and the second, 15–20 minutes.
[b]Scheduled only twice a month.

younger groups, materials related to familiarizing the children with their environment (nature and surrounding people) and with their native language are described together, a fact which reflects special characteristics in the development of conscious activity by preschool children at this age. For older groups, the program material is differentiated, i.e., the material related to familiarization with the environment and that related to studying the native language are separate units.

In the program are outlined the elementary skills and knowledge which the children are taught in a more or less systematic way in the course of activity periods.

In accordance with the wishes expressed by teachers, that part of the yearly instructional program related to familiarizing the children with their environment is divided into quarters. This approach provides for the repetition and reinforcement of skills; that is, teachers must plan for regular reviews of the material already covered.

In the following brief outline, we offer typical methodological approaches to each topic mentioned in the program. In familiarizing the children with a particular aspect of the environment, one should begin informally using a direct approach; the children are given the opportunity of observing the object or phenomenon: looking, listening, feeling, touching, smelling. If it is impossible to show the object itself, then teachers must use visual aids (pictures, slides, films).

The examples given do not include lists of literary works which are of value in helping the children to understand surrounding reality, but the teacher can make up for this easily on her own, since the program itself includes lists of suitable literature for each group.

Using her own judgment the teacher will select from the various trips, talks, slides, films, and educational games those which she considers are most suitable for introducing an environmental object or phenomenon; the others are then utilized in the following quarters for reviewing and supplementing the children's knowledge.

THE SECOND YOUNGER GROUP: FAMILIARIZATION WITH THE ENVIRONMENT AND THE NATIVE LANGUAGE

Activities include: Inspection of the common room and the objects it contains (furniture, dishes, toys, bedding); inspection of the cloakroom, the corridors, and the main hall; inspection of the grounds and the shrubbery; introduction to the personnel of the kindergarten and their work; observation of domestic animals; story telling by the teacher; discussions through pictures: "The Cat and the Kittens," "The Dog and the Puppies," "The Hens" (from S. A. Veretennikova, "Domestic Animals"), "The Family" and "The Vegetable Garden" (from F. F. Sovetkin and V M. Chistyakov, "Pictures of Rural Areas for Kindergartens"), "Our Tanya" (by O. I. Solovera); "Winter Sports" (from O. I. Solovera, "The Seasons"), "In the *Kolkhoz* Garden" (from O. A. Frolova and O. I. Solovera, "Pictures of Rural Areas for the Kindergarten").

Educational games for improving knowledge about household objects and domestic animals, and for increasing the active use of the related vocabulary; training in the proper pronunciation of standard speech; educational games involving sound imitation and the reading of nursery rhymes.

THE MIDDLE GROUP

Familiarization with the Kindergarten

Inspection of the kindergarten building: the rooms of the older groups, the main hall, and the corridors.
Examination of household objects.

Observation of the work of the kindergarten staff (how the assistant washes dishes, how the cook cleans the vegetables, and so forth).

Talk given by the teacher about the work of the kindergarten staff.

Educational games to reinforce knowledge about the objects located in the kindergarten and their properties; the names of objects, colors, sizes, and shapes.

Discussion of the picture entitled "The Kindergarten."

Familiarization with the Means of Transportation

Trip to the nearest street (to observe a bus or streetcar).

Trip to a railroad (to watch a train go by).

Trip to a river (to observe ships, launches, and little boats).

Discussion of the picture "On The River" (from the series "Pictures of Rural Life for the Kindergarten").

Familiarization with Nature

Trips to parks and woods with specific purposes in mind.

Observation of fish in an aquarium and subsequent discussion.

Showing of the slides entitled "Domestic Animals."

Observation of a bird in a cage.

Observation of field and garden flowers and subsequent discussion.

Talk given by the teacher about the seasons of the year.

Planting of onions.

Planting of radishes and peas (in boxes or in the ground).

Educational games to improve the children's recognition of vegetables and fruits from their appearance, their taste, and their feel, as well as from pictures.

Training in the proper pronunciation of standard speech: exercises for the development of the speech organs, educational games involving sound imitation, the reading of nursery rhymes, and educational games for the development of listening comprehension.

OLDER GROUP

Familiarization with the Kindergarten

The Preparation of Food

Inspection of the kitchen.

Conversation with the cook and observation of his work.

Discussion of the work performed by the cook and the other kitchen help.

Sewing Clothes

Observation of the work of the kindergarten staff: sewing underwear and outer clothing for the children.

Inspection of various items of clothing and discussion on this subject.

Talks given by the children about their mothers or grandmothers sewing underwear and other clothing.

Familiarization with the Home Town

The Neighborhood

Trips to nearby streets.

Familiarization with the appearance of various buildings (factories, schools, garages).

Trips to city streets just before holidays.

The Postal System

Trip to the nearest post office.

Inspection of a mail box.

Observation of how mail is dropped into the mailbox and how it is collected.

Meeting with the mailman.

Discussion of the postal system; composition of a letter to children in some other kindergarten.

Building Construction

Trip to the nearest construction site.

Talks given by the teacher about the things workers are constructing in their home town.

Trips to areas where trees, bushes, and flowers are being planted (along a street or boulevard or in a garden).

Discussion of the picture "At the Construction Site" (from L. A. Penevskaya and E. I. Radina, "Pictures for Kindergartens").

Means of Transportation

Trips through the streets to observe buses, streetcars, trains, taxis, bicycles, trucks (whatever is available in the home town).

Trips to bus or streetcar stops.

Trips to railroads.

Talks given by the teacher on the topic "How People Travel"; showing of the slides entitled "How People Travel."

Familiarization with the Occupations of the Collective Farm Workers

Trip to a grocery store.

Trip to a field or a meadow during the haying season.

Talks given by the teacher about the way in which the *kolkhoz* (collective farm) laborers do their work.

Showing of the slides entitled "At the Collective Farm."

Discussion about vegetables.

Discussions about the following pictures: "The Cow and the Calf," "The Horse and the Foal," "Sheep," "Rabbits," "Geese and Ducks" (from the series "Domestic Animals").

Educational games to improve recognition of the different vegetables by their appearance, their taste and their feel.

Familiarization with Nature

Trips to a park or to the woods at various seasons of the year, a trip to a river.

Observation of the planting of trees and bushes.

Inspection of branches and leaves, followed by a discussion of trees.

Observation of flowers, followed by a talk.

Observation of mushrooms followed by a talk.

Observation of insects (beetles, butterflies) and talk about them.

Stories about wild animals (based on pictures).

Discussion of the picture entitled "The Garden" (from the series "Domestic Animals").

Teaching Oral Self-Expression (Storytelling)

Paraphrases of fairy tales: "The Castle," "The Doughnut," "The Bear and the Little Girl," and "The Wolf and the Seven Kids."

Paraphrases of stories: "The Fire Dogs" by L. N. Tolstoy; "Is That the Way to Play?" by N. Kalinina, and by the same author, "How the Stinging Nettle Burned Sasha," "About the Beetle," and "Helpers"; also "Block on Block" by Ya. Taitz.

Telling of stories based on pictures: "Spring on the Boulevard" and "Summer in the Park" (from the series "The Seasons"), "Kindergarten on the Collective Farm" (from the series "Pictures of Rural Life for the Kin-

dergarten"), "The Cat and the Kittens" (from the Series "Domestic Animals"), "Mommy's Helper."

Descriptions of walks, trips, games.

Training in the proper pronunciation of standard speech.

Educational games to develop auditory phonemic discrimination:
"Echo," "Guess What I Said."

Educational games involving sound imitation and nursery rhymes.

Educational games for the formation of correct grammatical speech.

THE SCHOOL-PREPARATORY GROUP

Familiarization with the Home Town

Trips through various streets.

Trips to the main square.

Trips to the river.

Trips to monuments to outstanding people and to the graves of those
who gave up their lives for the freedom and happiness of the people; the
placing of flowers there.

Trips to buildings of interest (clubs, theaters, factories).

Talks by the teacher about the home town.

Discussion of the home town.

Storytelling by the children based on the theme "How to Get from
Home to the Kindergarten" (describing the way to the kindergarten).

Showing the slides entitled "Petya's Letter."

Trips through the streets of the town on days prior to special celebrations and holidays.

Familiarization with the School and the Pioneers

Trips to the nearest school with the purpose of inspecting the building,
the playground attached to it, and so on; discussion about things observed during the trips.

Familiarization with the Means of Transportation

Trips through the streets (to watch city transportation), to the
railroad, to a dock; oral descriptions by the children of what they have
seen during the trips.

Discussion of the picture "At the Dock."

Showing of the slides entitled "How People Travel."

Showing of the film entitled "The Young Travelers" and the film "What the Bus Told Us."

Discussion of the topic "How People Travel."

Familiarization with the Occupation of the Collective Farm Workers

Trip to a field in the fall and in the spring; to a fruit orchard or to an animal breeding farm in the summer.

Discussion about the things observed on the trip.

Talk given by the teacher about the growing of wheat by collective farmers.

Showing the slides entitled "At the Collective Farm."

Showing the films entitled "Visiting a Collective Farm" and "A Jug of Milk."

Discussion based on the pictures "Native Fields," "At the Docks," and "Warm Reception" (from the series "Pictures of Rural Life for Kindergartens"); "The Collective Farm Road" (from the series "Pictures for Kindergartens" by F. F. Sovetkin and V. M. Chistyakin); "The Sheep" (from the series "Domestic Animals"); and others concerning animals or animals and their young.

Familiarization with Nature

Numerous trips for nature study (several times to the place at different times of the year), to the park, the woods, to a river, a pond, a field, a meadow, a bird sanctuary.

Bird watching (pigeons, sparrows, crows, swallows).

Discussion about trees (examining and comparing branches, leaves, fruits).

Examination of house plants followed by discussion.

Discussion of the animals that inhabit the forest (based on pictures).

Showing of the slides entitled "Domestic Animals," "In the Woods" and "By the Pond."

Showing of the films entitled "Children are Friends of the Birds," "In the Zoo," and "Where Does the Table Come From."

Grafting of house plants.

Sowing of vegetable and flower seeds.

Gathering of the harvest in the vegetable garden; gathering of flower seeds.

Educational games to reinforce knowledge about plants, birds, domestic and wild animals.

Our Homeland

Talks given by the teacher about Moscow—based on pictures and scenes of Moscow.

Showing of slides entitled "In Our Moscow," "About the Subway—for Children," and "I Live in Uzbekistan."

Showing of the film entitled "Unusual Travelers."

Discussions and composing letters to children in a kindergarten in one of the other republics of the U.S.S.R.

Discussion based on the pictures, "Our Little Friends" (from the series "Pictures for Kindergartens").

Trips to the monument of V I. Lenin (placing of flowers) and to places connected with the life and activity of V. I. Lenin.

Talks given by the teacher about V. I. Lenin (based on pictures).

Training in Oral Self-Expression (Storytelling)

Paraphrasing fairy tales: "Little Red Riding Hood," "Geese and Swans," "The Snow-Maiden."

Paraphrasing the following stories: "The Fire Dogs," by L. N. Tolstoy; "The Chicken and the Ducklings" and "The Four Wishes," by K. D. Ushinsky; "The Talking Rock," by M. Prishvin; "The Snowball," by N. Kalinina; "Mill-cakes and Cottage Cheese," by L. Voronkova.

Telling stories based on the personal lives of the children (suggested themes: "What we did yesterday during the walk;" "What I did while I was on duty;" "How we spent the holiday;" "How we raised chickens;" "What I saw on the way to the kindergarten").

Creative stories (the children making up stories based on subjects suggested by the teachers, for example, "The little boy who found a puppy;" "The adventures of a kitten in the kindergarten;" "Animals on a visit to Belka and Strelka").

Telling of stories based on pictures: "The Balloon Flew Away," "The New One," "Presents for Mommy on the Eighth of March," "At the Demonstration" (from the series "Pictures for Kindergartens"); "They Brought the New Year's Tree" (from the series "Pictures of Rural Life for the Kindergarten").

Training in the Proper Pronunciation of Standard Speech

Education games for the development of auditory phonemic discrimination: "Echo"; "Guess What I Said."

Educational games for exercising the speech organs: games involving sound imitation, nursery rhymes, and tongue twisters.

Educational games for the development of correct grammatical speech.

LITERATURE

Literature for children contributes to the achievement broad educational goals and to the development of all aspects of a child's personality. It adds breadth and depth to the child's knowledge of people and life in general, and enriches the emotional experiences of the child. The feelings, experiences, and moods aroused in the children in the process of listening to literary works are the basis for the educational effect produced by the artistic imagery and expression of literature.

It is important for the child to experience joy and satisfaction in listening to poetry, stories, and fairy tales. The power to respond emotionally is an indication of the awakening ability to perceive the esthetic quality of a piece of literature, that is, to understand it as a work of art. It is also important that along with producing feelings in the children the literature helps to develop their ability to think and prompts them to ask questions; it is also important for a child not only to be interested in the facts and events about which he has heard, but also for him to try to penetrate deeper into the meaning of what he hears, whenever a story is told or read to him. If a literary work is fully and deeply perceived by the child, then it will have a real educational value.

Teachers develop the children's ability to listen attentively and to consciously strive to get the meaning of a literary work. These goals are attained by gradually increasing the challenge of the literary works, from simply exposing children of early preschool age to the habit of listening in groups all the way to developing the ability of the older children to evaluate correctly the actions or deeds of the heroes in the stories. Educating children through literature involves two objectives: teaching the children to listen to literary works so as to be able 1) to reproduce them, that is, be able to recite them by heart (in the case of poetry) or 2) paraphrase them (stories and fairy tales).

Reciting material learned by heart and paraphrasing require the acquisition of certain skills and the ability to speak expressively. These skills are described in the program of instruction, which indicates the specific requirements related to diction and to breathing. Other requirements, also outlined in the program, pertain to reading with comprehension and expressive intonation.

The education of children through literature cannot be separate from the graphic arts, since children's books combine the artistic word with the artistic illustration.

Illustrations, as a special form of art, help the children to assimilate the text more easily and more deeply, and also facilitate memorization; they depict the hero of a given literary work and the setting of the action. Very frequently, illustrations complete the text and help to present that which the author may possibly have only hinted at. Therefore, book illustrations must be examined with the children frequently; the teacher should stimulate them with questions and remarks to express their own opinions about the drawings, and thus teach the children to study and understand graphic art, and thereby develop their esthetic sensitivity.

TEACHING ARITHMETIC TO CHILDREN

Teaching children arithmetic requires a systematic and sequential approach in working with each age group, as well as articulation between groups.

In the 3-year-old group, preparatory work must be done which does not yet involve teaching the children to count using the actual word for the numerals. In this group, the basic objective is to get the children to form the idea of a set as an aggregate of like elements. The children must be taught to see the boundaries of a set, to distinguish all the elements in a set, to compare the elements of one set with the elements of another, and to recognize the equality or inequality of sets. Inasmuch as sets may be represented not only by objects but by sounds, the children must be taught to compare the elements of a set consisting of sounds with the elements of a set consisting of objects. Such preliminary work will stimulate in the children an interest in distinguishing between sets and in designating them by numbers; that is, it will arouse the children's interest in learning arithmetic through the use of numerals.

The basic objective in the middle group consists in teaching the children to count by the numerals. Experience shows that in groups of 4-year-old children, it is quite possible to teach the children to count up to five.

Besides learning the actual process of counting the children absorb the underlying meaning, that is, that counting results in a number which expresses a sum total. In teaching the children to count by the numerals, the teacher must make them aware of the difference between the sum total which is the result of counting and the actual process of counting. To make children understand why one set is designated as three geese and another as two geese, counting must always be taught using as a basis the contrast of the elements in one set with the elements in another; then the children observe visually the inequality of the two sets, consider the quantity of elements in one set and contrast this quantity with that of elements in the other set. It must be remembered that the essence of the operation of counting lies in establishing a one-to-one correspondence between elements of different sets; thus instruction of the children, even at the age of 3 years, must begin from this point of view. When adults count, they are actually applying the very same process of establishing one-to-one correspondences, but one of the sets involved now happens to be the series of natural numbers. Therefore, in the early stages of instruction, it is important always to compare two sets of concrete elements which may be designated by adjacent numerals. Such a comparison will enable the children to understand why the same geese are in one case designated "three geese" while in another case they are designated "two geese." Children begin to understand which of the adjacent numbers is the larger and which is the smaller.

By counting sets of objects which are equal in quantity but differ in the size of their respective objects, the children begin to understand that the number designating a set is independent of the spatial qualities of the objects in the set; they gradually begin to comprehend that a number merely reflects the quantity of elements (that is, the number is the power index of the set, as one would say in the theory of arithmetic).

4-year-old children learn to count not only objects, but also sounds and movements, and they learn to count objects by feel alone; in other words, they learn to count with various different sensory organs involved in the analysis. Thus, as the children get further and further away from sets of concrete objects, they gradually begin to grasp the abstract concept of a number.

In the older group, the concept of a number as the power index of a set is further developed, as the children develop greater ability in computational operations. 5-year-old children can master with relative ease the task of counting up to ten. Here again, the instruction must be based on the comparison of sets designated by adjacent numbers and on the establishment of one-to-one correspondences between their elements. Thus, the children learn on the basis of this type of perception which of the consecutive numbers is the larger, and which is the smaller. It thus becomes possible to get children to understand in a practical way the relationship between consecutive numbers. On the basis of this type of correspondence between the elements of sets, designated by the first five digits, the children learn to determine in a practical manner the equality of different sets and also to contrast two sets, one of which is either smaller or larger than the other by one element. Such comparisons between consecutive numbers based on contrasting the elements of the sets are conducted with the help of various "analyzers" (clapping hands one time fewer than the number of dolls on the shelf; moving one toy forward every time a sound is heard,—then counting the toys and announcing the number of claps).

Working with the first five digits, the children in the older group begin to penetrate the meaning of realtionships between numbers, not only when they are given in the natural order, but also in the reverse order; in this way they are approaching the study of numbers themselves. First they must be taught to understand the relationships between consecutive numbers (greater and smaller); then it becomes possible, using the same first five digits, to show the quantitative aspect of the numbers in terms of units, by utilizing sets of concrete objects and stressing their composition in terms of separate elements.

Thus, in the older group the children, while working only with the first five digits, begin to approach the study of the relationships between consecutive numbers and the relationship between numbers and units (the quantitative aspect of numbers in terms of units), and both these aspects of instruction are not only extremely elementary and basic but also most appropriate in terms of the work which has preceded.

Further development of this work in the school-preparatory group proceeds along the lines of having the children assimilate the relationships between consecutive digits up to ten, when presented both in the natural and in the reverse order; different relationships between consecutive digits are established ("by how much is one of the consecutive digits greater or less than the other?"), and the children assimilate the quantitative aspect of the remaining digits, from six to ten. On this basis, it becomes possible to differentiate the concepts of the cardinal and ordinal numbers, which the children normally will already be using, but the difference between which they do not perceive. Gradually, the children develop an understanding of the series of natural numbers as a definite system.

Relying on these concepts, the children in the school preparatory group can now freely progress to a new aspect of numerical study, that of computation. Within the sequence of preparation for this activity, it is important to show the children that any number can be formed out of two smaller numbers, each by itself designating a set. This leads to an understanding of the special characteristic of a sum and the way in which a sum thought of in these terms differs from a set thought of merely in terms of the units it contains.

The study of the formation of numbers from two smaller numbers represents the crucial step in the study of computation. In studying the composition of numbers in terms of two smaller numbers it suffices perfectly well to limit ourselves to the first five digits. There is no need to overburden the children with material that is not absolutely necessary for the immediate step in instruction and development. A knowledge of the composition of the second five digits only becomes necessary at the end of the second quarter in school, when the children become involved in addition and subtraction problems which transcend the first ten numbers.

At the conclusion of their study of the counting operation, the children become familiar with numerals as representations of numbers, a concept which comes easily to them and which may be introduced right along with their study of the formation of numbers from two smaller numbers. With this ends the children's study of counting, a process which is always concerned with sets of concrete objects, perceived through various analyzers; this study is thus differentiated from the new computational activity in which the children will be engaging in the future. From this point on, the work of computing will always be connected with numbers, which must be added or subtracted from each other (and later on, multiplied or divided). The methods and approaches to be used in this computational work are no longer qualitatively the same as those used by the children in counting, and they must therefore be taught to the children. These techniques are many and varied and must be introduced in a definite prescribed sequence. The task of the kindergarten is only to get children acquainted with the simplest of them all, that is, the techniques involved in adding or subtracting by units. These techniques are based on all the work conducted previously and described in the preceding sections of this commentary.

But completely new problems arise when introducing the children to computational work. These arise in connection with teaching the children to solve arithmetic problems. Here again, a gradual approach must be adopted and the continuity of the process maintained.

First of all, it is imperative that the children understand the essence of an arithmetical problem: (a) that they understand how an arithmetical problem differs from a story or a riddle; (b) that they comprehend the structure of the problem—what is given and what is asked for; (c) that they understand that in a problem quantitative relationships in the environment are always reflected, and that these relationships comprise the main ingredients in the problem; (d) that they understand that the question posed in the problem represents an integral part of the problem, and suggests to the solver where to look for the answer. For this, it is necessary to grasp the relationships between the numerical data in the problem, and to reflect these relationships in the formulation of a specific arithmetical operation. In performing the arithmetical operation of addition, the children should no longer use the previous method (counting up the elements of both addends) but the new computational technique, whereby since the first addend is known there is no necessity to count it up, and the child, relying on knowledge of the quantitative composition of the second given number in terms of units, then adds it on to the first addend by units. This process is based on what the child already has learned about the realtionship between consecutive numbers presented in the natural order. In doing subtraction, it would be wrong to limit the children simply to taking away, literally, the number indicated by the minuend and then counting up the number left to get the difference. Rather, the subtrahend should be divided into units, a process with which the children are already familiar (the quantitative composition of a number in terms of units), and then the subtrahend is counted off one by one, again a process familiar to the children inasmuch as they have learned the realtionship between consecutive numbers not only when presented in the natural order but also in the reverse order. Bearing all these things in mind, one can see that it is wrong to tackle all aspects of the program objectives simultaneously; a certain sequence is essential.

During the first stage, it is best to introduce the children to the structure of the problem. During the second stage, one should teach the formulation of arithmetical operations; in the third stage, the children are taught to use the computational techniques.

During the first and second stages, out of all the numbers from one to ten only the number one should be used as the second addend or as the minuend, and it is only during the third stage, when computational techniques are being learned, that the second addend or the minuend may be the number two, three, or even sometimes four. In this way the children learn to handle those cases in which a smaller number is being subtracted from a larger one. This will enable the children to learn those computational techniques and approaches which are practiced in school, and will insure that their preparation is fully integrated with the school work to come.

During the period of preparation for learning computational techniques, the children's concept of the series of natural numbers as a definite system is reinforced. The children give the numbers consecutively out loud, both forward and backward, name the numbers up to a given number or after an indicated number, and find the missing number among those named (four, five, seven, eight, and so on).

In this way, the entire arithmetic program studied in the kindergarten represents a domain of knowledge and skills which are of gradually increasing complexity and are presented sequentially, and which contribute first to developing the ability of the children to count (the various methods and approaches to counting), then to aiding them in forming the concept of a number through the notion of distinguishable sets, and finally to developing elementary computational skills based on solved arithmetical problems.

It is only when the sequential pattern and systematic nature of the structure of the program has been understood, that the teacher of any given group will know where to begin the work with her children and what material to use from that covered in the preceding group. She can then easily maintain the gradual rate of progress in the development of her children, and guide their development.

In accordance with the indicated principle of gradually increasing the complexity of the work, the program is subdivided to be applied specifically in the four age groups.

*Suggested Schedule of Arithmetic Activity Periods for the Second Younger Group
(prenumerical instruction of the children in the second semester)*

TOPICS	SUGGESTED NUMBER OF ACTIVITY PERIODS
1. Forming quantitative groups out of individual objects.	3
2. Finding sets of objects and individual objects in the environment (at first, a specific setting is provided, but then this is generalized to any environment at all: the room, the outdoors).	3
3. Comparing quantities of objects by establishing one-to-one correspondences between the objects of one and the objects of the other; arranging the objects in rows.	6
4. Working with the concept of a set of auditory stimuli (hand claps, taps with a hammer) and verifying that the number of circles depicted on a card is the same as the number of sounds perceived without actually counting; designating sets by numbers.	2
5. Comparing quantities on the basis of one-to-one correspondences of the objects, and determining whether one quantity is larger, smaller, or equal to the other.	3

*Suggested Year Schedule of Arithmetic Activity Periods for the Older Group
(instruction in counting with the use of words for the numerals—from the beginning of
the school year)*

TOPICS	SUGGESTED NUMBER OF ACTIVITY PERIODS
1. Demonstrating the technique of counting by comparing sets of concrete objects arranged in rows, with the objects placed side by side opposite each other. Teaching the children to count, and determining on the basis of a comparison between sets of objects which is greater and which is less.	6
2. Forming a quantitative group of objects on the basis of a model.	2

TOPICS	SUGGESTED NUMBER OF ACTIVITY PERIODS
3. Teaching the children to perceive and reproduce for themselves the quantitative equality of groups of objects of different sizes.	2
4. Teaching the children to perceive and to reproduce the quantitative equality of groups of objects arranged differently (and groups of objects of varying shapes).	2
5. Teaching the children to recognize the quantitative equality of groups of objects which have been arranged in rows with the distance between the objects in the first group different from that between the objects in the second group.	2
6. Practicing forming sets in accordance with a given model; counting off an indicated quantity of objects from the larger set.	3
7. Practicing counting objects of various sorts depicted on a card.	3
8. Practicing forming sets when a number has been designated orally, and learning to memorize the number given.	3
9. Learning to designate quantities of objects of varying kinds by one and the same number.	3
10. Learning to count objects by feel.	3
11. Learning to count sounds and to perform actions an indicated number of times.	4

Suggested Year Schedule of Arithmetic Activity Periods for the Older Group

TOPICS	SUGGESTED NUMBER OF ACTIVITY PERIODS
1. Practicing counting and counting off objects according to a model or a designated number.	2
2. Comparing sets representing consecutive numbers; introduction to the formation of a new number from the preceding one and the determination of the larger set and the smaller set, the greater number and the smaller number.	4
3. Distinguishing the independence of a number from the size of the objects (in a set representing it).	3
4. Counting by feel and counting the number of times an action is performed.	3
5. Counting by ear.	4
6. Forming sets which are greater or smaller by one, using "analyzers" of various types.	5
7. Reinforcing the concept that numbers are independent of the characteristics and spatial arrangement of the objects in the sets representing them.	5
8. Becoming familiar with some of the actual numerals. Understanding the independence of the number and the particular arrangement of the elements in the set.	3

TOPICS	SUGGESTED NUMBER OF ACTIVITY PERIODS
9. Developing the concept of a number on the basis of the equality relationship between sets (the ability to recognize one and the same number in groups of objects of different kinds and sets of varying types of elements).	4
10. Composing a number in terms of units, comparing of consecutive numbers, and counting up to five.	4

Note: Several of these topics may be covered in the same activity period.

Suggested Year Schedule of Arithmetic Activity Periods for the School Preparatory Group

TOPICS	SUGGESTED NUMBER OF ACTIVITY PERIODS
1. Counting of objects, remembering the number and forming sets according to a given model or designated number, and forming a set which contains one more or one fewer object than the designated number.	4
2. Comprehending the concept of the independence of the number from the spatial arrangement of the objects.	3
3. Counting by ear, counting by feel, and counting the number of times an action is performed.	3
4. Counting up to ten in order.	3
5. Composing numbers in terms of units.	3
6. Comparing sets representing consecutive numbers and determining which is the larger and which is the smaller set.	3
7. Comparing consecutive numbers and determining difference in relationships.	2
8. Making more precise the children's conceptions of geometric forms (squares, rectangles, circles, ovals, triangles); having the children draw these forms on graph paper.	3
9. Studying the composition of a number in terms of two smaller numbers.	2
10. Learning the actual numerals.	4
11. Introducing arithmetic problems: the structure of the problem; the formulation of the arithmetical operations of addition and subtraction; the techniques of adding on and subtracting one by one in solving problems involving addition and subtraction.	5
12. Practicing naming the numbers orally, forward and backward; practicing determining the number which was skipped.	2

INSTRUCTION IN THE GRAPHIC ARTS

In Soviet kindergartens the children's creativity develops under the influence of guidance and instruction. Activities in drawing, modeling and appliqué work contribute to the all-round education of the children. As graphic art reflects the real environment, it contributes to the perception of objects and events, and such properties of the world of material objects as shape, size, color, texture, structure and spatial orientation, through the development of the sensory organs which it promotes. The shape, structure and color of objects produce esthetic feelings and bring forth an esthetic and emotional evaluation.

Since they are conducted in groups, the activity periods devoted to drawing, modeling and appliqué work provide opportunities for developing friendly attitudes and cooperation; moreover, in the course of these activities important personal qualities develop: perseverance, initiative, perceptiveness and general work capabilities.

Drawing, modeling and appliqué work require special skills in handling materials, adroitness, gracefulness and coordination. In this way, the art activities contribute to the development of the skills and knowledge required in handicrafts. The practical, concrete character of this activity provides an opportunity for the children to develop the ability to plan their work, to overcome obstacles, to persevere until a particular project is finished, and to work accurately and carefully. These qualities are basic in training the children to perform work satisfactorily. In addition, graphic art activities enhance the development of the child's powers of thought and speech, his memory and his imagination.

.   .   .

If conditions are favorable in the child's life, his creative abilities will to a certain extent develop on their own. Drawing and modeling, just like playing, become necessary to the child; these needs he satisfies within the limits of his ability. However, this development will proceed in a more correct fashion, more intensively and more smoothly in relation to that of the rest of the children of a given age if a sensible program of instruction is applied.

During the preschool years, just as during the subsequent school period, the terminal goals of instruction in drawing, modeling and appliqué work are: To develop the ability to portray realistically and in considerable detail objects and events in the visually perceived world; to embody actively and creatively this world in one's consciousness; and to work out and express one's own relationship to it. These terminal goals are achieved by establishing and then carrying out a series of objectives commensurate with the age and ability of children. In relation to children of preschool age, these objectives must of necessity be extremely limited.

Step by step, the teacher guides the artistic activity of children—she sets before them the task of conveying the shapes of objects and their colors (and later, their texture, proportions, relative magnitude and spatial orientation). The reproductions produced by the children are true to life and sincere but incomplete, and, in this sense, unsatisfying.

Instruction brings in the necessary corrective factor to guide the self-development of the child and to bring forth and strengthen new positive elements which will raise the artistic activities of the children to a higher level, and work to eliminate the lifeless character of their work at an earlier stage in their development. The better and more accurately the teacher has planned the course to be followed, and the greater her assurance in applying it, then the more fruitful is the process of instruction for the development of the child's potential.

In drawing, modeling and appliqué work, the children deal with specific materials. They must be taught the proper use of these materials, as well as the use of pencils, brushes and scissors.

In the process of learning techniques for drawing, modeling, cutting and pasting, manual dexterity develops, as does visual control over force and direction. Training in the techniques of graphic arts is a subject of instruction for the final four years which the children spend in the kindergarten.

The general program requirements are spread out over all the age groups, forming a definite system of instruction; but for the children of a particular age group, certain goals are stressed and these are considered the essential objectives at the given stage of instruction. Thus, for the second younger group the primary goals are: to develop coordination and visual control of movements, and to develop an understanding of the general role of conveying the shape of objects when modeling, drawing or doing applique work.

In the middle group, along with conveying the proper shapes, it is important to teach the children to convey the color, structures and size of objects. To make the various parts of an object conform demands and understanding, however elementary, of relationships of size, shape and position.

A new goal is set for the older group: to position objects in space and to unify them through a single theme. As the children learn techniques for representing a series of objects, it becomes possible for them to use these techniques in various ways to express a particular theme. As far as modeling goes, the basic task is to form figures out of various parts which must be in correct relation to each other.

For the school preparatory group the primary objective is to teach the children to convey the individual features and qualities of concrete objects. Thus, in the activities involving drawing, modeling and appliqué work, a specific amount of time must be set aside in which the children work from real life models and then compare the things they have made with the real life model in order then to improve the resemblance in shape, structure and coloring. The teacher sets the object before the children either directly facing them or in profile, in such a way that they are not required to attempt to convey its depth.

Work aimed at developing the visual memory of the child and his ability to reproduce from memory any subject seen previously also continues in this group.

Decorative art (design work) contributes greatly to the development of the children. We have stipulated those goals which are common to drawing, modeling and appliqué work; however, each type of art involves its own individual specifications.

During each year of instruction the relationship between the general and special objectives of the various artistic activities differs. In the second younger group a single goal is achieved through drawing and modeling, and what is important is only to observe the proper sequence, to decide with which of these activities it is best to begin. The further one goes, the more manifest become the specific characteristics of each art form. Some goals are predominantly achieved through one medium, while others lend themselves more to realization through some other medium. Thus, for example, in activities in the older group, the children acquire skill in modeling, reproducing the shape and structure of living creatures, while in appliqué work they deal predominantly with rectilinear forms, their relative sizes and proportions; drawing gives the children an opportunity to convey related events in life, in simple poems and fairy tales and in scenes of nature, and to arrange the various objects in space and make their relative magnitudes conform.

Having acquired through modeling the ability to convey the form and structure of an animal or human being, this skill is carried over to drawing.

The program supplies suggested themes for drawing, modeling and appliqué work. Each teacher, taking into consideration the particular environment, assigns themes corresponding in difficulty and complexity to those indicated in the program.

The younger the age group, the simpler and more restricted is the program of instruction. Therefore, to assimilate its contents, only a relatively small number of activity periods is required. The remaining scheduled activity periods are used for practice and consolidation of the already acquired skills and for their utilization in more creative ventures. For the second younger group, it is desirable for approximately half of the assigned activities to be devoted to independent art work, without direct guidance from the teacher as to how or what things are to be done.

In all groups, including the school preparatory group, enough time must be assigned to independent creative work where the children depend entirely on their own inspiration, thus insuring the realization of another important educational objective and that of the all-round development of the children. In suggesting to the children a particular subject for their art work, the teacher must ascertain that the subject is familiar to them and that they have previously handled and played with the related objects.

The subject matter prescribed for modeling, drawing, or collage, in many cases assumes that the children will subsequently make use of their work in their games; for example, modeling objects for playing "bakery," "harvest," or "doll's tea party." The children make decorative designs on some of the things which they need for their role-playing and dramatization games (little carpets, table cloths, handkerchiefs, and so forth). The older preschool children may do a certain amount of art work in making and decorating things to be used in connection with their work duties: boxes for plants, pots for houseplants, spades, little buckets, sand containers.

Drawing, modeling and collage are activities which by their very nature are related to play. Expressing in a drawing or painting, or in modeling or appliqué work, a particular idea or theme, the child strives to reproduce the action which is taking place between the various characters. Not knowing how to attain his aim through graphic means, he starts actually engaging in play activities while in the process of creating his drawing, or while modeling; he gets completely absorbed in the situation he is trying to depict, and as he creates the situation he at the same time takes part in it with little comments and sometimes even actions. When a child in the older group creates a drawing based on a theme, while he is utilizing a variety of techniques of graphic art he is nevertheless also in the process of performing playful activity.

PHYSICAL DEVELOPMENT

As of the age of 3, physical education activities are conducted for all groups. In the course of these activities, the children are taught the correct way to perform physical movements: walking, running, jumping and climbing. The children are also trained to maintain correct posture and to be graceful and agile. Activities including exercises and active games serve as a safeguard against the detrimental effects of immobility.

With the groups of 5- and 6-year-old children, teachers must pay attention both to the further development of each of these basic motor skills (in accordance with the program of requirements), and to the speed and coordination with which they are performed. 6-year-old children are taught to respond not only to visual examples, but also to the spoken commands of the teacher. Therefore, children of this age must be able to orient themselves in space, distinguish the various directions, and know their left hands from their right and their left feet from their right.

Activities involving exercises and active games are valuable in that through them the children develop a sense of organization and the ability to coordinate their movements with those of the rest of the group. Children exercise in light clothing (shorts and undershirts), and this factor also contributes to conditioning their bodies.

Exercises and active games form the core of the physical activities. Considerable importance must be attached to developing the child's sense of balance and his ability to jump, climb, throw, and exercise the muscles of his feet (in order to prevent flat feet). For this purpose exercises and games are selected which involve objects (balls, hoops, sticks, ropes, sandbags) and special pieces of equipment (horses, ladders, gymnastic apparatus). The children high jump, broad jump, and throw at targets in turn, rather than at the same time, as in the case with walking, running, and gymnastics. To insure that each child has an opportunity to engage in these more demanding physical activities, that is, to jump or throw at a target two or three times, the most convenient and effective organizational scheme must be thought out in advance. For example, small groups of three, four, or five children might all jump at the same time over a rope.

Furthermore, in an attempt to increase the effectiveness of these activities, and specifically to enhance the development of physical movements, it is important to try and limit as much as possible the amount of time devoted to organizing the children and distributing and putting away the equipment. Everything needed must be prepared ahead of time by the teacher (prior to the children's arrival).

A typical pattern to follow for exercises and active games is as follows: first, there is a short walk and run, during which one might include exercises for alertness and spatial orientation; on a signal from the teacher, the children stop walking and form into pairs (according to the program for each age group); then come exercises for various muscle groups (arms, back, stomach, legs) and exercises in one of the basic physical movements—jumping, climbing or throwing. Following the exercises, the teacher organizes active games. The general activity and great emotional lift generated by the active games gives way to a quiet walking period or a quiet game (one involving little physical activity). With this the physical activity period ends.

For the groups of 3-year-old children, exercises for the development of physical movements are conducted in the form of games based on imitation (such games as "The Train," "The Bird," and so on) or in the form of playful exercises, for example, "Get the Ball" or "Crawl through the Hoop."

MUSICAL TRAINING

Musical training contributes to the general development of a child. The music conveys scenes from nature and expresses feelings, moods, thoughts. Listening to music, the child experiences the different feelings evoked by the various aspects of the music.

For a successful musical education, musical appreciation must be systematically developed in the children; that is, they must be taught to listen and respond emotionally to it. The development of musical perception proceeds through the learning of songs, musical games, and circle dances. In addition, the children listen to such musical works which they would find difficult to reproduce, but which enrich them with musical impressions and from which they derive great satisfaction. Thus, a portion of the time assigned to musical activities is specifically devoted simply to listening to music. Through listening to music, the child's perceptiveness and sensitivity to music develop, and the children acquire very elementary ideas about music. They begin to differentiate and to remember musical works, their contents, their character, and the means by which the music is expressed.

The program provides for a definite repertory, through which these educational goals are achieved in a systematic way. Through their musical training, the children must acquire certain knowledge and skills related to singing and performing musical-rhythmic movements. Instruction even in the simplest modes of singing and the most elementary musical-ryhthmic skills requires a definite systematic practice and constant review and reinforcement of the skills which have already been acquired. Thus, for example, from the time the children reach the younger group, their attention is repeatedly drawn to the fact that they should not begin singing until the introduction is over, By the time the children reach the school preparatory group, they are easily able to identify the introduction, to call it by the proper name, and to obey the instruction to begin singing or marching the minute the introduction has been played completely.

The leading musical activity is singing and much attention must be devoted to this. The program describes the particular singing skills to be developed; the children are trained to sing in a natural, resonant, and smooth voice, to pronounce the words distinctly, to sing on pitch, and to execute simple musical nuances. With each age group, more complexity is introduced into these basic skills. The children receive instruction in these skills as they learn songs, selected and arranged to be studied in the order of gradually increasing difficulty.

In teaching the children to sing, attention must be directed at developing their singing voices and their ear for music, while at the same time making certain that no child's voice is impaired. The vocal apparatus of a child is extremely vulnerable and tender, and excessive strain is harmful. The teacher must watch to make sure that in singing and in speech the children maintain a natural, unstrained voice. Under such conditions, the child's hearing will also develop normally, as it will not be subjected to sharp discordant sounds. The teacher should arrange for periodic inspections by an ear and throat specialist. In order for a child's singing to sound well, it is important that he observe the correct singing posture, that he stand erect and straight without bending the body or the head, and that he sit well back on the chair so that his feet rest on the floor and do not dangle (chairs must be provided of appropriate size for the children). It is useful to have the children sing familiar songs standing up. Children's voices are limited in their range. There should be no hurry to extend their range. After teaching the children to sing within the range most comfortable for them, one may very gradually extend the range slightly. Basically the songs are pitched in the range which is comfortable for children's voices, starting from the key *mi-la* of the first octave (for children of the younger group) and reaching *re-do* in the school preparatory group.

The children will develop an ear for melody if, starting from an early age, their attention is constantly attracted to the correct performance of the simplest songs. A child in the older group is already able to single out an introduction to a song, or its refrain, to notice who sang it correctly, to match his voice with those of the others, to distinguish which of two sounds is the higher or lower, and to determine whether the melody is rising or falling. All this testifies to a certain development in their ear for music, one of the basic musical abilities, and prepares the children for learning to read music.

Musical-rhythmic movements also contribute to the development of certain musical capacities, among which are emotional responsiveness to music and especially a sense of rhythm. Therefore, as the basis for this part of the program musical-rhythmic activities are prescribed; the children are taught how to move in accordance with the evolution of the musical images in a given piece of music, its character, dynamics, cadence, and changes of tempo.

Musical-rhythmic skills develop as the children perform various movements. Involved are such basic movements as walking, running, and hopping, and such qualities as will enable the children to convey the varied aspects of the music (happy, gay, calm, solemn). Some of the movements are of the type performed in physical exercises (with and without objects). The movements are executed both smoothly and abruptly; they are imitative and expressive in nature, and are indispensable to various circle dances, folk dances, musical games, and more formal dancing. Thus, at the basis of this part of the program in musical training lies the objective of a steady and sequential development of a sense of rhythm. The learning of musical games, folk dances, and exercises should be considered merely as the means of achieving this goal.

The program provides a recommended musical repertory. It includes for the most part national folk songs and round dances, works of Soviet composers and of classical composers. The selection of these works has been made on the basis of their artistic value, their appropriateness in relation to the children's ability, and the variety of genres they represent. A supplementary list of songs, games, dances, and musical compositions is also provided; these are meant for listening, and among these works some may be exchanged for others of similar content and level of difficulty. However, it must be remembered that a limited but stable repertory will enable the children to learn the music better and to perform the works properly.

Those songs and games which were learned in the previous age group must be reviewed when the children transfer to the next age group. In addition, many of the songs, which the children could not actually perform but merely listened to, may be sung by them in the following year. Gradually, singing, round dances, and games become a part of the daily life of the children.

Whenever assemblies or morning parties are planned, it may become necessary to teach the children an extra song or dance which was completely unknown to them, and this represents for them something new and unexpected—a surprise. Dances and songs for such occasions are selected from among the most simple, so that the children can learn them in a short while without great effort, and without disrupting the daily schedule.

Along with games, round dances, and folk dances, the children perform exercises. These may be of varying types. Some of them are introduced in connection with the dances and games which the children are learning. Others are introduced more independently for the purpose of developing more fully and systematically the musical-rhythmic skills of the children. Some of the exercises of this latter type are indicated in the suggested repertory.

Gradually, children accumulate a store of musical impressions and acquire the elementary skills involved in singing and performing musical-rhythmic movements. Through this activity, their individual interests and inclinations are revealed, their musical talents emerge and develop.

EDUCATIONAL WORK IN THE SCHOOL PREPARATORY GROUP

The Program of Instruction in the Kindergarten singles out the school preparatory group for special emphasis in order to insure that the children are successfully prepared for their subsequent instruction in school.

CONCERNING THE PREPAREDNESS OF THE CHILDREN FOR SCHOOL INSTRUCTION

The readiness of children for elementary school instruction must not be confused with instruction in the elements of reading and writing; it involves rather the complex of personal qualities in the child, the level of his mental development, and the condition of his health. Learning is hard work, demanding definite physical efforts and mental strain, as well as the ability to persevere until a particular task is brought to a conclusion. The things which will guarantee success in this work are, first of all, good health, good physical development, and the attainment of a definite level of resistance in the child's organism.

Secure and useful habits of personal hygiene acquired in the kindergarten (washing, combing one's hair, keeping one's clothing neat, and so forth), a high level of self-sufficiency, and an enjoyment of work will all help the children to adjust to new ways of doing things at school and to enter into the realm of academic work.

First grade instruction in reading, writing, and arithmetic requires that the children be equipped with a certain range of ideas about people, their work, and their immediate environment, plants and animals, and inanimate nature; and that they have an elementary knowledge of spatial, temporal, and quantitative relationships. The groundwork for the acquisition of school subjects has been laid in the program of the kindergarten familiarizing the children with the various aspects of their environment.

To master the school program the children must acquire the ability to hold a pencil correctly, to handle books with care, to listen to and understand the words of a teacher or friend, to carry out instructions given by the teacher, to answer a question intelligibly, to apply elementary skills in handiwork. These abilities must be developed in the child by the kindergarten. Along with all of these things, it is important to develop in the children an interest in books and in school, a desire to study and discover new things, a respectful attitude toward people and labor, and a devotion to their community.

In accordance with the new system of preparing the children for school, preliminary instruction in the elements of reading and writing has been introduced into the program. It must be remembered, however, that this instruction must not be included at the expense of the work on speech development, familiarization with the environment, literature, or the graphic arts, or by curtailing outdoor recreation time, excursions, play, or work training.

The school preparatory group has its own schedule of activities, and the contents of the educational-instructional work are determined. The difference between the kindergarten school preparatory group and the first grade in school is determined by the special characteristics of 6-year-old children and by the fact that children do not attend the kindergarten solely for instruction, but spend a significant portion of the day there.

The articulation between kindergarten and school consists not in having the kindergarten imitate the schedule and organization of the school, but in having the total experience of the preschool education and instruction prepare the children for new relationships and new responsibilities. The transition from the work of the kindergarten to that of the school must be examined from the point of view of achieving a unified educational impact upon the children—the realization of a communist education on contiguous age levels. In fulfilling the program of the kindergarten, the teacher must always bear in mind the special characteristics of 6-year-old children and not treat them in the manner which will be necessary and appropriate when they have reached the following age level.

THE FORMATION OF THE
SCHOOL PREPARATORY GROUPS

The program and the system of instruction in the school preparatory group are intended for children who are 6 years old, and who will, in one year's time, be transferred to the elementary school. Having children all of the same age is an absolute necessity for the work of the school preparatory group. It is not practical, in a group containing children of various ages, to follow the program completely and satisfactorily.

In preparing for the new school year, each kindergarten must check the ages of the children in the older group and then form the school preparatory group out of those children who will be 6 years old as of the first of September.

CARING FOR THE CHILDREN'S HEALTH:
THE DAILY SCHEDULE

In order to fulfill the instructional and educational goals as outlined in the program, the children in the school preparatory group will be required to exert considerable physical and mental effort, and to be persevering and attentive.

The condition of the children's health and the success of the educational-instructional work depend a great deal on the observance of the daily schedule. In arranging the day's activities, the need of a growing child to be sufficiently active must be provided for, a variety of activities must be assured; physical and mental activity, work and rest must be properly alternated; a maximum of time must be spent outdoors; and a proper diet and meal schedule must be established. The teacher is responsible for the strict adherence to all of the above required conditions.

While continuing training and reinforcing the self-sufficiency of the children, the teachers must strive steadily to decrease the amount of time devoted to routine activities in comparison with that spent in the preceding groups, without, however, interfering with the standard of performance of these habitual acts (eating, dressing and undressing neatly, washing thoroughly, and so on). The children must be taught to eat everything served to them and one must instill in them a proper attitude toward food in general.

CARE OF EYESIGHT

The setup in the common room, which is used for a great variety of activities, must be geared to instructional purposes while being in full accordance with health requirements. During the activity periods, the tables and chairs must be arranged in rows across the room. If there are windows on only two or three sides of the room, the side with the most windows should be to the left of the children. Each child must have his permanent place, his chair and table, corresponding in size to his own size; the chairs and tables should be labelled. When the children are arranged for activities, their eyesight must be taken into consideration, as well as their hearing and their general emotional stability. The most excitable children must be placed next to the quieter and more well-balanced children. Within the field of vision there must be no bright objects (toys, decorations, bookshelves lined with books) to distract their attention. If standards of artificial lighting are not adhered to strictly, the results will be very sad, indeed: the children's eyesight will begin to worsen while they are still of preschool age.

TEACHING PROPER POSTURE

Children in the school preparatory group must acquire the ability to sit correctly during the activity periods. The children's posture must correspond to the requirements of good health and be comfortable for the work in which they are engaged. The position in which the child sits during an activity influences greatly the formation of his general posture, and thus the teacher must observe carefully the position of the children throughout the activity and, in general, over the course of the entire day. The teacher must strive to have the children maintain a proper carriage while walking, running, working, and playing.

PLAY

In the building and on the playground the children should have ample opportunity to use play equipment and gymnastic apparatus. It should be kept in mind that games and physical exercises have a great influence on the development of the child and the molding of his volitional efforts. Games contribute to the development of action, decisiveness, daring, and sociability. Team games in which the children must act independently, as well as simply the idea of playing according to the rules, serve to organize and discipline the children and teach them to subjugate their personal interests to the general will. The efforts of the teacher must be directed at getting the children to join in a variety of games of their own free will and to acquire the ability to follow the rules and play a leading role in any game. It is important to inculcate a love of sports in every child. . . .

WORK

In the school preparatory group significantly greater stress must be put on the various types of work, since the educational influence of work training increases in connection with the preparation of the children for study in school. For this group, it is important to attain definite results in the work through execution and increased skill in using tools and materials.

THE INSTRUCTION OF CHILDREN
IN THE ACTIVITY PERIODS

In the school preparatory group, the process begun in the previous group of children's study habits continues; this involves the ability to listen attentively, to comprehend the teacher's speech, and to know what to do with the material which is presented to them. In some cases, the children's activity is manifested physically; they sketch, model, make stick figures, do gymnastics, sing, dance, and so forth. In other cases, the active involvement of the children is not expressed in physical activity with objects of any kind; it manifests itself rather in mental activity and in comprehending what the teacher is saying. To teach children to think independently is the most important objective of the teacher, and it is significantly more difficult than teaching them to give routine answers, which, unfortunately, is a circumstance encountered much too often in practice.

Children must be taught to start and finish their work on time (that is, to work at approximately the same speed), to carry out exactly the teacher's instructions, to work on their own without disturbing others, to evaluate their own work and the work of others from the viewpoint of the instructions given by the teacher and the results achieved. More attention than in the previous groups must be given to training the children to restrain their impulsive physical reactions (standing up at the wrong time, turning around, handling various objects) and to developing in them the habit of controlling their movements. This is important with regard to preparing the children to write (knowing how to hold a pencil and being able to draw lines in a limited space, for example, between two lines or within a small square) and to handle everyday objects (being able to place a chair down or move it, or to close a door quietly).

Teachers must be thoroughly prepared for the day's work in order to conduct the activities and lessons in a lively manner, without prolonged pauses; they must strive intently to make the children understand, remember the things they have learned, and acquire new skills and knowledge.

There is no sense in requiring the children to raise their hands at every question, as the teacher should call on the children according to her own best judgment. Some teachers, after each question wait for all or the majority of children to raise their hands. But it must be kept in mind that not every child, far from it, raises his hand deliberately and with an assurance that he is prepared to give a correct answer. The teacher calls on the children, observing to what extent each child is attentive and whether he is participating actively in the work at hand. Children must get accustomed to raising their hands whenever the teacher poses questions such as the following: "Who noticed the error in the answer (or in the work) of a particular classmate?" "Who can add to what this classmate just said?"

The whole of the material indicated in the program of activities must be covered in such a way that the children form correct and clear ideas about the world surrounding them. Teachers must exploit to the maximum the broad opportunities offered by the way of life in the kindergarten to make trips through the nearby streets and to various places of interest; in this way, on the basis of vivid and concrete observations and an expanding vocabulary, the children will acquire knowledge and skills and develop their ability to use more intricate thought processes: comparison, establishing similarities or differences among objects and ideas, judgment, and deduction. If within a particular group there are still children with incorrect speech, then during the first quarter it is important to overcome the faults in their pronunciation, so that none of the children will encounter difficulties when they are introduced to work involving sounds and letters. In this connection also, there should be more frequent practice exercises for the development of distinct pronunciation (good diction) in all of the children.

Beginning with the first quarter (and continuing throughout the year) it is important to develop systematically the children's spatial orientation during the physical exercise activity periods: to the right, forward, back, in the middle. Children must be taught to carry out instructions not only imitating visual examples, but also obeying oral commands (turn to the right, raise your right hand). The children must know which is their right hand and which is their left, their right foot and their left foot, and the names of the fingers of their hands.

During activities devoted to the reading of literature, the children must be familiarized with books (the cover, the binding, the right or left-hand page, the lines); the children must know how to express in words where a particular picture is located in the book (on the first page, at the top corner of the left-hand page, and so forth). During activity periods devoted to art, collage, and construction, the time must be found to teach the children to identify the various parts of a sheet of paper and to describe the position of a drawing or design (at the top, at the bottom, on the left or right side, in the middle, in the upper corner, in the right corner), to note the composite parts of an object, their arrangement, and the way they are related in size.

In order to prepare the children for reading and writing, their ability to analyze the whole visually must be developed (drawings, designs, pictures); this ability will be important in distinguishing the different letters when the children learn to read and write. For this purpose, systematic exercises with tables, the so-called visual dictation exercises, are needed. These tables represent a set of combinations of lines and geometric forms (squares, rectangles, triangles, circles, and ovals), beginning with extremely simple patterns and going on to more complicated ones. The teacher shows the table to the children and explains which parts the pattern is made of; then the children reproduce the drawing from memory on their own paper with the help of little sticks or cutouts, or else work with color pencils.

Similar exercises are conducted using the method known as aural dictation, whereby the teacher does not show the pattern, but describes it; the children must visualize this pattern from the oral description, keep it in their minds, and reproduce it with sticks, triangles, or other geometric figures, or else draw it.

PREPARATION FOR READING AND WRITING

In the program of preparation for reading and writing, a so-called preparatory period is included in a somewhat more expanded form than that for the preparatory period in the school proper.

From the psychological point of view, the first period of instruction in reading and writing is a period in which a new attitude toward speech is being formulated. Speech itself, in its external sound aspect, becomes an end of conscious activity, whereas previously, the child's use and perception of speech was directed at the identification of objects.

In the kindergarten, a large role is given to the development of aural phonemic discrimination, that is, the ability to differentiate and to isolate the individual sounds of speech. Phonemic discrimination is developed through exercises involving oral-aural analysis and synthesis. All these exercises are designed to isolate individual words in a short meaningful sentence, combine a number of them together, and form sentences out of given words; all this must serve to direct the attention of the child to the word itself. For the first time, the children begin to regard speech as an object of instruction.

Through concrete examples involving the analysis and synthesis of oral speech, the children evolve a correct impression of the basic parts of speech: a sentence, a word, a part of a word, a syllable, a sound, a letter. The children must learn accurately what must be called a letter and what a sound. The teachers in their own speech must not confuse the meanings of these terms.

About ten to fifteen minutes must be devoted to the development of aural phonemic discrimination during each activity period in the native language (about twice a week).

At first, only one activity a week is devoted to the introduction of the sounds and letters (out of the five devoted to native language instruction, familiarization with the environment, and literature)—in all, 28-30 activity periods over the course of the entire school year.

TYPES OF WORK INVOLVED IN THE PREPARATION FOR READING AND WRITING

First Quarter

Putting together sentences of two, then three words (without conjunctions or prepositions): the boy sits, the bird flies; determining the order of the words in the sentence: name the first word in the sentence; the second word.

Dividing words into parts (syllables): *ma-ma, Li-da, She-nya*. Educational games involving the division of words. ("Finish the Word.")

Composing words out of syllables.

Gradually introducing the following sounds and letters: *a, u, o, m, sh,* [and an additional hard vowel without English equivalent].

Identifying a particular sound in a word.

Devising educational games (thinking up words containing the sound being studied).

Analyzing words by sounds.

Second Quarter

Continuing with exercises for the development of aural phonemic discrimination. Gradual introduction to the following sounds and letters: *s, p, l, n, r;* identifying the sounds in words. Analyzing words containing the sounds *a, u, o, m, sh, s, p, r, l, n* (*mama, Masha, Ura*).

Finding examples of words where these particular sounds occur at the beginning, in the middle, or at the end of the word.

Composing syllables and words from the sounds being studied.

Getting acquainted with the notebook used in the first grade (sheet, page, line, ruler).

Tracing and drawing designs in the notebook with rulers. Writing the basic elements of letters.

Third Quarter

Putting together syllables and words from a cut-out alphabet with a previous analysis of the sounds and a subsequent analysis of the letters (two syllable words with open syllables: *mama, papa, Sasha, luna*).

Continuing the work designed to prepare the children for writing. (One activity period a week is devoted to arithmetic—in all, 36 activity periods during the year to cover the material in the program.)

HOLIDAYS AND CELEBRATIONS

National holidays, in which the patriotism of the Soviet people, their feelings of international solidarity, and their pride in Soviet achievements in all fields of life are all strongly reflected, are triumphantly celebrated in the kindergartens as well. The deep patriotic feelings which are experienced by adults enter into the consciousness of the children through happy experiences linked with preholiday activities and with the special day itself. Children enjoy preparing presents, learning songs, poems, and dances, and decorating the building.

In the kindergartens, special assemblies are organized for the children. An indispensable part of the program at such assemblies is the active participation of the children: they sing, dance, read poems, perform dramatic scenes, and do gymnastics, all of which require special preparation. Unrehearsed games are also included in the program. In addition, the assembly programs include various acts in which the children are merely spectators: dances are performed by adults, and dramatizations, puppet shows, and the like are put on by school children. The younger the children, the simpler the performances they put on; the program of assemblies represents for them mainly a spectacle to watch (for example, dances and dramatizations done by older children). The active participation of the very young children in the assemblies is for the most part in the form of games and unrehearsed dances involving imitation.

It is important that no child be overlooked during the preparations for assemblies. The teacher should not allow a case where the same children always perform at the assemblies. An institution for children is not a theater where there are actors of varying talents. A festive assembly in a kindergarten is a source of joy to each child, independent of his abilities or talents. The task of the teacher is to select suitable material for each child's performance, material which he can master successfully and rapidly, so that he will not feel left out.

For an assembly program, the teacher should select songs, dances and other material with which the children are already familiar or which they will be able to learn without much strain. The children greatly enjoy familiar games when the teachers set them up in a slightly different fashion; for example, for the game "the hen and the chickens" (in the younger group) yellow caps are added to represent the chickens.

If it is not feasible to select only musical and literary compositions which are linked by their subject matter to the particular holiday, then it is best to include in the program such compositions as are devoted to children's games, amusements, and nature, rather than using material which is more appropriate for children of school age.

In arranging the program for a morning assembly, knowledge on the part of children, proficiency and ingenuity on the part of the teacher, and artistic taste are all required. If the program is organized with all these things in mind, then the children may be prepared for their performances within the allotted time, and there will be no need for either the teacher or the music instructor to disrupt the daily schedule.

A festive mood must be created for the children from the moment they arrive at the kindergarten: the whole building is decorated in a festive and tasteful manner; the costumes are cleaned, pressed, and ready for the performance; and the teachers and all the staff greet the children with best wishes for the holiday. Each group, along with the teacher, gives holiday greetings to the children in all the other groups and to the kitchen staff, the doctor, and all others who work in the kindergarten.

Guests come to the assembly—the parents of the children (depending on the size of the building all those who wish to come or merely certain ones designated as representatives), representatives from nearby organizations, and representations from the nearest school. Any of the workers at the kindergarten whom the children know well also come to their assemblies. Occasionally it happens that the directress of a kindergarten will neglect the personal interests of the children. Waiting for the representatives of some organization or for representatives from the national department of education who are late in arriving, she will considerably delay the beginning of the assembly and the children will get tired and become extremely restless. Or in another case, the best seats may have been reserved for guests, and the children of some group are seated in such a way that they can only see the backs of the children who are performing. The directress, the teachers, and the music instructor must all remember that the holiday is supposed to be a source of joy to the children, and that anything that may cloud their happiness must be foreseen in advance and prevented.

In addition to the national holidays, other events are celebrated in the kindergartens (for example, an anniversary of the city or of some industrial or other enterprise to which the kindergarten is attached), as are days commemorating particular professions. Thus, in kindergartens located by railroads, the Day of the Railroad is celebrated, and the children of miners celebrate Miner's Day. In the program for such assemblies, a puppet show, games familiar to the children, songs and dances, poems, and adult performances involving singing and dancing might all be included.

The children remember for a long time those assemblies which are organized for all the groups together on the grounds of the kindergarten: the winter festival with Grandfather Frost, sleigh riding on decorated sleighs or in troikas, lively active games, and the summer holiday with athletic events, round dances, singing, and dancing.

In many kindergartens the good tradition of celebrating the children's birthdays has been adopted. This is done in the following manner: once a month a festive tea is held (during snack time), with a birthday cake and small presents and greetings for the children who were born during that month. After the tea, the children sing, dance, and play games. In the younger groups, the teachers themselves prepare the presents for the children and also decorate the room. In the older groups, the teachers invite the children to participate in the preparations, encourage initiative on their part and stimulate in them a desire to try to please their classmates. The children enjoy and are even delighted by the fact that they are preparing as a surprise certain presents which they know will please their friends, and that for several days they must keep it secret from those whose birthdays are going to be celebrated. All of this has an extremely positive influence in rallying the friendly group spirit of the children and in forming kind and friendly attitudes in the children toward each other.

In addition to the assemblies on national holidays and on other celebration days, the children greatly enjoy puppet shows, "magic lantern" shows, performances by animals dressed up in costumes, and concerts.

The contents of a program and the level of the performance must correspond to the objectives of a communist education: to awaken in the children good feelings toward people, to teach them to value the beauty of labor, to engender in them a love for what is dear to the Soviet people (nature in their homeland, songs, and literature), and to develop good taste and a sense of humor.

For the preparation of concerts, Pioneers may be called upon, or else students at music schools and performers in "variety shows" at clubs or "palaces of culture." The teacher must explain to the invited performers exactly what is appropriate for their young audience and what is not and what objectives the kindergarten is trying to attain when concerts are organized for the children. The entire program as prepared by the guest performers should be previewed by the directress of the kindergarten and the teachers, as some part of it may possibly have to be excluded or revised; moreover, the duration of the concert must be determined.

Concerts organized around a particular theme are interesting to the children; for example, concerts can be dedicated to the seasons, to Russian fairy tales and songs, to the fairy tales and songs of other lands, or to the works of particular composers or writers (A. S. Pushkin, P. I. Tchaikovsky, or other Soviet writers and composers).

Children may take an active part in such concerts: they can read poetry, sing songs, dance, and participate in dramatizations. Preparations for concerts, like preparations for festive assemblies, must in no way, however, upset the daily routine of the kindergarten. It is the responsibility of the directress not to permit detrimental situations such as the following: cancelling outdoor recreation periods or activities for the sake of rehearsals and special work with the children on their performances or giving the parents the assignment of teaching the children the words to songs or poems. If the teacher is unable to find sufficient time to prepare the material needed, with the children at the proper times, this merely testifies to the fact that the selected material is unsuitable for the children, or that the teachers do not know how to organize correctly the children's activities and the routine procedures: dressing, undressing, washing, and eating are dragged out and as a result very little time remains for the various types of games and other activities which are conducted outside of the regular activity periods.

The success of special assemblies and entertainment does not depend solely on the teacher and on her abilities and ingenuity, but rather on the concerted initiative of the entire staff. From among the staff and the parents of the children, it will always be possible to find people who are endowed with a good voice and true ear, who know dances, who can recite poetry, or who can play some musical instrument. When they perform pieces from the children's repertory, either in solo or group performances, it is particularly satisfying to the children in the kindergarten.

PLANNING EDUCATIONAL WORK
FOR THE CHILDREN

The Program of Instruction in the Kindergarten reflects new requirements and new goals as indicated in the previous pages. The successful attainment of new goals depends in the final analysis on the teacher: on the extent to which she has studied the program in depth and on the extent to which she has studied the program in depth and on the extent to which she has prepared herself to achieve it. The program indicates what she must do over the course of the year; that is, the above-mentioned document includes the totality of educational objectives, describes the sum of knowledge and skills (by quarters) and defines the organization of life within the group and the various types of activities to be conducted with the children.

The teacher is guided by the program and achieves its aims through the process of daily instruction. She must have confidence that, working from day to day and solving the innumerable number of little problems daily which comprise the pedagogical process, she will reach the end of the year having fulfilled all the requirements of the program; also that the children in her group will have acquired the needed knowledge, skills, habits, and behavioral patterns to live, play, and work within a group of children of their own age. Such results are obtained when the teacher progresses each day, even if by a very small amount, toward the accomplishment of the year's program.

This purpose is served by the planning of the teacher's work. The form and contents of the plan must be evaluated in terms of the extent to which the plan helps the teacher in her daily work. The best means of planning are those which, all other conditions being equal, insure that the teacher's work is of the highest possible quality and produces the most results.

A "calendar plan" for a period of one or two weeks is an absolute necessity for teachers in all groups. A plan for each day will help the teacher to manage her activity and introduce purposeful direction into the pedagogical process.

The material needed to draw up the calendar plan is in all cases taken from the "Program": a preliminary outline of problems, habits, skills, and so forth for an extended period is unnecessary since the instructional part of the program is outlined in quarters, which in itself helps the teachers to distribute the material evenly. But the nature of the educational training the children are to receive is given for the year as a whole, rather than being broken up into shorter periods of time. This is by no means accidental; educational goals cannot be achieved in short periods of time and they cannot be taken in any particular order. They are being fulfilled simultaneously, little by little, from day to day.

The calendar plan must be worked out jointly by both teachers, since the educational objectives are being applied to the same children. In drawing up the schedule the teachers must exchange impressions of the children over the two-week period just completed: to what extent the children have absorbed the material presented in the activity periods, the manner in which they carried out their obligations, who played with whom and how they played. The children's work must also be examined and the daily notes made by the teacher read through. As a result of such an exchange of opinions, the teachers decide what must be deleted from the program for the next two-week period of the calendar-plan, what must be reviewed, and what measures should be taken to promote the fulfillment of the most urgent educational aims in relation to the children in their particular group at a given time.

What does the teacher need for successful planning?

(1) Basic knowledge of the program of the kindergarten as a whole and of the program for the particular group with which the teacher is working in the course of the current school year. To achieve this, the teacher must,

after having studied the "Program" on her own, discuss it thoroughly in a pedagogical group (in courses, seminars, faculty meetings, or method-study groups) in order to receive answers to all the questions and problems which may arise afterwards, and she must constantly refer to this document both when drawing up a schedule of work and when analyzing the results of her work over a fixed period of time.

(2) Knowledge of the children in her own particular group. General age characteristics are indicated in the program, but knowledge of the children in a particular group is acquired through constant and attentive observation. In the person of the teacher must be united the observer and the teacher—to divide these functions is impossible. Through systematically sharing their observations, the teachers of a particular group will gain answers to such questions as: What are the inherent traits of each child? What features are beginning to appear in the personalities of a child? What are his relationships with other children and with adults? How is each child assimilating the material in the program? How are the children reacting to the various types of activities? What interests are developing and which are disappearing?

The teachers must view the children in their group within the dynamics of their development and within the process of becoming a real group, or collective; they should not regard educational objectives as static entities, fixed once and for all and unchangeable. They must, correspondingly, plan their work according to the program while also insuring that the work planned is in conformity with the development of the children.

(3) Knowledge of the methods applicable to the education of children, knowledge of preschool educational methodology, constant improvement of one's own pedagogical knowledge (supplemented constantly by reading methodological literature and by learning and borrowing from the experiences of outstanding teachers).

THE CONTENTS OF THE EDUCATIONAL WORK AND THE PLAN

What is to be included in the work calendar? Things which are repeated every day are not included in the plan, but those which are not repeated every day and must be adapted by the teacher must be planned. Let us examine from this point of view the outline of the children's life in the kindergarten.

Daily, throughout the week, the nature and type of the regular activities change; consequently, the regular activities must be planned so that a gradual and sequential approach is maintained and so that by the end of the year the children will have been given the projected knowledge and skills and will have learned them thoroughly.

Active games are conducted every day. To develop uniformly the different basic physical movements, these active games must be varied: in some, running is predominant; in others, jumping, crawling, and so on. If children were to play the same game every day, then the physical development would be limited. Consequently, the proper alternation of various active games must be observed, and the calendar must stipulate the specific active games to be played.

The program to broaden the children's perspective and develop their speech (we have in mind here the program of educational-instructional work within the daily routine) demands systematic observations of the environment; the teacher must plan each day what is to be observed on the walks, and sometimes even indoors. Morning exercises are conducted daily, according to the schedule, but the exercise patterns change only once a week. This means that on the calendar-plan, notes concerning a new set of exercises and details about the exercises will be included only once each week.

Some types of activities are not engaged in by the children every day, but rather less frequently. Among these activities are periodic jobs (for example, cleaning up the common room, transplanting house plants, making scenery for dramatizations) and entertainment (concerts, puppet shows, fun games). Things like these are periodically set down in the calendar-plan for a particular day of the week.

Games occupy a large place in the daily lives of the children. Some of the games are organized by the teacher, while others develop through the initiative of the children themselves. The techniques of supervising the children in the different types of games vary, but to a certain degree all the children's games are guided directly or indirectly by the teacher. The teacher's own participation and activity in regard to the children's plan must be thought out and outlined in the calendar-plan.

In the calendar-plan for a day or for a week provisions are made for working with the entire group, with subgroups, and with individual children if the necessity arises. For instance, if a particular child has missed an entire month of school due to illness, then in planning the activity period devoted to drawing, the teacher must provide for an especially easy subject for this child. If within the group there are children with pronunciation faults who require special drills, the teacher must plan for individual work with these children. An over-excitable child requires more individual attention, and for such a child it would be best to plan for the play period a table game, looking at illustrations, or some other quiet activity involving the teacher's own participation.

THE TEACHER'S CALENDAR-PLAN

Activities

To insure the success of the activities, there must be proper preparation, and this means thorough planning: determining the program material to be covered, deciding upon a proper order of presentation, and selecting visual aids and educational equipment to be used.

The same type of notes cannot be used in the plan for all types of activities. The plan for discussions is not like the plan for an activity period devoted to physical exercises, and a plan for the reading of literature is not like the plan for appliqué work. For some activities it is important to describe in detail the first part—for example, in drawing, the introductory talk with the children when the teacher gives instructions, gives explanations, shows examples and models, asks questions, and so forth; for other activities the entire procedure must be completely worked out in the plan (musical training and physical education exercises). There must be no stereotyped notes in the plan, and concrete plans for a given activity must not be replaced by vague schematic outlines. For example, of what benefit to the teacher is a plan such as the following?

Painting theme: Ducks
Program content: Teaching the children to portray the characteristics of a duck by stressing the bill and the legs.
(1) Explanation and demonstration by the teacher
(2) Work by the children
(3) Summary remarks by the teacher
Material to be used: Paper, paints, brushes and model

The listing of the three stages of work is superfluous, since this represents no more than the typical outline of work in any activity period devoted to graphic art. Providing a list of the materials to be used is also of no use since it would suffice to merely indicate "painting." But what should have been indicated in the plan? A more concrete description of the first stage of the activity: precisely what is to be explained and shown to the children. The most important thing for the teacher to remember in planning an activity is to provide a concise and concrete note which will make it easy for her to prepare and conduct the activity.

Games

The program defines in detail the objectives and contents of the play activity of the children at various periods of the day, and makes provisions for a variety of games: role-playing games, games with rules (active, educational, musical), and building games.

In games involving rules, the teacher assumes the role of the spontaneous organizer, as well as that of a frequent participant; consequently, these games are simpler to plan. As to role-playing games, the teacher must bear in mind that the character of the play activity of the children changes with the development of the children, and changes under the influence of the educational efforts of the staff. The way the children are grouped for games changes, as do their interrelationships and their attitudes toward each other, the themes upon which the games are based, their contents, their duration, the toys and play material used, and the type of actions and roles performed.

In planning the supervision of children's games, this dynamic quality in the evolution of their games must be taken into consideration and recognized as one aspect of the way in which the children's lives are organized. In the younger as well as in the older groups which have just been formed (this occasionally takes place, for example, just before the children leave for vacation), the teacher will organize, more often than is usually the case, games involving the entire group and involving rules so that the children have a chance to get acquainted with each other and to get accustomed to doing things in groups. There are a great number of games involving rules from which to make a selection: active games, educational games, table games and musical games. The teacher can plan such games for the entire group or just for those who wish to take part, or for small subgroups. For the younger groups, the teacher has to plan the organization of elementary role-playing games, which might, for example, be based on a bus ride, a boat trip, and so on.

Gradually, within the larger group, smaller groups will begin to evolve through the initiative of the children themselves and on the basis of their interest in the same toys, their shared interests, their favorite fairy tales, and their friendships.

Changes in the character of the play activity of children will require other techniques of influencing the contents of their games, expanding the size of the groups involved, and encouraging sociability. The following is a list of suggestions, by no means exhaustive, of various ways of influencing the evolution of the children's games as a form of life organization: suggest to the children a new idea for games, remind them about what they have seen during a walk or about a book which has been read, give them friendly advice regarding the choice of a structure to build, give them an album with illustrations in it such as "The Beautiful Buildings of Our City," show them how to build a bridge with a double arch or some other type of construction, or talk to the children for a while about what, how, and with whom they wish to play on that day or on the following day. A knowledge of the "Program" and corresponding methodological commentary will help the teacher to determine her role in the development of games and to set forth definite goals in the calendar-plan.

Of course, all possible instances of the supervision of children's play cannot be foreseen and provided for in the plan, and one should not require the teachers to plan all play periods. The teacher must acquire such a mastery of the various methods which can be used and must observe all the children to such a degree that in any particular situation which may arise, however unexpectedly, she will be able to suggest to the children a suitable game, take part in it herself if need be, get the children playing together, and so on.

Work

Routine daily work, such as being on duty at some point or performing a particular task every day, need not be mentioned in the daily plan. The teacher puts down in the plan something new which she is about to include among the responsibilities and work obligations of the children, since anything new will require and explanation or demonstration. Such entries would appear in the calendar-plan whenever the need arises.

Types of work which are performed periodically it is best to plan, that is, to set down in writing in the calendar-plan: what the children will do, how the group of children will be organized (all with the same work to perform or with different tasks distributed among them), and what kind of equipment must be prepared in advance. A precise plan for the organization of the children will help the teacher to do the job quickly and smoothly, avoiding unnecessary waste of time and foolish activity on the part of the children, where some are actually doing something while others do not know where to start, and still others are duplicating the work being done by the first group of children.

ART IN THE LIFE OF THE CHILDREN

Esthetic education in a variety of different forms must enter into the daily life of the kindergarten. In the second half of the day, and in the summer even before the mid-day dinner, the teacher may suggest to the children that they listen to records, read a book, or listen to a fairy tale; she organizes them to look at reproductions of the works of classical and contemporary artists, examples of folk art, and slides based on fairy tales or literary works; she has the children sing favorite songs and gives them an added opportunity to draw and model.

Artistic activity organized for the children outside the regular activity periods is designed to get them to enjoy art and experience happiness when they come in contact with something beautiful, to stimulate the emergence of creative initiative, and to inculcate artistic taste. These objectives also determine the way of organizing the children which is different from that of the regular activity periods.

During activity periods devoted to graphic art, literature, and music, the goals listed above represent only one aspect of the totality of objectives, of which the central one involves developing the child's ability to sing, dance, draw, paint, or recite poetry, as well as training him in how to study. The objectives indicated require a definite organization of the learning process and of the behavior of the children.

The teachers must plan to develop the children's interest in art outside of the regular activity periods, and periodically put down in the calendar-plan what should be suggested to the children. The one thing which it is most important to remember is that the number and duration of these extra activities should not be strictly regulated, and there should be no obligation for every child to participate; that is, some of the principles guiding the organization of the regular activity periods do not apply in relation to these extra activities. Moreover, it must be remembered that the children must have enough time left for games.

In planning work involving esthetic instruction outside the regular active periods, the teachers should not be guided by any quantitative norms, but rather by the educational objectives for the particular group of children. In some groups, and at a given period of the year, the teachers will plan more frequent extra "art appreciation" sessions of the type described.

In relation to the intellectual and esthetic development of children, the teacher assigns more room for independence and initiative on the part of children, while the actual number of projects undertaken by the teacher decreases. The teacher more frequently assumes the role of advisor to the children rather than their immediate organizer. In the calendar-plan of the teachers will appear such entries as "Discuss with the children what films they want to see next week" (older groups) or "Work out together with a group of children a program of records to comprise a surprise concert for the rest of the children."

Thus, a teacher's calendar-plan for a week will include, besides scheduled activities, a whole series of activities determined by the program: games, observations, work functions, entertainment, listening to music, or listening to artistic works of literature. The number of such things during the week and on any given day does not depend on what has been previously decided and planned, but rather on circumstances which develop, situations, and demands: the teacher must give the children that which they need most at a given time.

A concrete meaningful plan for each day will help the teacher to cover the necessary work in an organized fashion and in a way which will be beneficial to the children. To require the teacher to plan in accordance with a rigid pattern (that is, to determine exactly how many minutes are to be spent on the morning walk or in the afternoon recreation period) would involve squeezing the live pedagogical process into a formalized framework. She would be forced to plan according to a schematic design rather than with the benefit of the inspiration provided by the life of the children and by the program itself.

CONCERNING LONG-RANGE PLANS

Some teachers not only make out a calendar-plan, but also make entries concerning a much longer period of time. For example, they write down for themselves what to do during the summer in relation to familiarizing the children with nature and the cultivation of plants. Making out a long-range plan of activities must be left as a matter of judgment to the individual teacher. Some are helped by such a plan at particular periods; for example, by a long-range plan for the month before the New Year or for the summer, or for the month of September (the beginning of the school year). Others will make out long-range plans for each one- or two-month period. Still others will make no long-range plans for the group as a whole, but will make note of some measures to be adopted regarding individual children. To establish required procedures regarding long range planning would not be wise at the present. It is all the more inappropriate to demand the type of long-range plan which as far as the teachers were concerned would take the place of the program itself; that is, one where the teachers would select sufficient materials from the program for the coming month, and then from the material selected would take material for the calendar-plan. Each time a calendar-plan is made out, the teacher must on the contrary consult the Program directly; if the teachers want to make out a long-range plan, then it must be a list of concrete measures to realize the objectives in the program.

EVALUATING THE EDUCATIONAL WORK

The educational process requires on the part of the teacher a constant analysis and evaluation of her own acts from the point of view of their influence and effect upon the children. What have the children learned and how? How do they show up in games, in work, in their relationships with each other and with adults? How is the speech development of the children progressing? How are their interests evolving? Each teacher writes down daily in the calendar-plan her observations regarding the children, her evaluation of the work covered that day from the point of view of the results achieved (how did the children respond, and how well did they learn the material taught that day?), and, if she is able to do it, makes notes regarding future work (with the whole group or with individual children).

The entries must be brief and to the point. They should be concerned with the actual subject matter of the children's activities and with behavioral manifestations which the teacher considers important to remember, ones which attest to specific results of instruction (regardless of whether they are positive or negative).

The entries must not be limited simply to confirming that something set down in the plan was actually carried out, as in this example:

Entry in the plan: In the evening show slides.
Entry in the evaluation: In the evening slides were shown.

Is such a formal entry of any use? Will it help to evaluate the progress in the development of individual children, in the development of interrelationships between children, in the evolution of interests? Of course not.

After the afternoon nap the children had an hour and a half at their disposal; showing slides probably took some twenty minutes. And what did the children do in the remaning one hour and ten minutes? Not a word is said about this by the teacher. But most likely children played various games, entered into a variety of different relationships with each other and with the teacher, experienced happiness or sorrow, quarrelled, and perhaps even discovered something brand new to them. These isolated facts must be remembered by the teacher, since it is in summarizing and comparing an accumulation of data that it becomes possible to formulate meaningful conclusions regarding the further educational and instructional work.

To observe all the children at the time when they are busy in a variety of different ways is a much harder thing to do than to observe them while they are all engaged in a given activity. Teachers must develop the ability to keep the whole group in view even at a time when the children are playing in small groups or individually. They must learn to write down only what is really essential, as this will be in their own best interests. When it becomes necessary to make out a plan for the next period of time, and doing so requires looking back over the work done previously, then if there are no notes in the daily record it will be extremely difficult to remember the significant things which occured in the course of several days in the life of some twenty-five to thirty children.

VII

Play and the Organization
of the Children's Lives

Play is the basic aspect of child activity at a preschool age and forms a characteristic pattern in child development. It is considered a need for the growing organism and a necessary precondition for becoming a man and a member of the society.

The play activity of children has for many years been utilized for the fulfillment of education objectives. In preschool educational psychology play is considered from various points of view: first, as a vehicle for educational-instructional work, through which it is possible to give the children definite knowledge and skills, and to contribute to the development of qualities and potentialities observed at an earlier stage; second, as a form of the organization of the life and activity of preschool children when, in freely chosen and freely evolving play activity guided by the teacher, play groups develop among the children and they form definite relationships, personal likes and dislikes, and social and personal interests. Taking her inspiration from the daily life of the children and from their activities, the teacher has an opportunity to fulfill broad educational objectives in developing the consciousness of the children and in molding their behavior.

In the given methodological commentary, the characteristics of a particular game are presented for the most part from a single point of view— that of their significance for the organization of the lives of the children in the kindergarten. This does not mean that we overlook other aspects of these games or do not fully appreciate their value. We merely feel that these other aspects must already be well known to the kindergarten teachers, while the question of the significance of play for the organization of the children's lives has not been sufficiently clarified.

The lives of children of preschool age and their activity may be most effectively organized in the form of play, since this will enable the children to satisfy basic needs. It is a well known fact that preschool children live in their games and come to the kindergarten with definite ideas and projects which they endeavor to realize. A. S. Makarenko said: "A child has a passion for games, and it must be satisfied. The child must not only be permitted to play, but his entire life must be nourished by his play. His whole life is his play!"

But merely to recognize the rights of children to engage in play activity and then to leave the whole process to chance development would be incorrect. It is essential that the children's games be given a certain character and that they be controlled with respect to time and contents in order that the lives of the children and their activity may be organized in the spirit of a communist education.

What must be done in order for play in the kindergarten to become a form of organization of the life and of activities of the children? The following are essential: first, those specific educational objectives on the basis of which the children's lives and activities will be organized in play must be determined; second, play must be strengthened through greater organization and by emphasis placed upon it in the daily schedule of the kindergarten, similar to the way in which other aspects of the children's lives and of the educational process are organized; third, we must establish how the teacher is to play with the children, how and by what means her participation and guidance are to manifest themselves.

THE SIGNIFICANCE OF PLAY IN THE ORGANIZATION OF THE LIFE AND ACTIVITY OF THE CHILDREN

In pedagogical literature, the role of play in the development of children of preschool age has been rather extensively discussed and clarified. The outstanding Soviet educators, N. K. Krupskaya and A. S. Makarenko, examine the meaning of play in a broader sense than merely as an education tool. They see in play first of all the tangible manifestation of the life of the child, his immediate interests and his potentialities. N. K. Krupskaya wrote: "For the youngsters of preschool age, play is exceptionally meaningful. To them play represents learning; play for them is work, and play for them is a serious form of education."

The famous Soviet educator and physician, E. A. Arkin, writes: "There cannot be any healthy development without an active and interesting life. Such an active, absorbing life the child experiences in free and self-created play or in games involving rules. I, as a doctor, praise play, not only in that the child creates, but also in that play has a favorable influence on the child's health. Play is the unique form of activity which in all cases corresponds to the proper organization of his life. Play never makes demands of him of the kind he cannot fulfill, while at the same time it always requires from him a certain degree of effort and challenge which is linked with a healthy feeling of well-being and cheerfulness. And happiness and cheerfulness are a guarantee of good health."

Organization of the life and the activity of children through play becomes possible only insofar as the child's play evolves along lines which reflect the level of development determined by the child's age and individual growth characteristics.

Play does not originate spontaneously in the child. For the emergence of play activity, a whole series of external conditions is necessary: the presence of impressions of the surrounding world, the availability of toys, and contact with adults, in which the role of play occupies a significant place. Let us remember the *ku-ku* which accompanies an adult's disappearance and reappearance before the baby in the first months of his life, the *ladushki* ("clap hands") which stimulates the baby to move his hands in a definite rhythm, and so on. But all these involve joint action between the child and the adult in which the adult, so to speak, "amuses" the child by playing some sort of game with him. The child himself remains at the level of handling objects, without distinguishing those objects which have a special purpose—the toys.

As the child grows, his desire to act independently increases; the first way in which this endeavor manifests itself is in handling objects independently. At this point, the adults very deliberately give the child the toys he needs in order to separate them in his mind from ordinary household objects. The child learns to perform simple actions with these toys—to roll them, throw them, and so forth. The child obviously experiences a great sense of joy in the mastery of these actions and the fact that the toys or objects are thus subjected to his will. However, these games represent the individual world of the child in which a considerable role is played by the adult, since the child can only occupy himself for a very short span of time.

But already from the beginning of his third year of life, a new element introduces itself into the child's play with increasing persistence. Rather than simply handling an object, the child begins to see the possibilities of accomplishing some action with it (and to recognize himself as the agent performing the action: "I am preparing dinner," or "I am taking care of the child"); the child begins to use a rule as the point of departure in his play. From that time on and during all of the preschool years, wide possibilities open before the child for playing "everything" which he sees and which makes a deep impression upon him. Adult life and adult activities are introduced wholesale into the children's games. It is, therefore, fully understandable that the child quickly realizes the necessity of including some other person in his game, the person linked with the role he is performing: if there is a "doctor," then a "patient" is needed; if there is a "mommy," then there must be a "baby."

In their fifth year of life, the children master the positions required by games, and later use them quite freely. Now games with rules are accessible to the children, as is the performance of the roles involved in these games: cats and mice, the hunter and the rabbit, and so on.

The most characteristic stages in the development of play as an activity are, consequently, the appearance in the child of the ability to act out a definite role (for himself) and then, for the creation of a necessary situation, the involvement of other people, mainly children (someone to feed, dress, transport). A typical type of independent activity appears in which the child more deliberately goes about involving other children in his play. His need of their participation becomes more urgent. Children by this time are already capable of organizing a game by themselves along very definite lines, coming up with an idea or theme for the game, and then carrying it through.

In playing, the children live a full life and enjoy life. At each step they discover something new in their environment, and while playing they acquire the habits and skills required in life. S. A. Marshak is right when he writes that childhood, almost from the very first steps a man takes, is a time of steadily increasing comprehension of the world. Although this is a joyful time, it is also a difficult one, as there are a multitude of concepts, feelings and relationships to be assimilated. From time to time adults have to guide the child, warn and protect him, teach him, lead him by the hand. If all this is done in a harsh, admonishing manner, without a smile, there can be only one result: the complete loss of friendly contact with the child as he grows up. And the younger the child, the more he needs a smile and the more he needs a gay and fanciful game.

Through play, the little man may be made ready for great deeds. However, such an attitude toward play is often considered as a recognition of the special age characteristics of children which must be taken into account and which must be satisfied by leaving time for games too. But must these views be looked upon only in this light?

We suggest that in them must be seen possibilities for educating children of a certain age on the basis of an organization of their lives around play. And the possibilities which are pointed out by outstanding educators must be transformed into educational reality; that is, the children's lives must be organized in such a way as to prepare "the little man for great deeds" in the ordinary conditions in which the child lives, which are, without a doubt, the very same conditions in which he plays.

For the kindergarten this is an important goal. It is not enough to have respect for the children's desire to play—it is essential to arrange things in such a way that the organization of play in the kindergarten will unconditionally guarantee the children an interesting, meaningful life and will satisfy their need to play; at the same time the play will develop in the children patterns of social behavior and personality characteristic of the Soviet people.

In play, we are dealing with a society of children, and consequently with social education. To consider the life of a child at play in terms of the isolated existence of a separate personality is simply impossible. Consequently, one should not be concerned with exerting an influence upon a separate child. One must not limit oneself to developing his individual qualities. We must concern ourselves only with the lives of children within the society and with their acquisition of social patterns of behavior. We must give to their games such contents and such a character that they will encourage the children to positive forms of behavior and to positive relationships among themselves.

If for the children play represents life in its most direct form, then for the teacher it represents an opportunity to form the Soviet man with his characteristic attributes, in the conditions which prevail naturally at this age and stage of development. The significance of games for the organization of the lives of children and for their education within the spirit of the rules and norms of Soviet behavior and interrelationships have long interested kindergarten teachers. For it is quite obvious that Soviet pedagogy cannot use play only for purely didactic purposes.

The themes of some of the following articles written by kindergarten educators are characteristic: "Play as a means of bringing the child closer to the children's collective," (Z. V. Obydova), "The training of friendly reciprocal relations through creative games," (V. P. Zalogina), and others. Such themes as the following have appeared in research papers: "Concerning the formation of children's collectives through the process of play," (A. V. Cherkov), "The role of play in the formation of the social behavior of a child," (A. V. Cherkov), "The role of play in the formation of the child's personality," (P. I. Zhukovsky).

It is a significant fact that the solution of educational problems regarding the development of social qualities and forms of child behavior is being sought in connection with role-playing games, which evolve from the inspiration of the children themselves. There have been considerably fewer attempts to adopt a broad educational plan with respect to games of an instructional nature (active and mental games), but experience does already exist even in this area. With regard to role-playing games, opinions are divided. Some consider that they must be subjected to an instructional plan; that is, to be steered in such a direction that the children will acquire through them certain skills. Others consider that these games should be utilized for the purpose of bringing about the fulfillment of a broad educational plan. It is evident that inasmuch as instruction *per se* is carried out during regular activities periods in Soviet kindergartens, role-playing games must serve broad educational purposes for the most part; but, granted this fact, it is nevertheless obvious that the perceptional character inherent in these games cannot and should not be ignored.

The educational objectives in building games can also be significantly broadened (contact between children, development of friendly relationships). What are the main aspects of a child's life around which his play is organized?

In the first place, of course, there is the organization of the children's interests. Everything that attracts and absorbs the children is expressed by them in their play and makes their lives joyful. And as the child is an active being, his interests are therefore distinguished by his active character, and at an early stage this is more often than not expressed in his play. These interests, naturally, are not nourished solely by games but have a broader foundation comprising the contact of the child with the environment and with surrounding people as well as observations made by the child himself. But it is nevertheless characteristic that while playing, a child is most likely to express that which interests him, absorbs him, or inspires his life at any given moment. At the same time the children's interests are growing. Hence, it is only by correctly coordinating both these factors that good results can be attained.

In games, joint projects arise naturally: building something together, going somewhere, and so forth. Gradually, common interests develop and, on the basis of these, the children form into groups. Some are interested in running games, others prefer role-playing games, still others musical games. One can always see in kindergartens such groups of children united by common interests.

In organizing the children's lives around play, one must have a clear idea in mind of what character the games should take and what significance they will have.

During the entire duration of the preschool period, the games invented by the children themselves will always delight them and give them the opportunity to express their interests, for in such games the child himself easily reconciles his capabilities with the demands of the game. He stops playing "movies" when he is no longer interested in the game and is able to think up something else immediately. The obligations imposed upon the group of children in their play are not very demanding and can always be well motivated by the children themselves. All this not only does not interfere with, but rather helps them to enjoy the game and become more interested in it.

Despite all their positive qualities and despite the fact that games of this kind are in fact the products of a definite level of child development in the preschool stage of childhood, such games nevertheless contain weaknesses, reflecting precisely this level of development in the child. While recognizing the great value of these games in orienting the child within the environment and developing his ability to fantasize and to conform to the interests of a group, it must be realized that here the child is too free from outside circumstances—these circumstances do not control him. To "deliver up" someone in a role-playing game is often simply a question of imagination, whereas to save oneself, the "wolf," in the active game called "The Sheep," is a much more complicated affair, as it requires action. Therefore, it would be wrong to organize the life of children in kindergartens only on the basis of the games devised by the children themselves.

Games with rules (active games, educational games, musical games) are of great significance for the children's collective. The rules in those games determine for the children certain norms of activity—they determine what may and what may not be done or said. Also, they impose a form of external regulation. The children must learn to use these rules and to conform to them, for it is only when these conditions are satisfied that the game can take place. These requirements represent something new for the preschool child. As he was free to act within the framework of games of his own invention, he now becomes dependent on rules in these new games. Mastering the rules of the games (whether active or educational) is an important factor in introducing greater organization into the life of the child and that of the children's collective. These qualities require training and have their own age profile.

Here is an example. 4-year-old children pretend to be birds, and on a given musical signal are supposed to leave their "little houses" and "fly." Knowing that a "cat" is lying in wait for them, they do not leave their little houses. The musical signal does not have any effect upon them. Therefore, the rules of the game do not work. The children have not as yet attained that level of development at which a rule can have any regulatory significance for them.

Mastering games with rules has great organizational significance on the individual child not only in a personal way, but also in his capacity as a member of a group. For older children, the rule of the game becomes a definite norm in their relationships with each other within the collective, through its control over oneself and the other players. Submitting to the rules of the game is facilitated by little hints and reminders from the teacher.

It is characteristic for the children to be interested in the children's collective, since it represents the source of their games. The child is not at all indifferent as to whom he is actually going to play with. On the contrary, the interest of children becomes quite selective at an early age, and this fact must be the subject of considerable attention.

While playing, the child always finds himself in a definite relationship with the collective, even in such cases when children are playing in twos and threes. The social influence of the game and the feelings aroused by it enter into the relationships which are formed through the game. This is the essence of life, that which leads to the formation of human relationships. Whether it be a game which is created by the child or the collective, or whether it be a game worked out for the children, in both cases there will be revealed those interrelationships between children which in fact make the game possible. Experience shows that where such interrelationships do not develop for some reason or other, the game is impossible.

Play, more than any other activity during the preschool years, necessarily involves the performance of definite actions on the part of the child and the emergence of personal characteristics and qualities. Here the child makes his first steps toward establishing relationships with children of the same age group—herein lies the child's first training for social behavior. Meeting each other daily in the kindergarten, the children have contacts with each other at different moments in their lives; this happens most actively in the process of playing. Social feelings, habits, the ability to act in common, and the understanding of one's own as well as extremely basic general interests all develop on the basis of these interrelationships. The degree of purposefulness in the performance of actions is increased, and the evaluation both of one's personal achievements and also common achievements is promoted. In addition, a feeling of friendship, interdependence and equality arises. All this requires guidance.

We all know children whose exuberance often overflows. This is particularly noticeable in games. Such children become real tyrants. A false image of them as "good organizers" develops. In fact, they do achieve some kind of organization of the children in general play, but it is far from being of a positive nature. These are important facts in the lives of children; moreover, when they are repeated daily, they reinforce in the children totally undesirable forms of personal and social behavior. What teacher does not know cases where groups of children are held together through the despotism of a single child, through his undisputed authority? "I said so," "I want it to be that way," says one of these "organizers"; and in answer one hears, "Kolya said to do it that way," or "Kolya wants it to be that way."

The best that can happen is that the teacher limits this despotism for a time by giving the leading role over to some other child. But the system of interrelationships already established between the children continues to exist and have its effects. Only persistent educative work of a very delicate and sequential nature can succeed in changing the character of the interrelationships between the children. Here, a simple command to the children forbidding them to play with each other will not work. If they do not continue openly, they will nevertheless continue to play together in secret.

The personal contact between children in play gives rise to the performance of specific *acts*. In his play, the child is always doing something, and in doing something he acts in a definite manner. This is a particularly basic characteristic of the games of preschool children. Right at the start of the game the child is performing an act already. He needs a toy, and can either take it away from his neighbor or ask for it. He can call to someone to play with him or, on the contrary, refuse to join in a game. In the process of the children's play, we encounter at every step acts performed by the children—whether they are quarrelling or acting in a friendly manner, whether they are acting fairly or unfairly, and whether they are acting in an organized or disorganized manner. But an act is not merely the isolated action of one child (or group). The committed act always involves someone else and has a certain import. Therefore, it is more important than anything else to help the children in the organization of their actions—to teach them how to behave, how to act. Without this, the more organized of children may perform actions which will have a disorganizing effect.

In one of the kindergartens, children in the middle and older groups are allowed to use balls, not only on the playground, but also in the common room. It is often asked whether some glass has not been broken or something or other knocked to the ground. But the fact of the matter is that before these games were permitted children were shown how they must play with a ball, and they were warned about the various possibilities for accidents if the rules were not observed. In this way alone, incidents where the ball might have broken glass or crashed into the flowers, were prevented. Children were not told, "Do not break the glass," or "Do not hit the flowers," but were simply and in a kindly fashion shown how well everything could work out if they merely observed the rules.

Usually, 5-year-old children are already allowed to play independently on the playground, but in order to prevent undesirable actions on their part, groups of children are given an interest in particular games and sometimes specific details are even arranged (such as who is to "count"). Thus when the children go out to play, they already have definite intentions.

.   .   .

A variety of different games is essential for the proper organization of the children's lives in the kindergarten, since it is only under such conditions that the children will be guaranteed interesting and meaningful activity.

We are convinced of the fact that, by relying on play as a form of organization of the lives and of the activity of children in the kindergarten routine, the situation described in the following words by A. S. Makarenko will be achieved: "Play must, without fail, be present in the children's collective. A children's collective where play is absent is not a true children's collective."